THE ART OF
WORLDLY WISDOM

中英對照全譯本

智慧書

與世推移・佈局人生・善謀能斷

300篇
亙古不朽的睿智箴言

17世紀西班牙智者
巴爾塔沙・葛拉西安 著
Baltasar Gracián

前　言

PREFACE

巴爾塔沙・葛拉西安，1601年出生於西班牙。是十七世紀著名的思想家。青少年時期，他就開始修習哲學與文學。歷任軍中神父、告解神父、宣教師、教授及行政人員等職。他從未出任重要公職，但是常與政治人物交遊往來，這些人生經驗都成為他寫作思考的源泉。

1637年，其處女作《英雄》問世，旋即引起轟動。1640年討論領袖資質的《政治家》出版。1643年，《詩之才藝》出版。1647年，其巔峰之作《智慧書》問世。因其筆鋒犀利、譏諷政治，被耶穌會警告，未獲批准出版。1651年，寓言小說《批評家》問世。為此，他被耶穌會解除了教席，放逐到一個鄉下小鎮，直至1658年終老於此。葛拉西安生活的年代正處於宗教改革浪潮之中，其一生與耶穌會有著千絲萬縷的關係，這兩個事件對葛拉西安思想有著重要的影響。

《智慧書》文風簡練辛辣，多暗含典故。葛拉西安的文風使得其與讀者的關係處於一種很微妙的關係之中。作者如擊劍般與讀者周旋進退，他的意圖多方巧飾，避免手中之牌一次攤盡，保持延宕懸疑，

以隱曲幽微引人傾羨與尊敬。他在文中寫到：「謹慎之人雖然自己十分清楚，卻總是說一半留一半」。葛拉西安的這種文風除了有審美上的追求，還有自我保護的考量。葛拉西安的文風顯示了其經驗之深厚，處事之周到圓滑，思想之獨到深刻。

《智慧書》300箴言述說處事智巧，與《論語》、《老子》有異曲同工之妙，待人接物講究圓而不方，欲臻於完美，人必須識實務而與世推移。全書警語多有交錯、對立之處，但可方便從多角度觀察人的處事之道。一個片段教我們如何以某種策略與人周旋，另一片段就交我們如何防禦這種巧計。生活本身就是黑白交錯而成，沒有誰的世界是純白或純黑的，箴言採取這種策略是極高明的生活智慧，沒有什麼處事原則是不需要變通的。

善惡是人居於人世間不得不面對的永恆話題，關於這個話題卻從來沒有一個定論，向來是見仁見智。要成為一個大器之人，在善惡這個問題上，每個人都應該有自己的獨到見解，明辨善惡是智慧的表現。善惡之路何其漫漫，何其艱難！

先賢之道讓我們領略前人之智慧，聖人之書讓我們日進千里。有此捷徑，何當獨行？讓我們與之同行，共勉之！

本書英譯本採用的是Joseph Jacob 1927年的版本，鑑於譯者能力有限，書中若有不足之處，敬請指正。

目　錄

CONTENTS

1・世間萬象已達極致

尤其是立身處世之道。如今世界造就一位賢人比古代造就希臘七賢更為不易；如今對付一個人所要付出的代價比過去對付整個民族所付出的代價還要大。

2・性格與智能

乃人發揮才能之依託，二者缺其一，人生就無法完美。只靠智慧是不夠的，還必須有一個適合於你的性格。此外，愚人是不幸的，因為他無法透過二者獲得與其適合的地位、職業、鄰里及朋友。

---

1. Seven Sages 希臘七賢，指古希臘人所說的最有智慧的7個人。指的是普林納（小亞細亞）的拜阿斯（Biass）、斯巴達的開倫（Chilon）、林都斯（羅得島）的克利奧布拉斯（Kleoboulos）、科林斯的拍立安得（Periandros）、密提利那（列斯保島）的庇達卡斯（Pittakos）、雅典的梭倫和米利都的泰勒斯。

2. sufficeth 是古英語 suffice 的第三人稱單數形式。

i Everything Is at Its Acme,

e specially the art of making one's way in the world. There is more required nowadays to make a single wise man than formerly to make **Seven Sages**[1], and more is needed nowadays to deal with a single person than was required with a whole people in former times.

ii Character and Intellect:

t he two poles of our capacity; one without the other is but halfway to happiness. Intellect **sufficeth**[2] not, character is also needed. On the other hand, it is the fool's misfortune to fail in obtaining the position, the employment, the neighbourhood, and the circle of friends that suit him.

3・勿使所行之事公開亮底

出人意料的成功增加了成功的價值。把什麼事情都擺到明處是無用且愚蠢的。如果不急於表態，你就會讓人滿懷期待——尤其當你地位顯赫、成為眾人關注的焦點時。讓你的每件事都有點神秘色彩，這種神秘會讓你贏得別人的敬重。當你解釋時不要解釋得太過明白，正如你在平常聊天時不會洩露自己內心深處的想法一樣。**大智慧需要謹慎的沉默來體現。**你決心要做的事一旦被披露，不但很難獲得尊重，而且只會招致批評，萬一失敗就會更加不幸。更何況，如果你能讓人們好奇並且觀察你，那你就在行神明之道。

4・知識和勇氣

是成就豐功偉業的條件。它們會讓你變得不朽，因為它們本身就是不朽的。知識可以成就一個人，一個智慧之人幾乎無所不能。一個人沒有知識正如世界沒有陽光。才智與力量好比人的雙眼與雙手。有識無膽者，其知識無法結出成功的果實。

---

1. insipid [ɪn`sɪpɪd] adj. 乏味的，缺乏風格的，單調的
2. play with the cards on the table 攤牌，將想法或打算全盤托出
3. veneration [ˌvɛnə`reʃən] n. 尊敬
4. Divine way 指像神那樣的做法。英語中凡特指上帝及和上帝相關的詞一般首字母大寫。如 Divine Wisdom, Creator, His property, God Almighty 等。

iii Keep Matters for a Time in Suspense.

Admiration at their novelty heightens the value of your achievements, It is both useless and **insipid**[1] to **play with the cards on the table**[2]. If you do not declare yourself immediately, you arouse expectation, especially when the importance of your position makes you the object of general attention. Mix a little mystery with everything, and the very mystery arouses **veneration**[3]. And when you explain, be not too explicit, just as you do not expose your inmost thoughts in ordinary intercourse. Cautious silence is the holy of holies of worldly wisdom. A resolution declared is never highly thought of; it only leaves room for criticism. And if it happens to fail, you are doubly unfortunate. Besides you imitate the **Divine way**[4] when you cause men to wonder and watch.

iv Knowledge and Courage

are the elements of Greatness. They give immortality, because they are immortal. Each is as much as he knows, and the wise can do anything. **A man without knowledge, a world without light. Wisdom and strength, eyes and hands.**[5] Knowledge without courage is **sterile**[6].

---

5. 這兩句均為省略句。完整的句子應該是："A man without knowledge is like a world without light. Wisdom is like eyes; strength is like hands."

6. sterile [ˈstɛrəl] adj. 無效果的，無結果的

5．培養建立別人對你的依賴心理

神之所以成為神，並不在於人們把他做成飾物隨身佩戴，而在於人們對他的敬畏。聰明人寧願看到人們需要他，而不是感謝他。讓人們一直存有希望是精明的做法，相信人們會一直感激你則是笨拙的做法。當人心有所求時，他便能銘心不忘，感謝之辭除了會促其忘卻恩情外一無用處。與其讓人對你彬彬有禮，不如讓人對你有依賴之心。人喝飽了水就會離井而去，吃過的橘子會被人從光鮮的水果盤扔到垃圾桶裏。一旦別人不再依賴你，他就不再對你畢恭畢敬。把這作為最重要的經驗之談吧：維持別人對你的依賴心理，不要完全滿足其需求。運用此法就連君王也可以輕鬆應付。但踐實此法需把握適度，不可過分，若只是引而不發，則會使你誤入歧途，萬不可只為一己之利而無視他人的艱難處境。

---

1. on the threshold of 在⋯的開頭，在⋯快要開始的時候，在⋯前夕
2. boorish [`bʊrɪʃ] adj. 鄉土氣的，粗野的，粗鄙的
3. courtesy [`kɝtəsɪ] n. 謙恭，禮貌
4. platter [`plætɚ] n. 大淺盤
5. patron [`petrən] n. （對某人、某種目標、藝術等）贊助人，資助人

v Create a Feeling of Dependence.

Not he that adorns but he that adores makes a divinity. The wise man would rather see men needing him than thanking him. To keep them **on the threshold**[1] **of** hope is diplomatic, to trust to their gratitude **boorish**[2] ; hope has a good memory, gratitude a bad one. More is to be got from dependence than from **courtesy**[3]. He that has satisfied his thirst turns his back on the well, and the orange once sucked falls from the golden **platter**[4] into the waste-basket. When dependence disappears, good behaviour goes with it as well as respect. Let it be one of the chief lessons of experience to keep hope alive without entirely satisfying it, by preserving it to make oneself always needed even by a **patron**[5] on the throne. But let not silence be carried to excess lest you go wrong, nor let another's failing grow **incurable**[6] for the sake of your own advantage.

---

6. incurable [ɪnˋkjʊrəbl] adj. 不能治癒的

6 · 至善至美

人非生而完美。每天，我們需堅持德業兼修，不斷進取，從而最終達到盡善盡美之境界，修行會使你秉性圓滿，聲名顯赫。完美之人品味高雅，才智精純，判斷老練，意志堅定。有些人永遠難以達到完美，總是有些缺憾。還有一些人則需要很長時間的修煉才會初見成效，取得進步。至善至美的人，言語中透露著智慧，行為中透露著謹慎，上流社會仁人志士願與之結交，樂與之為伍。

---

1. awanting [əˋwɑntɪŋ] adj. <古>缺乏的

vi A Man at His Highest Point.

We are not born perfect: every day we develop in our personality and in our calling till we reach the highest point of our completed being, to the full round of our accomplishments, of our excellences. This is known by the purity of our taste, the clearness of our thought, the maturity of our judgment, and the firmness of our will. Some never arrive at being complete; somewhat is always **awanting**[1] : others ripen late. The complete man, wise in speech, prudent in act, is admitted to the familiar intimacy of discreet persons, is even sought for by them.

7．不要顯得比上司高明

顯得比別人高明往往會招致怨恨，若是顯得比你的上司還要高明，那不但愚蠢，也可能致命。自以為高明的人總會招人厭惡，更容易招惹上司和人們的嫉恨。因此，應學會明哲保身，小心掩飾自己的優點，例如：天生麗質的人衣著打扮可以隨意一點。也許有人不會在意你在運氣或性格方面比他們好，但是絕對不會有一個人（更別說是王子了）能夠容忍你在智商上超越他們。智商被認為是人格特徵之最高代表，冒犯別人智商無異於犯下滔天大罪。王公貴族更是希望在一切重大事情上顯示出他有比別人更高的智商。他們允許被人輔佐，而不是被超越，所以，當你想向他們提出忠告和建議時，你應該表現得好像是提醒他們忘掉的事，而不是指導他們做沒考慮到的事。此中處事之奧妙亦可從天上群星之狀況悟得，雖然星星是太陽的子民，也像太陽一樣明亮，但卻沒有哪顆星星敢和太陽爭輝！

---

1. gloss over 簡略的、或敷衍地處理某事（以求避開難堪的細節）
2. attire [əˋtaɪr] n. 服裝
3. precedence [prɪˋsidns] n. 優先，居先
4. least of all 最不
5. prerogative [prɪˋragətɪv] n. 特權

vii Avoid Victories over Superiors.

All victories breed hate, and that over your superior is foolish or fatal. Superiority is always detested, let alone superiority over superiority. Caution can **gloss over**[1] common advantages; for example, good looks may be cloaked by careless **attire**[2]. There be some that will grant you **precedence**[3] in good luck or good temper, but none in good sense, **least of all**[4] a prince; for good sense is a royal **prerogative**[5], any claim to that is a case of majesty. They are princes, and wish to be so in that most princely of qualities. They will allow a man to help them but not to surpass them, and will have any advice **tendered**[6] them appear like a recollection of something they have forgotten rather than as a guide to something they cannot find. The stars teach us this finesse with happy **tact**[7] ; though they are his children and brilliant like him, they never rival the brilliancy of the sun.

---

6. tender [`tɛndɚ] v. 正式提出
7. tact [tækt] n. 機智，手法

8 · 擺脫一切衝動的激情

這 是思維的最高境界。自我克制能使你免於被轉瞬即逝且庸俗的衝動左右。沒有一種勝利比戰勝自己及自己的衝動情緒更偉大——因為這是自由意志的勝利。當情緒衝動時，要學會克制，千萬不要讓它影響你的地位，特別是當你的地位對你很重要時。這是能使你避免麻煩的唯一明智之舉，也是你獲得良好聲譽的捷徑。

9 · 避免受到環境的負面影響

河 水總會受到河床土質的影響；人也會受到其出生地氣候好壞的影響。有的人會比其他人多蒙其故土的恩澤，因為那裏氣候更加宜人。但即使是那些文明最發達的國家，也有其特有的缺陷，讓其他國家幸災樂禍或引以為戒。若有誰能克服或至少掩飾住這些民族的弱點，那他就比別人高明一籌。如果你在你的同胞中與眾不同，你就會受到大家的推崇，而且，你越是出人意料，你就會越受人尊重與推崇。還有一些其他缺陷源於人們的出身、地位、職業或是所處的時代。如果這所有的缺陷都集中在一個人身上而未被小心防範，那這個人就成了一個令人難以忍受的怪物。

---

1. 'Tis 是古英語中 It's 的拼寫方法。
2. eminence [`ɛmənəns] n. 出眾，顯赫，崇高
3. redeem [rɪ`dim] vt. 挽回，補償
4. strata [`stretə] n. stratum 的複數 stratum [`stretəm] n. 地層
5. zenith [`zinɪθ] n. 頂點，頂峰，天頂，最高點

viii To be Without Passions.

❯ Tis[1] a privilege of the highest order of mind. Their very **eminence**[2] **redeems**[3] them from being affected by transient and low impulses. There is no higher rule than that over oneself, over one's impulses: there is the triumph of free will. While passion rules the character, no aiming at high office; the less the higher. It is the only refined way of avoiding scandals; nay, 'tis the shortest way back to good repute.

ix Avoid the Faults of Your Nation.

Water shares the good or bad qualities of the **strata**[4] through which it flows, and man those of the climate in which he is born. Some owe more than others to their native land, because there is a more favourable sky in the **zenith**[5] . There is not a nation even among the most civilised that has not some fault peculiar to itself which other nations blame by way of boast or as a warning. 'Tis a triumph of cleverness to correct in oneself such national failings, or even to hide them: you get great credit for being unique among your fellows, and as it is less expected of you it is esteemed the more. There are also family failings as well as faults of position, of office or of age. If these all meet in one person and are not carefully guarded against, they make an intolerable monster.

10 · 好運與名聲

好運流轉不定，名聲歷久不衰。前者是為了今生，後者是為了來世。好運須防他人嫉妒；名聲須防湮沒無聞。**好運可遇而不可求；然而名聲則要靠艱苦努力才能獲得。**佼佼者對名譽的追求來自人類自身的願望。從古至今，名聲總是與巨人為伴，且總會造就極端的人才：不是奸雄怪傑，便是英才豪傑；不是臭名昭彰，便是美名遠揚。

11 · 與可師者為友

朋友間的交往可以成為你知識的泉源，交談可提高你的文化修養。你要尊朋友為師，在愉快的交談中學習其過人之處。理性的人會享受其中不同的樂趣，不但他們說的話會博得聽者喝彩，他們還會從別人的話中得到啟發。我們總是為了自身利益而被別人吸引，但如果是為了學習，這種吸引就提升到更高的層次。智者常常拜訪偉人，不是為了滿足虛榮心，而是因為可以看到許多具有良好修養的人。有人以處世智慧而聞名遐邇，他們不但以身作則、行為示範，他們身邊的人也充滿無上智慧、具有高尚情操和教養。

---

1. fickle [`fɪkl] adj. （在感情等方面）變幻無常的
2. oblivion [ə`blɪvɪən] n. 遺忘，淹沒
3. prodigy [`prɑdədʒɪ] n. 驚人的事物，天才（特指神童），奇觀，奇事
4. vanity [`vænətɪ] n. 虛榮心，浮華，無價值的東西。Vanity 還指英國作家班揚（John Bun yan）在宗教小說《天路歷程》（Pilgrim's Progress）中所寫的浮華市集。
5. oracle [`ɔrəkl] n. 神使，哲人，聖賢

x Fortune and Fame.

W here the one is **fickle**[1] the other is enduring. The first for life, the second afterwards; the one against envy, the other against **oblivion**[2] . Fortune is desired, at times assisted: fame is earned. The desire for fame springs from man's best part. It was and is the sister of the giants; it always goes to extremes – horrible monsters or brilliant **prodigies**[3] .

xi Cultivate Those Who Can Teach You.

L et friendly intercourse be a school of knowledge, and culture be taught through conversation: thus you make your friends your teachers and mingle the pleasures of conversation with the advantages of instruction. Sensible persons thus enjoy alternating pleasures: they reap applause for what they say, and gain instruction from what they hear. We are always attracted to others by our own interest, but in this case it is of a higher kind. Wise men frequent the houses of great noblemen not because they are temples of **vanity** [4], but as theatres of good breeding. There be gentlemen who have the credit of worldly wisdom, because they are not only themselves **oracles**[5] of all nobleness by their example and their behaviour, but those who surround them form a well-bred academy of worldly wisdom of the best and noblest kind.

12・自然與人工

素材與修飾。一切美都需要修飾和襯托。自然美若沒有能工巧匠的修飾加以昇華，也會變得野蠻粗俗。修飾會使惡者變善，而善者更善。自然幾乎從沒有給過我們最好的，我們必須依靠藝術加工對其進行修飾改變。若無人為修飾，再好的天然條件也會顯得粗俗而失去雅致之姿，完美事物若缺乏文化薰陶，其光輝也會大打折扣。若不加以訓練，人們都會顯得有些粗魯無禮。因此，盡善盡美之物均需人為加以雕飾。

---

1. barbaric [bɑr`bærɪk] adj. 野蠻的，粗野的
2. artifice [`ɑrtəfɪs] n. 技巧
3. recourse [rɪ`kors] n. 求援，求助
4. unpolished [`ʌn`pɑlɪʃt] adj. 未磨練的，粗魯的

xii Nature and Art:

m aterial and workmanship. There is no beauty unadorned and no excellence that would not become **barbaric**[1] if it were not supported by **artifice**[2] : this remedies the evil and improves the good. Nature scarcely ever gives us the very best; for that we must have **recourse**[3] to art. Without this the best of natural dispositions is uncultured, and half is lacking to any excellence if training is absent. Every one has something **unpolished**[4] without artificial training, and every kind of excellence needs some polish.

13・有時要三思而行，有時要憑藉直覺

人生就是一場與人類邪惡較量的戰爭。狡詐者的武器無非是玩弄心計——它常常表裏不一，聲東擊西，假裝瞄準一個目標，然後煞有其事佯攻一番，但其實心底卻在暗自鎖定別人不留心的靶子，然後伺機施以致命一擊，總是要隱藏自己的真實意圖。有時它會故意洩露自己的心思來吸引對手的注意，然後突然出奇制勝。明察秋毫之人對此種伎倆往往靜觀默察，然後加以阻攔，審慎伏擊。觀其表面張揚之意而逆向操作，可即刻識破其虛假意向。聰明人常常會忽略對方的第一意圖，以便引出其第二乃至第三意圖。玩弄詭計者一旦發現自己的陰謀敗露，便立刻偽裝得更精巧，往往以吐露真言而引人上鉤。他們改變戰術，故作憨厚誠實之態，有時會假意使用推心置腹的坦誠態度，然而骨子裏藏著的卻仍是狡詐之心。不過，其對手會越來越小心防範，總能洞察其每一步行動光鮮外表下的陰暗之處，因為**越是簡單的東西就越是複雜**。蛇怪皮宋竭其心智與阿波羅的洞察之光搏鬥的情形就是如此。

---

1. dexterity [dɛksˋtɛrətɪ] n. 靈巧，機敏
2. strike home　擊中要害
3. game [gem] n. 獵物，為食用或娛樂而捕獵的野生動物、飛禽或魚
4. lurk [lɝk] vi. 潛藏，潛伏，埋伏
5. feint [fent] n. 假象，偽裝，假裝
6. guile [gaɪl] n. 狡詐，詭計

xiii Act sometimes on Second Thoughts, sometimes on First Impulse.

Man's life is a warfare against the malice of men. Sagacity fights with strategic changes of intention: it never does what it threatens, it aims only at escaping notice. It aims in the air with **dexterity**[1] and **strikes home**[2] in an unexpected direction, always seeking to conceal its **game**[3]. It lets a purpose appear in order to attract the opponent's attention, but then turns round and conquers by the unexpected. But a penetrating intelligence anticipates this by watchfulness and **lurks**[4] in ambush. It always understands the opposite of what the opponent wishes it to understand, and recognises every **feint**[5] of **guile**[6] . It lets the first impulse pass by and waits for the second, or even the third. Sagacity now rises to higher flights on seeing its artifice foreseen, and tries to deceive by truth itself, changes its game in order to change its deceit, and cheats by not cheating, and founds deception on the greatest **candour**[7] . But the opposing intelligence is on guard with increased watchfulness, and discovers the darkness concealed by the light and **deciphers**[8] every move, the more subtle because more simple. In this way the guile of the **Python**[9] combats the far **darting**[10] rays of Apollo.

---

7. candour [ˈkændɚ] vt. 直率，公正
8. decipher [dɪˈsaɪfɚ] vt. 譯解（密碼等），解釋
9. Python 皮宋，古希臘神話中從丟卡利翁大洪水的污泥裡孵出的蛇怪，後來被阿波羅神殺死在希臘帕爾納索斯山腳下。
10. dart [dɑrt] v. 飛奔，投擲

14 · 事情本身與做事方法

有真才實學還不夠,正如經院哲學家們所說,你還需要點「運氣」。一個人如果態度不好,他做什麼事都不會成功,甚至連理性與正義都會被扭曲變質。**一個人如果態度很好,做什麼事都會事半功倍**,即使你對別人說「不」,也會讓人樂意接受你的理由。好的態度能使年長的人顯出獨特的魅力。做事的方式非常重要,良好的舉止往往令人傾倒。高雅的行為會為生活帶來許多樂趣,令人愉悅的言行往往能以絕妙的方式幫你脫離困境。

---

1. scholastic [skə`læstɪk] n. 經院哲學家,學究,墨守成規者
2. gild [gɪld] v. 鍍金,虛飾,粉飾

xiv The Thing Itself and the Way It Is Done.

CC Substance" is not enough: "accident" is also required, as the **scholastics**[1] say. A bad manner spoils everything, even reason and justice; a good one supplies everything, **gilds**[2] a No, sweetens truth, and adds a touch of beauty to old age itself. The how plays a large part in affairs, a good manner steals into the affections. Fine behaviour is a joy in life, and a pleasant expression helps out of a difficulty in a remarkable way.

15・廣納智士

強者周圍多有謀臣略士，使之諸事順達；一旦強者由於自己的無知而陷入困境時，這些謀士自然會助其化險為夷，並代為辛勞苦戰。讓智者為我所用是一種難得的大德大才，遠遠勝過提格拉涅斯的野蠻趣味，提格拉涅斯總想讓被他征服的君主成為他的奴僕。最巧妙的方法就是讓那些在天賦上比你優越的人臣服於你，這是生活能給你的最好禮物。人生苦短，知海無涯，沒有知識的人生算不上是真正的人生。能夠不經苦讀便學有所成是大智慧的表現，即藉眾家之長擴展自己的才識，最後達到集眾家之大成。在這之後，你就可以代表大多數人在議會上發言，像多位智者透過你的嘴提供建議一樣，別人的辛苦成就了你的名聲。這樣的人會從那些最好的書中提煉出智慧的精髓。但是，如果你無法讓那些賢人成為你的奴僕，那就讓他們成為你的朋友。

---

1. minister [ˋmɪnɪstɚ] vt. 供給
2. champion [ˋtʃæmpɪən] n. 擁護者，戰士
3. extricate [ˋɛkstrɪˌket] vt. 使解脫，救出
4. moot [mut] adj. 未決議的，無實際意義的
5. barbarous [ˋbɑrbərəs] adj. 野蠻的，殘暴的，粗野的

xv Keep Ministering[1] Spirits.

I t is a privilege of the mighty to surround themselves with the champions[2] of intellect; these extricate[3] them from every fear of ignorance, these worry out for them the moot[4] points of every difficulty. 'Tis a rare greatness to make use of the wise, and far exceeds the barbarous [5]taste of Tigranes[6], who had a fancy for captive monarchs as his servants. It is a novel kind of supremacy, the best that life can offer, to have as servants by skill those who by nature are our masters. 'Tis a great thing to know, little to live: no real life without knowledge. There is remarkable cleverness in studying without study, in getting much by means of many, and through them all to become wise. Afterwards you speak in the council chamber on behalf of many, and as many sages speak through your mouth as were consulted beforehand: you thus obtain the fame of an oracle by others' toil. Such ministering spirits distil[7] the best books and serve up the quintessence[8] of wisdom. But he that cannot have sages in service should have them for his friends.

---

6. Tigranes 提格拉涅斯，公元前1世紀亞闗尼亞君主，曾征服帕提亞。對所有俘虜的君主十分輕慢、殘暴，常驅使他們為侍從。

7. distil [dɪˋstɪl] v. 提取…的精華

8. quintessence [kwɪnˋtɛsns] n. 精萃，精華，典範

16．知識與善念

會讓你不斷獲得成功。擁有聰明才智卻心術不正的人會變成一個惡魔。惡意常常毒害所有傑出人才，若又有知識助紂為虐，則危害更甚，縱然你智慧超群，也只會落得失敗的下場。有知識而無理智的人更是愚蠢至極。

17．變換做事風格

不要讓你的做事方式總是一成不變，這樣才能分散人們的注意力，尤其在有對手的情況下。不要總是憑第一反應行事，否則別人很快就會發現它們的相似之處，預知你的行動，從而挫敗你的計畫。直線飛行的鳥兒很容易被射殺，而要射殺一隻總是變換飛行路線的鳥兒就很難。但你也不要總是三思而後行，下一次別人就會識破你的意圖。你的敵人總是很警覺，所以你務必慎謀能斷，才能棋高一著。棋藝高超者絕不會走正中對方下懷的路數，更不會讓對手牽著自己的鼻子走。

---

1. continuance [kənˋtɪnjʊəns] n. 持續，繼續
2. wed [wɛd] vt. 使緊密結合
3. envenom [ɪnˋvɛnəm] v. 毒害
4. subtlety [ˋsʌtltɪ] n. 微妙
5. on the wing 在飛行中

xvi Knowledge and Good Intentions

together ensure **continuance**[1] of success. A fine intellect **wedded**[2] to a wicked will was always an unnatural monster. A wicked will **envenoms**[3] all excellences: helped by knowledge it only ruins with greater **subtlety**[4] . 'Tis a miserable superiority that only results in ruin. Knowledge without sense is double folly.

xvii Vary the Mode of Action;

not always the same way, so as to distract attention, especially if there be a rival. Not always from first impulse; they will soon recognise the uniformity, and by anticipating, frustrate your designs. It is easy to kill a bird **on the wing**[5] that flies straight: not so one that **twists**[6] . Nor always act on second thoughts: they can discern the plan the second time. The enemy is **on the watch**[7], great skill is required to **circumvent**[8] him. The **gamester**[9] never plays the card the opponent expects, still less that which he wants.

---

6. twist [twɪst] vi. 扭動，呈螺旋形
7. on the watch 留心，注意
8. circumvent [ˌsɝkəmˈvɛnt] vt. 智取
9. gamester [ˈgemstɚ] n. 體育比賽中不屈不撓者

18・實幹與實力

如果一個人沒有實力也沒有實幹精神，那他就無法出人頭地；如果一個人二者兼備，就會聲名顯赫。一個資質平庸的人如果具有實幹精神，會比一個天資聰穎但眼高手低的人更有成就。**努力工作是成名的代價**，不需要怎麼努力就能獲得的東西也沒什麼價值。有時候，一個人不能擔任要職往往並非由於缺少才幹，而只是因為缺乏實幹的精神。選擇在大事適度表現也不願在小事上嶄露頭角，這樣的人可以以性格豁達為藉口。可是如果你可以有所作為卻甘於平庸，這就沒有藉口可以辯解。因此，除了天賦和後天培養之外，實幹精神是確保成功的關鍵。

---

1. mediocrity [ˌmidɪˋɑkrətɪ] n. 平常，平庸之才
2. seal [sil] n. 封鉛，封條

xviii Application and Ability.

There is no attaining eminence without both, and where they unite there is the greatest eminence. **Mediocrity**[1] obtains more with application than superiority without it. Work is the price which is paid for reputation. What costs little is little worth. Even for the highest posts it is only in some cases application that is wanting, rarely the talent. To prefer moderate success in great things than eminence in a humble post has the excuse of a generous mind, but not so to be content with humble mediocrity when you could shine among the highest. Thus nature and art are both needed, and application sets on them the **seal**[2] .

19・做事之初，勿讓人抱過高期望

成名之後的發展難以滿足人們之前的期望，這是在有成就者身上常見的不幸。現實永遠都比不上想像，完美的東西很容易想像但很難實現。想像與希望的結合會孕育出比事物本身更多的東西。不管這東西多麼美好，總是不能達到人們的期望。而當人們發現自己過高的期望沒有被實現時，他們就很容易幻滅，而不是產生崇拜之情。希望是真實的偽裝，須要明察秋毫，以便讓實際的快樂超過我們原有的期望。一開始的幾次良好嘗試就足夠喚起人們的好奇心，但不保證一定會達到最終目標。如果現實比我們計畫的好，或比我們原來預想的要好，會有出人意料的驚喜。此法則不適用於惡的事物，同樣誇大的期望對它們來說反而是莫大的幫助：當一種惡被事先誇大，而人們後來發現後果並非如此嚴重時，就會轉而對它抱寬容態度。於是原以為具有毀滅性的事物後來倒變得似乎可以忍受了。

---

1. exorbitant [ɪgˋzɔrbətənt] adj. 過度的，過高的
2. disillusionise [ˌdɪsɪˋluʒənaɪz]v. 使幻滅，使覺醒
3. falsifier [ˋfɔlsəˌfaɪɚ] n. 弄虛作假者，偽造者，撒謊的人
4. pledge [plɛdʒ] vt. 保證，使發誓

xix Arouse No Exaggerated Expectations on Entering.

It is the usual ill-luck of all celebrities not to fulfil afterwards the expectations beforehand formed of them. The real can never equal the imagined, for it is easy to form ideals but very difficult to realise them. Imagination weds Hope and gives birth to much more than things are in themselves. However great the excellences, they never suffice to fulfil expectations, and as men find themselves disappointed with their **exorbitant**[1] expectations they are more ready to be **disillusionised**[2] than to admire. Hope is a great **falsifier**[3] of truth; let skill guard against this by ensuring that fruition exceeds desire. A few creditable attempts at the beginning are sufficient to arouse curiosity without **pledging**[4] one to the final object. It is better that reality should surpass the design and is better than was thought. This rule does not apply to the wicked, for the same exaggeration is a great aid to them; they are defeated amid general applause, and what seemed at first extreme ruin comes to be thought quite bearable.

20・人需生逢其時

時勢造英雄。並非每個人都覺得自己生逢其時，即使他知道自己
生逢其時，也未必明白如何伺機而動。有些人如果生在一個更
好的時代或許會更有價值，因為善良美好的事物並不總是獲得勝利。
世間萬事皆有其時，識時務者為俊傑。智者有一個優勢：智者是永生
的。縱然一時不得志，總還會有許多別的機會可讓他一展風采。

21・好運與成功之道

運氣自有其規律。對智者來說，運氣並非都是機遇，也可以藉助
努力獲得。有些人僅僅滿足於滿懷信心地守在命運女神的門
口，等待她打開大門。有些人做得好一些，他們昂首闊步邁進命運之
門，憑藉美德與勇氣贏得智慧女神的青睞。真正的成功哲理是依靠智
慧與謹慎——因為世間沒有好運與厄運之分，只有聰明與愚蠢之別。

---

1. press forward 奮力向前
2. valour [`vælɚ] n. 英勇，勇猛
3. umpire [`ʌmpaɪr] n. 仲裁人，裁判員

xx A Man of the Age.

The rarest individuals depend on their age. It is not every one that finds the age he deserves, and even when he finds it he does not always know how to utilise it. Some men have been worthy of a better century, for every species of good does not always triumph. Things have their period; even excellences are subject to fashion. The sage has one advantage: he is immortal. If this is not his century many others will be.

xxi The Art of Being Lucky.

There are rules of luck: it is not all chance with the wise: it can be assisted by care. Some content themselves with placing themselves confidently at the gate of Fortune, waiting till she opens it. Others do better, and **press forward**[1] and profit by their clever boldness, reaching the goddess and winning her favour on the wings of their virtue and **valour**[2] . But on a true philosophy there is no other **umpire**[3] than virtue and insight; for there is no luck or ill-luck except wisdom and the reverse.

22 · 學以致用

智者用高雅趣味和滿腹學識來武裝自己，其所言不是市井瑣談，而是經世致用之學。他們妙語如珠，行為勇武，懂得適時而言、適時而行。有時透過詼諧玩笑的方式比一本正經的教誨更有效。閒聊之中傳達出的智慧雖然隨意，但比高雅的論道更有用。

23 · 白璧不可有微瑕

這是稱為完美的必需條件。世人都不免有某些身體上或道德上的缺陷，他們對此聽任，因為他們覺得自己可以輕而易舉地將之克服。但觀察敏銳的其他人卻經常因發現一個品格高尚的人也有細微的缺陷而為之惋惜。就算是一抹流雲也能遮住整個太陽的光輝。同樣地，那些不懷好意的人很快就會發現我們榮譽上的弱點，並持續關注，以期有利可圖。最高超的技巧就是把這些弱點變成裝飾，所以凱撒大帝才用桂冠來掩飾他天生的缺陷。

---

1. erudition [ˌɛrjʊˋdɪʃən] n. 博學
2. copious [ˋkopɪəs] adj. 很多的，豐富的，廣識的
3. jest [dʒɛst] n. 笑話，俏皮話
4. seven arts「七藝」，指大學文科包括的七門課程：邏輯、語法、修辭、數學、幾何、天文、音樂。

xxii A Man of Knowledge to the Point.

W ise men arm themselves with tasteful and elegant **erudition**[1] ; a practical knowledge of what is going on not of a common kind but more like an expert. They possess a **copious**[2] store of wise and witty sayings, and of noble deeds, and know how to employ them on fitting occasions. More is often taught by a **jest**[3] than by the most serious teaching. Pat knowledge helps some more than the **seven arts**[4], be they ever so liberal.

xxiii Be Spotless:

t he **indispensable**[5] condition of perfection. Few live without some weak point, either physical or moral, which they **pamper**[6] because they could easily cure it. The keenness of others often regrets to see a slight defect attaching itself to a whole assembly of elevated qualities, and yet a single cloud can hide the whole of the sun. There are likewise **patches**[7] on our reputation which ill-will soon finds out and is continually noticing. The highest skill is to transform them into ornament. So **Caesar hid his natural defects with the laurel**[8] .

---

5. indispensable [ˌɪndɪsˈpɛnsəbl] adj. 不可缺少的，絕對必要的

6. pamper [ˈpæmpɚ] v. 縱容

7. patch [pætʃ] n. 斑紋，斑點

8. 凱撒曾以桂冠掩飾禿頭。

24 · 控制你的想像力

有時你需要矯正它，有時需要激發它。這對我們的幸福甚為重要，甚至能把理性引入正途。有時候，想像力就像是暴君，不滿足於僅僅做個旁觀者，而會影響，甚至經常主宰你的生活，讓你的生活變得時而愉快時而痛苦。它會讓我們自滿或不知足。有些人一直在承受自己行為帶來的惡果，想像力便讓他們不得解脫。對另一些人來說，想像力用充滿喜悅的幻境給他們承諾了幸福和奇遇。如果我們不用最謹慎的自制來羈束想像力，那它什麼都做得出來。

25 · 見微知著，自有方寸

演說的藝術曾一度被視為最高的藝術，但現在看來，這已經不夠了，我們還須見微知著——特別是需要我們自己解開謎團的時候。對於自己很難理解的東西，也很難拿出來說服別人。但另一方面，也有些人假裝善於窺測他人內心，讀懂別人的心思。與我們相關的最重要的真相往往只是冰山一角，只要留心，我們就能完全明白話中的意思。對你看起來有利之事寧可信其無；而對你看起來不利之事寧可信其有。

---

1. tyrannize [ˋtɪrəˌnaɪz] vi. 施行暴政，實施集權統治，橫行霸道
2. mortify [ˋmɔrtəˌfaɪ] vt. 使感到羞辱，使蒙受屈辱
3. delusion [dɪˋluʒən] n. 錯覺　4. subjection [səbˋdʒɛkʃən] n. 征服
5. hint [hɪnt] n. 暗示，提示 take a hint 暗示
6. diviner [dəˋvaɪnɚ] n. 占卜者，占卦的人　7. lynx [lɪŋks] n. 山貓

xxiv Keep the Imagination Under Control;

S ometimes correcting, sometimes assisting it. For it is all-important for our happiness, and even sets the reason right. It can **tyrannize**[1], and is not content with looking on, but influences and even often dominates life, causing it to be happy or burdensome according to the folly to which it leads. For it makes us either contented or discontented with ourselves. Before some it continually holds up the penalties of action, and becomes the **mortifying**[2] lash of these fools. To others it promises happiness and adventure with blissful **delusion**[3] . It can do all this unless the most prudent self-control keeps it in **subjection**[4] .

xxv Know How to Take a Hint[5].

❯ T was once the art of arts to be able to discourse; now 'tis no longer sufficient. We must know how to take a hint, especially in disabusing ourselves. He cannot make himself understood who does not himself easily understand. But on the other hand there are pretended **diviners**[6] of the heart and **lynxes**[7] of the intentions. The very truths which concern us most can only be half spoken, but with attention we can grasp the whole meaning. When you hear anything favourable keep a tight rein on your credulity; if unfavourable, give it the spur.

26 · 洞察他人的弱點

這是讓意志力付諸行動的訣竅，除了決心之外，更需技巧。你必須知道如何洞察他人的內心。一個人自願做一件事的時候一定有他特別的動機，這動機根據個人品味不同而有所差別。人皆有所求，有人重名，有人重利，而大多數人都重享樂。技巧便在於弄清楚究竟哪一種事物可以令哪些人趨之若鶩。知道一個人最主要的動機，就等於拿到了打開他心靈之門的鑰匙。好好利用這種「原動力」，它不一定總是其本性中最高尚的，反而經常是最卑下的部分，因為世上心術不正者總是多於循規蹈矩者。首先，你要揣測他的興趣主要在哪裡，然後用言語試探他，再施以誘惑，就一定會讓他上鉤。

---

1. thumbscrew [`θʌm͵skru] n. 拇指夾（過去使用的一種用於壓迫拇指的刑具）
2. volition [vo`lɪʃən] n. 意志（力），決心，決斷
3. idolater [aɪ`dɑlətɚ] n. 偶像崇拜者，皈依者，追星族
4. mainspring [`men͵sprɪŋ] n. （主要）動力，主要動機
5. have resort to 採用，使用（手段）

xxvi Find out Each Man's Thumbscrew[1] .

❯ Tis the art of setting their wills in action. It needs more skill than
resolution. You must know where to get at any one. Every **volition**[2] has
a special motive which varies according to taste. All men are **idolaters**[3],
some of fame, others of self-interest, most of pleasure. Skill consists in
knowing these idols in order to bring them into play. Knowing any man's
mainspring[4] of motive you have as it were the key to his will. **Have resort
to**[5] primary motors, which are not always the highest but more often the
lowest part of his nature: there are more dispositions badly organised
than well. First guess a man's ruling passion, appeal to it by a word, set it
in motion by temptation, and you will **infallibly**[6] give **checkmate**[7] to his
freedom of will.

---

6. infallibly [ɪnˋfæləblɪ] adv. 絕對無誤地
7. checkmate [ˋtʃɛkˋmet] n. 擒王棋；完全失敗

27·與其博，不如精

要想有所成就應重質而非量。物以稀為貴，量多則降價。就連人類社會中的偉人在真實生活中也往往是矮子。有些人以厚度評價一本書的好壞，好像它們不是為了鍛鍊我們的智力而是為了鍛鍊我們的臂力。博而不精永遠無法擺脫平庸，不幸的是，世界上有很多天才總想門門皆精，結果卻往往未能如願。如果你專精於某一方面，必能成為這一方面的專家；若專攻於重要的事務，則必得美名。

28·萬事須求超然脫俗

首先，品味必須脫俗。啊，偉大的智者，當你發現你的行為取悅大眾的時候，你能不坐立難安嗎？明智的人從來不會滿足於世俗間冗餘的掌聲。有些人就好像仰人鼻息的變色龍，情願吞食眾人吐出的濁氣，卻不肯呼吸阿波羅的和煦輕風。其次，在見識上也不要從眾。對於庸眾驚歎的事情無須津津樂道，因為這種驚歎不過是源於無知。**當庸眾大驚小怪時，有智慧的人總會冷眼旁觀，像是在看一齣鬧劇。**

---

1. intensity [ɪn`tɛnsətɪ] n. 強度，密度
2. brawn [brɔn] n. 強壯的肌肉，體力，腕力
3. at home 精通的
4. 本句意為：Unfortunately, most geniuses try to do well in everything, but as a result they do well in nothing.

xxvii Prize Intensity¹ more than Extent.

Excellence resides in quality not in quantity. The best is always few and rare: much lowers value. Even among men giants are commonly the real dwarfs. Some reckon books by the thickness, as if they were written to try the **brawn**² more than the brain. Extent alone never rises above mediocrity: **it is the misfortune of universal geniuses that in attempting to be at home³ everywhere, are so nowhere.** ⁴Intensity gives eminence, and rises to the heroic in matters **sublime**⁵ .

xxviii Common in Nothing.

First, not in taste. O great and wise, to be **ill at ease**⁶ when your deeds please the **mob**⁷ ! The excesses of popular applause never satisfy the sensible. Some there are such **chameleons**⁸ of popularity that they find enjoyment not in the sweet savours of **Apollo**⁹ but in the breath of the mob. Secondly, not in intelligence. Take no pleasure in the wonder of the mob, for ignorance never gets beyond wonder. While vulgar folly wonders wisdom watches for the trick.

---

5. sublime [sə`blaɪm] adj. 崇高的，卓越的
6. ill at ease 不安的
7. mob [mɑb] n. [集合名詞]暴徒，烏合之眾，（賊等的）一群
8. chameleon [kə`miljən] n. 變色龍
9. Apoll n. 阿波羅，美男子，太陽神

29 · 剛正不阿的品德

　　一個剛正不阿的人會堅定地站在正義的一方，無論是被大眾輿論施壓還是暴君以武力威脅，都無法讓他放棄正義。可誰願意為了正義而甘願像鳳凰一樣涅槃呢？正直剛正之人真是寥寥無幾！確實，有很多人讚揚這種品德，但是——只是讚揚別人，讓別的人堅持正義。有危難來臨時，虛偽的人會否認它，而政客會隱藏它。當友誼、權力甚至個人利益與堅持正義相悖時，很多人寧願不要這種品德。狡猾的人會找一些似是而非的藉口替自己辯解，不與上司或大眾作對。但是，那些誠實的、一貫堅持正義的人會覺得掩飾是種背叛，情願做光明磊落的剛正不阿者而不願做所謂的聰明人，他們總是選擇和真理站在一起。如果他們脫離了某個團體，並不是因為他們善變，而是因為這個團體裏的其他人先拋棄了真理。

---

1. rectitude [ˋrɛktəˌtjud] n. 正直，公正，清廉
2. sect [sɛkt] n. 部分，段　　3. tenacity [tɪˋnæsətɪ] n. 堅韌
4. transgress [trænsˋgrɛs] vt. 違反，犯罪
5. Phoenix 鳳凰，傳說中阿拉伯地區的一種鳥。在希臘神話中，這種鳥在生活一段時間後，便會用香料築成一個巢，把自己燒成灰燼。從灰燼中飛出一隻新的鳳凰。Phoenix 也是耶穌復活的象徵。

xxix A Man of Rectitude[1]

C lings to the **sect**[2] of right with such **tenacity**[3] of purpose that neither the passions of the mob nor the violence of the tyrant can ever cause him to **transgress**[4] the bounds of right. But who shall be such a **Phoenix**[5] of equity? What a scanty following has rectitude! Many praise it indeed, but – for others. Others follow it till danger threatens; then the false deny it, the **politic**[6] conceal it. For it cares not if it fights with friendship, power, or even self-interest: then comes the danger of **desertion**[7] . Then astute men make plausible distinctions so as not to stand in the way of their superiors or of reasons of state. But the straightforward and constant regard **dissimulation**[8] as a kind of **treason**[9], and **set more store on**[10] tenacity than on **sagacity**[11] . Such are always to be found on the side of truth, and if they desert a party, they do not change from **fickleness**[12], but because the others have first deserted truth.

---

6. politic [ˈpɑləˌtɪk] adj. 策略性的   7. desertion [dɪˈzɝʃən] n. 丟掉，遺棄
8. dissimulation [dɪˌsɪmjəˈleʃən] n. 掩飾，虛偽，裝糊塗
9. treason [ˈtrizn] n. 叛逆，通敵，背信   10. set store on 重視，喜歡
11. sagacity [səˈɡæsətɪ] n. 睿智，聰敏
12. fickleness [ˈfɪkəlnəs] n. 浮躁，變化無常

30 · 不要做出有損聲譽的事情

千萬不要做那些只會讓你聲名狼藉而非聲名遠播的狂熱之事。一個謹慎的人應擺脫一切任性。有些人品味很奇怪，對於智者所拒斥的一切東西都來者不拒，任何奇癖怪行都讓他們引以為樂。這樣確實會讓他們聲名大噪，但多半只是淪為笑柄，而並非交相稱讚。即便是追求智慧的時候，聰明謹慎之人也應該避免矯揉造作和拋頭露面，更不要說在那些會使他們的跟隨者顯得滑稽的場合了。這些無須具體舉例，因為許多司空見慣的嘲諷事例已足以說明問題。

31 · 走運者，交之；霉運者，斷之

厄運通常是由愚蠢所招致。沒有什麼疾病比霉運傳染得更快了。所以即便對於小惡也不能開門，因為門外潛伏著更多的大惡。打牌時最厲害的技巧就在於知道什麼時候該扔牌。現在手裏最小的牌也比最後可能出現的大牌要好得多。如果你還存有疑慮，那就跟隨那些聰慧謹慎的人吧，因為這些人或早或晚都會走運的。

---

1. naught [nɔt] n. 零　2. fad [fæd] n. 時尚，一時流行的
3. notoriety [ˌnotəˈraɪətɪ] n. 惡名，醜名，聲名狼藉
4. bizarre [bɪˈzɑr] adj. 奇異的（指態度、容貌、款式等）
5. repudiate [rɪˈpjudɪˌet] v. 批判　6. make profession of 公開宣稱
7. single out 挑選

xxx Have Naught[1] to Do with Occupations of Ill-repute,

S till less with **fads**[2] that bring more **notoriety**[3] than repute. There are many fanciful sects, and from all the prudent man has to flee. There are **bizarre**[4] tastes that always take to their heart all that wise men **repudiate**[5] ; they live in love with singularity. This may make them well known indeed, but more as objects of ridicule than of repute. A cautious man does not even **make profession of** [6] his wisdom, still less of those matters that make their followers ridiculous. These need not be specified, for common contempt has sufficiently **singled them out**[7] .

xxxi Select the Lucky and Avoid the Unlucky.

I ll-luck is generally the penalty of folly, and there is no disease so **contagious**[8] to those who share in it. Never open the door to a lesser evil, for other and greater ones invariably **slink in**[9] after it. The greatest skill at cards is to know when to **discard**[10] ; the smallest of current trumps is worth more than the **ace**[11] of trumps of the last game. When in doubt, **follow the suit**[12] of the wise and prudent; sooner or later they will win the odd trick.

---

8. contagious [kən`tedʒəs] adj. 傳染性的，會感染的
9. slink [slɪŋk] v. 潛逃　slink in 偷偷進入
10. discard [dɪs`kɑrd] vt. 丟棄，拋棄　　11. ace [es] n. （紙牌或骰子）么點
12. follow the suit 跟著做，跟著出同花色的牌

32・贏得樂善好施的美譽

對那些位高權重的人來說，樂善好施是最高的榮耀，有了它，國王就能獲得眾人的好感與讚譽。對一個統治者來說，他有一個好處就是比別人都有能力行更多的善。所謂朋友無非是那些能夠幫助你做事的人。另一方面，也有人故意不想幫助別人，倒不是因為怕麻煩，而是因為這種人性格怪異。不管做什麼事，他們都與神聖的、與人為善的準則背道而馳。

---

1. gracious [ˋgreʃəs] adj. 親切的，高尚的
2. prerogative [prɪˋrɑgətɪv] n. 特權
3. lay themselves out 竭盡全力的
4. on account of 由於

xxxii Have the Reputation of Being Gracious.

❯ Tis the chief glory of the high and mighty to be **gracious**[1], a **prerogative**[2] of kings to conquer universal goodwill. That is the great advantage of a commanding position – to be able to do more good than others. Those make friends who do friendly acts. On the other hand, there are some who **lay themselves out**[3] for not being gracious, not **on account of** [4] the difficulty, but from a bad disposition. In all things they are the opposite of Divine grace.

33 · 知道如何退出

如果說學會如何拒絕是人生中很重要的一堂課，那麼學會如何把自己從事物和人中抽離出來則更為重要。有些事情並不重要，卻要耗費寶貴的時間。忙著做一些與己無關的事情比什麼都不做還要糟糕。一個小心謹慎的人不但要做到不管他人的閒事，還需確保別人不會來管他的閒事。如果你太依賴他人，你就會失去自我。對朋友也是這樣，你不能濫用朋友提供的幫助，也不能要求提供過分的幫助。過猶不及，與人交往時尤其如此。如果你能夠明智地掌握其中的分寸，你就能得到他人的青睞與尊重。能做到有理有節是難能可貴的，這將使你受益無窮。因此，你能自由地選擇那些美好事物，而決不會違反那未曾形成書面文字的高雅準則。

---

1. extraneous [ɛkˋstrenɪəs] adj. 無關係的，外來的
2. goodwill [ˋgʊdˋwɪl] n. 善意，親切
3. esteem [ɪsˋtim] n. 尊敬，尊重
4. boon [bun] n. 恩惠，實惠，福利

xxxiii Know How to Withdraw.

If it is a great lesson in life to know how to deny, it is a still greater to know how to deny oneself as regards both affairs and persons. There are **extraneous**[1] occupations which eat away precious time. To be occupied in what does not concern you is worse than doing nothing. It is not enough for a careful man not to interfere with others, he must see that they do not interfere with him. One is not obliged to belong so much to all as not to belong at all to oneself. So with friends, their help should not be abused or more demanded from them than they themselves will grant. All excess is a failing, but above all in personal intercourse. A wise moderation in this best preserves the **goodwill**[2] and **esteem**[3] of all, for by this means that precious **boon**[4] of courtesy is not gradually worn away. Thus you preserve your genius free to select the elect, and never sin against the unwritten laws of good taste.

34 · 瞭解己之所長

要瞭解什麼是自己最重要的才能,如果將之加以培養,其他才能也會跟著發展。如果世人都知道自己的強項,他們定都能夠在某方面取得卓越成就。要留心自己在哪一方面超越別人,然後專攻這一方面。有些人明察善斷,有些人勇氣過人。大多數人浪費了自己天生的才能,結果一事無成。隨著時間的流逝,那曾經點燃我們激情的東西慢慢成空,悔之晚矣。

---

1. aptitude [ˈæptəˌtjud] n. 智能,自然傾向

xxxiv Know Your Strongest Point –

Your pre-eminent gift; cultivate that and you will assist the rest. Every one would have excelled in something if he had known his strong point. Notice in what quality you surpass, and take charge of that. In some judgment excels, in others valour. Most do violence to their natural **aptitude**[1], and thus attain superiority in nothing. Time disillusionises us too late of what first flattered the passions.

35 · 遇事謹慎權衡，
尤其是那些最重要的事

愚人之所以失敗，就是敗在缺乏慎重思考。他們對事情的思考總是不透徹，看不出其中的利弊，更別說下苦工去做了。也有人本末倒置，往往忽略重要的大事，卻重視那些雞毛蒜皮的瑣事。還有很多人絕不會昏了頭，因為他們本來就沒有頭腦。有些事情需要我們細心觀察，才能謹記在心。聰明人事不分大小，必審慎對待，但其中又有分別，對特別困難的事情尤其會詳加斟酌，想想是不是還有自己沒有想到的地方。只有這樣，他們的分析能力才能與理解能力一起發展。

---

1. come to grief 遭難，受傷，失敗
2. import [ɪmˋport] vi. 有關係，有重要性
3. thenceforth [ˌðɛnsˋforθ] adv. 從那時，其後

xxxv Think over Things, Most over the Most Important.

A ll fools **come to grief** [1] from want of thought. They never see even the half of things, and as they do not observe their own loss or gain, still less do they apply any diligence to them. Some make much of what **imports**[2] little and little of much, always weighing in the wrong scale. Many never lose their common sense, because they have none to lose. There are matters which should be observed with the closest attention of the mind, and **thenceforth**[3] kept in its lowest depths. The wise man thinks over everything, but with a difference, most profoundly where there is some profound difficulty, and thinks that perhaps there is more in it than he thinks. Thus his comprehension extends as far as his apprehension.

36 · 對自己的時運心中有數

這比弄清你的性格還要重要。比如人到40歲時還要向醫聖希波克拉底要健康，可謂愚蠢；若此時還要向塞內加要智慧，那就更加愚不可及。在等待時來運轉的時候，學會如何引導你的時運需要高超的技巧。雖然我們無法預測它的路線，因為它讓人捉摸不定，但是既然它不時地會給人機會，那我們就可以一邊等待一邊有所作為，才能在時機到來的時候抓住它。當你發現命運之神垂青於你的時候，就要勇敢地大步前進，因為命運之神喜歡勇敢的人，而且，作為一個女神，她也喜歡年輕人。但是，如果你運氣不佳，那就韜光養晦，等待時機，不要讓自己變得更加不幸。

---

1. refrain [rɪ`fren] vi. 節制，避免，制止
2. Hippocrates [hɪ`pɑkrə,tiz] n. 希波克拉底（約公元前460年~約公元前370年，古希臘醫師，稱醫藥之父）
3. Seneca [`sɛnɪkə]：　塞內加（約公元前4年～公元65年）古羅馬政治家、哲學家、悲劇作家。生於西班牙。受過很好的修辭教育，對哲學也頗有興趣，是晚期

xxxvi In Acting or Refraining[1], Weigh Your Luck.

More depends on that than on noticing your temperament. If he is a fool who at forty applies to **Hippocrates**[2] for health, still more is he one who then first applies to **Seneca**[3] for wisdom. It is a great piece of skill to know how to guide your luck even while waiting for it. For something is to be done with it by waiting so as to use it at the proper moment, since it has periods and offers opportunities, though one cannot calculate its path, its steps are so irregular. When you find Fortune favourable, stride boldly forward, for she favours the bold and, being a woman, the young. But if you have bad luck, keep retired so as not to redouble the influence of your unlucky star.

斯多噶派的代表。他官至元老，公元41年被流放科西嘉島，49年被召回，成為皇儲尼祿的教師。54年尼祿即位後輔佐朝政，62年退出政界，65年因涉嫌反尼祿陰謀受命自殺。他一生撰寫過不少倫理哲學著作，寫有一篇諷刺散文《克勞狄烏斯變瓜記》和《瘋狂的赫拉克勒斯》、《特洛伊婦女》、《美狄亞》等9部悲劇。

37 · 學會諷刺，知道如何使用它們

與人相處時此點最為奧妙。人們經常用諷刺的言語來試探別人的情緒如何，並經常由此而洞見對方的心思。有些諷刺是惡毒的、無禮的，出於嫉妒和衝動，這就像是讓人意想不到的閃電一樣，可立即讓你身敗名裂。許多人就因為聽到這種諷刺的言語而和親密的上司或下屬斷交，而他們之間的關係本來是連公眾的諷刺或私底下的陰謀都無法撼動的。另一方面，有些諷刺卻對我們有利，能鞏固並提高我們的聲望。但是說這些話的時候技巧越是高超，我們聽的時候就越是要謹慎，越要有預見力。通曉關於惡的知識本身就是一種防禦，預見到子彈飛來，常常可以免受其害。

---

1. touchstone [ˈtʌtʃˌston] n. 試金石，標準
2. malicious [məˈlɪʃəs] adj. 懷惡意的，惡毒的
3. insolent [ˈɪnsələnt] adj. 傲慢的，無禮的，侮慢的
4. insinuation [ɪnˌsɪnjʊˈeʃən] n. 暗示，暗諷
5. malevolence [məˈlɛvələns] n. 惡意，狠毒

xxxvii Keep a Store of Sarcasms, and know How to Use Them.

This is the point of greatest tact in human intercourse. Such sarcasms are often thrown out to test men's moods, and by their means one often obtains the most subtle and penetrating **touchstone**[1] of the heart. Other sarcasms are **malicious**[2], **insolent**[3], poisoned by envy or envenomed by passion, unexpected flashes which destroy at once all favour and esteem. Struck by the slightest word of this kind, many fall away from the closest intimacy with superiors or inferiors which could not be the slightest shaken by a whole conspiracy of popular **insinuation**[4] or private **malevolence**[5]. Other sarcasms, on the other hand, work favourably, confirming and assisting one's reputation. But the greater the skill with which they are launched, the greater the caution with which they should be received and the foresight with which they should he foreseen. For here a knowledge of the evil is in itself a means of defence, and a shot foreseen always misses its mark.

38 · 功成身退，見好就收

所有最出色的玩家均奉行不悖。退得妙恰如進得巧。一旦獲得足夠的成功，即便是尚有更多的成功在等待，那也必須見好就收。長時間的好運總是不可靠的。比較安全的情況是好運和厄運交錯而至，如果苦中有樂就更好了。爬得越高，摔得越慘。有時候幸運女神越是寵幸你，那麼成功持續的時間就越短。如果她把某個人長時間扛在肩上，那她一定很快就會感到疲倦。

39 · 知道事物何時成熟並享受之

自然界的一切事物都會有成熟的一天，在這之前，它們會一直不斷地成長進步，在這之後，它們就會漸趨衰弱凋敗。至於人工之作，能臻於至善者，萬中無一。品味高雅的人懂得如何欣賞每一件臻於完美的東西。並非人人都會這樣做；也並非人人都能知道其中奧妙。理智也有其成熟之時，不論是瞭解其價值而善加利用，還是將其用來交換別的東西，在這個時刻都最合適。

---

1. gallant [ˋɡælənt] adj. 英勇的，豪俠的
2. infusion [ɪnˋfjuʒən] n. 灌輸
3. heap [hip] n. 堆，大量，許多

xxxviii Leave Your Luck While Winning.

A ll the best players do it. A fine retreat is as good as a **gallant**[1] attack. Bring your exploits under cover when there are enough, or even when there are many of them. Luck long lasting was ever suspicious; interrupted seems safer, and is even sweeter to the taste for a little **infusion**[2] of bitter-sweet. The higher the **heap**[3] of luck, the greater the risk of a slip, and down comes all. Fortune pays you sometimes for the intensity of her favours by the shortness of their duration. She soon tires of carrying any one long on her shoulders.

xxxix Recognise when Things are Ripe, and Then Enjoy Them.

T he works of nature all reach a certain point of maturity; up to that they improve, after that they degenerate. Few works of art reach such a point that they cannot be improved. It is an especial privilege of good taste to enjoy everything at its ripest. Not all can do this, nor do all who can know this. There is a ripening point too for fruits of intellect; it is well to know this both for their value in use and for their value in exchange.

40・人們的善意

獲得普遍尊敬固然是一件大事，但獲得眾人的善意卻更為重要。要想達到這一目的，一方面要靠天賦，但更要靠實踐。天賦是基礎，而實踐則在此基礎上蓋起了高樓大廈。人們常常認為，只要有了名聲，就會很容易獲得人們的好感，但單靠才華是遠遠不夠的，還要行善才能讓人們對你產生好感。用雙手做一切善事，不但要善言，更要善行。要想人愛己，己須先愛人。謙恭是偉人們的魅力之一。行之在前，言之在後。先解甲，後為文，如果你贏得文人雅士的好感，這種好感就會永恆不滅，亙古長存。

---

1. suffice [sə`faɪs] vt. 使滿足，滿足…的需要

xl The Goodwill of People.

❯ Tis much to gain universal admiration; more, universal love. Something depends on natural disposition, more on practice: the first founds, the second then builds on that foundation. Brilliant parts **suffice**[1] not, though they are presupposed; win good opinion and 'tis easy to win goodwill. Kindly acts besides are required to produce kindly feelings, doing good with both hands, good words and better deeds, loving so as to be loved. Courtesy is the politic witchery of great personages. First lay hand on deeds and then on pens; words follow swords; for there is goodwill to be won among writers, and it is eternal.

41.勿誇大其辭

特別注意不要濫用誇張的言辭，這樣才不會有違真理，也不會使人對你的判斷心存疑慮。誇大其辭是對判斷力的濫用，只會暴露出你知識和品味的欠缺。對事物的讚揚會引起人們對該事物的好奇，滋生欲望，但如果被讚美之物的價值與稱讚不匹配——一般情況都是這樣——之後人們就會感到被欺騙與愚弄，便會生出報復心理，對讚美者和被讚美者都不屑一顧。所以謹慎之人懂得慎言，與其言過其實，不如言之未逮。卓越非凡的事物十分少見，所以你不宜濫下褒辭。言過其實是一種謊話，不僅會讓別人覺得你沒有品味，而且更糟的是會失去人們對你的好感。

---

1. in superlatives 誇張地，言過其實地，過火的
2. prodigality [ˌprɑdɪˈgælətɪ] n. 浪費，揮霍
3. beget [bɪˈgɛt] vt. 招致，產生，引起
4. deception [dɪˈsɛpʃən] n. 欺騙，詭計
5. 被讚美的事物和讚美者

xli Never Exaggerate.

It is an important object of attention not to talk **in superlatives**[1], so as neither to offend against truth nor to give a mean idea of one's understanding. Exaggeration is a **prodigality**[2] of the judgment which shows the narrowness of one's knowledge or one's taste. Praise arouses lively curiosity, **begets**[3] desire, and if afterwards the value does not correspond to the price, as generally happens, expectation revolts against the **deception**[4], and revenges itself by under-estimating **the thing recommended and the person recommending**[5] . A prudent man goes more cautiously to work, and prefers to err by omission than by commission. Extraordinary things are rare, therefore moderate ordinary valuation. Exaggeration is a branch of lying, and you lose by it the credit of good taste, which is much, and of good sense, which is more.

42 · 生而為王

生而有治人之術是一種超凡的神秘力量，這種力量不是來自後天的苦心經營，而是與生俱來的王者天性。所有人都會莫名地臣服於他，尊崇他神秘的力量和天生的權威。這種人具有貴人氣概，其才德可以為人君，其天運可以成獅王。他們令人敬畏，心悅誠服。如果他們還有別的天賦，那他們就會是天生的政治界風雲人物。別人的長篇大論還不如他們一個手勢來得有效。

---

1. connatural [kə`nætʃərəl] adj. 先天的，固有的
2. magisterial [ˌmædʒɪs`tɪrɪəl] adj. 官氣十足的，有權威的
3. by merit 根據優勢，優點
4. harangue [hə`ræŋ] n. 尤指指責性的長篇大論，誇張的話

xlii Born to Command.

I t is a secret force of superiority not to have to get on by artful trickery but by an inborn power of rule. All submit to it without knowing why, recognising the secret vigour of **connatural**[1] authority. Such **magisterial**[2] spirits are kings **by merit**[3] and lions by innate privilege. By the esteem which they inspire, they hold the hearts and minds of the rest. If their other qualities permit, such men are born to be the prime motors of the state. They perform more by a gesture than others by a long **harangue**[4] .

43・心隨少數，言隨大眾

逆潮流而動很難發現真理，且危機四伏，只有像蘇格拉底這樣的人才能做到。與他人的觀點相左等於是對別人的變相侮辱。想到被批評的事物和原本稱讚它的人，當事人對批評他的人就更加厭惡了。真理只屬於少數人，而粗鄙大眾經常犯錯。你很難憑某些人在大庭廣眾之下所說的話來判斷他們是不是智者，因為他們往往在此種場合下不會說真心話，而是說蠢材們才說的話，儘管他們內心對此亦深惡痛絕。謹慎之人既避免被人反駁，也避免反駁他人。他可能本來敏於責難，但卻不輕易在大庭廣眾之下這樣做，因為人們的思想是自由的，不能也不應該受到侵犯。智者會保持緘默，只有在私下少數幾個志趣相投的人面前才會表露一番。

---

1. Socrates [`sɑkrə,tiz] n. 蘇格拉底（469BC～399BC, 古希臘哲學家）他是著名的古希臘哲學家，他和他的學生柏拉圖及柏拉圖的學生亞里士多德被並稱為「希臘三賢」。他被後人廣泛認為是西方哲學的奠基者。
2. dissent [dɪ`sɛnt] v. 不同意
3. gainsay [gen`se] v. 否認

xliii Think with the Few and Speak with the Many.

By swimming against the stream it is impossible to remove error, easy to fall into danger; only a **Socrates**[1] can undertake it. To **dissent**[2] from others' views is regarded as an insult, because it is their condemnation. Disgust is doubled on account of the thing blamed and of the person who praised it. Truth is for the few, error is both common and vulgar. The wise man is not known by what he says on the house-tops, for there he speaks not with his own voice but with that of common folly, however much his inmost thoughts may **gainsay**[3] it. The prudent avoid being contradicted as much as contradicting: though they have their censure ready they are not ready to publish it. Thought is free, force cannot and should not be used to it. The wise man therefore retires into silence, and if he allows himself to come out of it, he does so in the shade and before few and fit persons.

44 · 與偉人惺惺相惜

英雄所見略同是一種英雄般的美德,這可以說是人世間的一大奇觀,既神秘又有益。世上有相似相通的心靈與氣質,其心心相印的效果可與俗世無知之輩心目中的靈丹妙藥的效果相比。這種共鳴不僅給我們帶來聲名、別人的善意,有時候還會使別人對我們傾心。這種能力靜默無言但雄辯滔滔,不事誇耀但成就顯赫。這種共鳴有時候是積極的,有時候是消極的,但都能讓人感到幸福。它越是這樣就越顯得崇高。要瞭解它們,區別它們並利用它們,需要很高的技巧。如果沒有這種天賦,那麼怎麼努力都是不夠的。

---

1. scent [sɛnt] vt. 聞出,嗅,發覺
2. witchcraft [ˋwɪtʃˌkræft] n. 魔法,魔力
3. felicific [ˌfilɪˋsɪfɪk] adj. 產生幸福的,帶來幸福的

xliv Sympathy with Great Minds.

I t is an heroic quality to agree with heroes. 'Tis like a miracle of nature for mystery and for use. There is a natural kinship of hearts and minds: its effects are such that vulgar ignorance **scents**[1] **witchcraft**[2]. Esteem established, goodwill follows, which at times reaches affection. It persuades without words and obtains without earning. This sympathy is sometimes active, sometimes passive, both alike **felicific**[3] ; the more so, the more sublime. 'Tis a great art to recognise, to distinguish and to utilise this gift. No amount of energy suffices without that favour of nature.

45 · 狡猾，但不要過度

一個人不應該為自己的狡猾沾沾自喜，更不應對此進行吹噓。所有虛偽的事物都應該被隱藏起來，尤其是狡猾，因為這會招人怨恨。詐欺行為十分常見，務必小心防範，但你卻又不能讓人知道你的防範心理，否則可能會使人對你產生不信任的態度。有時人們若知道你有戒心，就會感到自己受了傷害，反而會尋機報復，導致意想不到的後果。凡事三思而後行，總會讓你受益良多，也是智慧的最好表現。一項行動是否能圓滿成功，取決於實現行動的手段是否縝密周全。

46 · 掌控你的反感情緒

我們經常在還沒認識某個人的時候就會討厭他。有時候，這種內心的卑劣的反感是針對某些傑出人物的。對這種負面情緒我們要小心地加以控制，因為對優秀人物抱有厭惡情緒是最有損自己人格的。正如和偉人惺惺相惜讓我們變得高尚一樣，對他們產生反感只會使我們墮落。

---

1. consist in 存在於
2. aversion [əˋvɝʃən] n. 厭惡，討厭的事和人

xlv Use, but Do Not Abuse, Cunning.

O ne ought not to delight in it, still less to boast of it. Everything artificial should be concealed, most of all cunning, which is hated. Deceit is much in use; therefore our caution has to be redoubled, but not so as to show itself, for it arouses distrust, causes much annoy, awakens revenge, and gives rise to more ills than you would imagine. To go to work with caution is of great advantage in action, and there is no greater proof of wisdom. The greatest skill in any deed **consists in**[1] the sure mastery with which it is executed.

xlvi Master Your Antipathies.

W e often allow ourselves to take dislikes, and that before we know anything of a person. At times this innate yet vulgar **aversion**[2] attaches itself to eminent personalities. Good sense masters this feeling, for there is nothing more discreditable than to dislike those better than ourselves. As sympathy with great men ennobles us, so dislike to them degrades us.

47・避免從事那些「光榮的使命」

此點是小心謹慎的關鍵所在。對有能力的人來說,兩個極端之間的距離很遠,而他們又總是在跨越這兩極的過程中小心謹慎,因此需要很長時間。事先躲避這些事情總比陷入之後再從中全身而退要容易。這是對我們判斷力的考驗;避免它們比征服它們要好得多。要知道「光榮的使命」一件接著一件,最後有可能讓你名譽掃地。有的人因先天或後天的原因很容易就會承擔這種責任。但是對理性的人來說,像這樣的事情需要謹慎地加以思考。放棄做這件事比完成這件事更需要勇氣。如果已經有人蠢到願意去冒險犯難,你就不用去做第二個了。

---

1. asunder [əˋsʌndə] adv. 分離,成碎片

xlvii Avoid "Affairs of Honour" –

O ne of the chiefest aims of prudence. In men of great ability the extremes are kept far **asunder**[1], so that there is a long distance between them, and they always keep in the middle of their caution, so that they take time to break through it. It is easier to avoid such affairs than to come well out of them. They test our judgment; it is better to avoid them than to conquer in them. One affair of honour leads to another, and may lead to an affair of dishonour. There are men so constituted by nature or by nation that they easily enter upon such obligations. But for him that walks by the light of reason, such a matter requires long thinking over. There is more valour needed not to take up the affair than to conquer in it. When there is one fool ready for the occasion, one may excuse oneself from being the second.

48・做一個思想深刻的人

每個人思想的深刻性都不一樣，但至少內在要和外在一致。有的人完全是金玉其外，敗絮其內，好像一棟房子，入口處像宮殿一般金碧輝煌，但內部卻像草棚一樣粗糙簡陋。雖然他們也在忍受你，但你不必忍受他們，因為除了一開始的問候語外，你們就無話可談了。雖然他們最初的招呼應酬話活潑生動得像西西里的駿馬一樣，但接下來他們便會變得安靜，因為他們想不到要說什麼。別人也許會被這種人所吸引，因為他們自己只看表面，但這卻無法騙過那些謹慎的人。他們會看透這種人的內心，知道他們的內在深處空空如也。

---

1. frontage [ˋfrʌtɪdʒ] n. 房子的正面，前方
2. portico [ˋportɪˏko] n. （有圓柱的）門廊，柱廊
3. flag [flæg] v. 失去興趣　　4. salutation [ˏsæljəˋteʃən] n. 招呼
5. prance [præns] vi. 騰躍，歡躍，昂首闊步
6. Sicilian barbs 西西里的駿馬，很活潑

xlviii Be Thorough.

H ow much depends on the person. The interior must be at least as much as the exterior. There are natures all **frontage**[1], like houses that for want of means have the **portico**[2] of a palace leading to the rooms of a cottage. It is no use boring into such persons, although they bore you, for conversation **flags**[3] after the first **salutation**[4] . They **prance**[5] through the first compliments like **Sicilian barbs**[6], but silence soon succeeds, for the flow of words soon ceases where there is no spring of thoughts. Others may be taken in by them because they themselves have but a view of the surface, but not the prudent, who look within them and find nothing there except material for scorn.

49．觀察力和判斷力

一個有觀察力和判斷力的人可以駕馭事物，而不是被事物所駕馭。他可以洞察事物最深處的本質，像面相學家一樣一眼看穿一個人。不論是誰，他一看就能看穿並把握其最真實的本質。經過幾次觀察，無論多麼隱密的事物，他都能破解。他觀察細微，思考嚴謹，推理清晰，因此他能發現、注意、把握和理解所有的事物。

50．永遠不要失去自尊

或對自己過於隨便。要讓你自身的正義之心做為評判正義的標準。你應該盡可能嚴格地要求自我，而不應寄望於外部的清規戒律。要避免所有不得體的言行，這倒不是出於對法律和權威的恐懼，而是出於自尊。如果你能注意這一點，那麼就不需要塞內加所謂的虛擬證人——良心了。

---

1. phrenologist [frɛˋnɑlədʒɪst] n. 顱相學者
2. physiognomy [ˌfɪzɪˋɑgnəmɪ] n. 相貌
3. subtile 是古英語中 subtle 的拼寫方法
4. judicious [dʒuˋdɪʃəs] adj. 明智的
5. inference [ˋɪnfərəns] n. 推論

xlix Observation and Judgment.

A man with these rules things, not they him. He sounds at once the profoundest depths; he is a **phrenologist**[1] by means of **physiognomy**[2].On seeing a person he understands him and judges of his inmost nature. From a few observations he deciphers the most hidden recesses of his nature. Keen observation, **subtile**[3] insight, **judicious**[4] **inference**[5] : with these he discovers, notices, grasps, and comprehends everything.

l Never Lose Self-respect,

O r be too familiar with oneself. Let your own right feeling be the true standard of your rectitude, and owe more to the strictness of your own self-judgment than to all external **sanctions**[6]. **Leave off**[7] anything unseemly more from regard for your own self-respect than from fear of external authority. Pay regard to that and there is no need of Seneca's **imaginary tutor**[8].

---

6. sanction [ˋsæŋkʃən] n. 制裁
7. leave off 停止，避免
8. imaginary tutor 虛擬證人，被稱為良心。典出塞內加的《道德書簡》一書。

51・學會正確選擇

生活中的大多數時候需要你做出正確的選擇。這需要良好品味和正確的判斷，只靠智力或學習是不夠的。要有良好的品味和正確的判斷，你必須學會選擇，這就需要滿足兩個條件：即能夠選擇，然後能作出最佳選擇。有許多人雖然聰慧多智，判斷嚴謹，博學多聞，觀察力強，可他們卻不知道如何做出正確的選擇。他們總是選擇最壞的，就好像他們是故意要犯錯一樣。學會正確選擇是上天給予我們的最重要的禮物之一。

---

1. thereon [ðɛr`ɑn] adv. 在那上面
2. fecund [`fikənd] adj. 生殖力旺盛的

li Know How to Choose Well.

Most of life depends **thereon**[1]. It needs good taste and correct judgment, for which neither intellect nor study suffices. To be choice, you must choose, and for this two things are needed: to be able to choose at all, and then to choose the best. There are many men of **fecund**[2] and subtle mind, of keen judgment, of much learning, and of great observation who yet are at a loss when they come to choose. They always take the worst as if they had tried to go wrong. Thus this is one of the greatest gifts from above.

52·切莫惱怒

謹 慎的人總是努力不讓自己變得難堪。這樣的人才是真正的人，才是高尚的人，因為胸襟寬大的人不會輕易受情緒制約。激情是靈魂生出的古怪念頭，稍稍過量便會削弱我們的判斷力。如果人們從你的話中聽出了這一點，那你的名聲就岌岌可危了。你需要徹底地把持住你自己，要做到不管是春風得意還是厄運連連，都不會因擾亂自身而使名聲受損，相反會因為這些事而提升名聲，顯示你的優越之處。

53·勤奮與智力

聰 明的人往往優柔寡斷，勤奮的人卻能快速實現聰明人一直在醞釀卻遲遲不行動的事情。傻瓜喜歡速決，因為他們不知道其中的關鍵，毫無準備就開始工作。另一方面，智者卻常常由於遇事猶豫不決而導致失敗。他們的先見之明讓他們必須深思熟慮，卻因此而錯失良機。敏捷行事是幸運之母。一個從不把今天的事情留到明天的人必有所成。有句話說得極妙：忙裏須偷閒，緩中須帶急。

---

1. magnanimity [͵mægnə`nɪmətɪ] n. 寬宏大量
2. excogitate [ɛks`kɑdʒə͵tet] vt. 想出，研究出，設計
3. procrastination [pro͵kræstə`neʃən] n. 延遲，拖延
4. remiss [rɪ`mɪs] adj. 怠忽職守的
5. nullify [`nʌlə͵faɪ] v. 無效
6. celerity [sə`lɛrətɪ] n. 敏捷，快速

lii Never Be Put out.

❥ Tis a great aim of prudence never to be embarrassed. It is the sign of a real man. of a noble heart, for **magnanimity**[1] is not easily put out. The passions are the humours of the soul, and every excess in them weakens prudence; if they overflow through the mouth, the reputation will be in danger. Let a man therefore be so much and so great a master over himself that neither in the most fortunate nor in the most adverse circumstances can anything cause his reputation injury by disturbing his self-possession, but rather enhance it by showing his superiority.

liii Diligent and Intelligent.

D iligence promptly executes what intelligence slowly **excogitates**[2]. Hurry is the failing of fools; they know not the crucial point and set to work without preparation. On the other hand, the wise more often fail from **procrastination**[3] ; foresight begets deliberation, and **remiss**[4] action often **nullifies**[5] prompt judgment. **Celerity**[6] is the mother of good fortune. He has done much who leaves nothing over till to-morrow. "make haste slowly" is a royal motto.

54 · 懂得如何亮出你的武器

即使是兔子也敢去拔死獅的鬍鬚。不能對一個人的勇氣隨便開玩笑，只要你屈服過一次，就會有第二次、第三次……最後，要克服它比第一次所要付出的努力多得多。道德上的勇氣遠勝過肢體上的勇敢，它應該像一把被小心地插入鞘中，卻伺機而用的劍一樣。勇氣是你的自衛武器，因此道德上的軟弱比肢體的軟弱更讓人不堪。許多人雖然有傑出的品質，但卻缺乏一顆勇敢的心，所以他們一生庸庸碌碌，在散漫懶惰中過了此生。冥冥之中自有絕妙的安排：蜜蜂身上既有甘甜的蜂蜜也有螫人的蜂刺。

---

1. show your teeth　露出牙齒，作威脅姿態；發怒
2. mane [men] n. 鬃毛
3. scabbard [ˋskæbɚd] n. 鞘
4. stout [staʊt] adj. 勇敢堅定的
5. sloth [sloθ] n. 怠惰，懶惰

liv Know How to Show Your Teeth[1].

E ven hares can pull the **mane**[2] of a dead lion. There is no joke about courage. Give way to the first and you must yield to the second, and so on till the last, and to gain your point at last costs as much trouble as would have gained much more at first. Moral courage exceeds physical; it should be like a sword kept ready for use in the **scabbard**[3] of caution. It is the shield of great place; moral cowardice lowers one more than physical. Many have had eminent qualities, yet, for want of a **stout**[4] heart, they passed inanimate lives and found a tomb in their own **sloth**[5]. Wise Nature has thoughtfully combined in the bee the sweetness of its honey with the sharpness of its sting.

55．學會等待

　　一個具備耐心的人心靈是高尚的，他從不匆忙行事，也不會受情緒左右。能制己者方能制人。在觸及機會的核心之前，不妨先在時光中漫遊等待。明智的人會充分利用時機，明確自己的目的，完善自己的方法。時光的拐杖比大力士赫克琉斯的鐵棒還要管用。上帝不是拿著棍棒來懲罰人，而是用時間。主曾經說過：時間與我作伴，則天下無敵矣。命運也總是把獎賞最先留給那些耐心等待的人。

---

1. dower [`daʊɚ] vt. 賦予（才能等）
2. circumference [sɚ`kʌmfərəns] n. 圓周，周圍
3. season [`sizn] n. 通常會發生某事的時期
4. crutch [krʌtʃ] n. （跛子常用的）拐杖，幫助
5. iron club of Hercules 大力士赫克琉斯的鐵棒

lv Wait.

I t's a sign of a noble heart **dowered**[1] with patience, never to be in a hurry, never to be in a passion. First be master over yourself if you would be master over others. You must pass through the **circumference**[2] of time before arriving at the centre of opportunity. A wise reserve **seasons**[3] the aims and matures the means. Time's **crutch**[4] effects more than the **iron club of Hercules**[5]. God Himself **chasteneth**[6] not with a **rod**[7] but with time. He **spake**[8] a great word who said, "Time and I against any two." Fortune herself rewards waiting with the first prize.

---

6. chasteneth 是 chasten 的古英語第三人稱單數形式　chasten v. 磨煉
7. rod [rɑd] n. 杆，棒
8. spake 為古英語中 speak 的過去式

56 · 要適時行動

快樂的心靈往往思維敏捷。多虧了這種生氣和活力,才不用害怕發生危險或不幸。許多人雖然想得很多,可往往最後都會出錯;還有些人雖然事先沒有經過深思熟慮,卻達到了自己的目標。有的人潛在抗壓能力特強,往往困難越大,其能力發揮得反而越好。他們都是一些怪傑,即興所作都會成功,但對再三思量的事情卻會失敗。如果他們當時沒有想到某一件事,那他們事後也絕不會想到,即使故意去想,也沒有用處了。行事敏捷能贏得人們的喝彩,因為這是能力超凡,思想精微,行動謹慎的表現。

57 · 做事要又慢又準

事情如果要做好,那就要早做。若只圖成事快,則敗事亦快。凡能留存久遠者,必費長久之功。只有傑出的表現才會受人矚目,只有成功才能長存不朽。深厚的智力才是探索永恆和不朽的根基。**越有價值的事物其代價也越大**。最珍貴的金屬往往也是最重的。

---

1. promptitude [`prɑmptɪˌtjud] n. 敏捷,迅速
2. Antiperistasis [`æntɪˌpɛrɪˋstælsɪs] n. 是亞里士多德提出的,被定義為:一種特性的增加,是由於它被另一相反特性包圍。例如,當周圍突然變冷時,溫暖的身體會變熱。
3. offhand [`ɔfˋhænd] adv. 即時地,隨便地　　4. in aught 無結果的,徒然的

lvi Have Presence of Mind.

The child of a happy **promptitude**[1] of spirit. Owing to this vivacity and wide awakeness there is no fear of danger or mischance. Many reflect much only to go wrong in the end: others attain their aim without thinking of it beforehand. There are natures of **Antiperistasis**[2] who work best in an emergency. They are like monsters who succeed in all they do **offhand**[3], but fail **in aught**[4] they think over. A thing occurs to them at once or never: for them there is no court of appeal. Celerity wins applause because it proves remarkable capacity; subtlety of judgment, prudence in action.

lvii Slow and Sure.

Early enough if well. Quickly done can be quickly undone. To last an eternity requires an eternity of preparation. Only excellence counts; only achievement endures. Profound intelligence is the only foundation for immortality. Worth much costs much. The precious metals are the heaviest.

58・做事恰到好處

你不需要在每個人面前都顯露出你的才華；做事亦如此，只要付出所需的努力就可以了。不要浪費你的知識和才能。比如優秀的養鷹者養的鷹不在多，只要夠他打獵就可以。如果你今天展露了過多的才能，那你明天就沒有什麼能拿得出手。所以你總是要保留一點新鮮感來迷惑眾人的眼睛。假如你每天都能帶來新鮮的表演，那人們就會對你抱有期望，因為他們看不清你的能力極限。

59・收場好才算好

在造訪命運之宮時，如果你從快樂之門進，那必定從悲哀之門出；反之亦然。你應該考慮如何收場，一個瀟灑的退場比掌聲如雷的進場更為重要。不幸的人往往是開頭很熱烈，但收場卻是很悲慘。因此重要的不是你到場時大家鼓掌歡迎——這幾乎沒什麼意義，而是你走後人們還能對你念念不忘。生命中只有少數幾個人在退場後還能讓人念念不忘。幸運女神很少會把你一直陪送到大門口，在歡迎你時她可能非常熱情，但送你去時卻冷若冰霜。

---

1. falconer [`fɔlkənɚ] n. 以鷹狩獵者，養鷹者，放鷹者
2. dazzle [`dæzl] v. （使）眼花，眩耀
3. outset [`aʊtˌsɛt] n. 開端，開始
4. encore [`ɑŋkor] n. 再演唱的要求，經要求而再唱

lviii Adapt Yourself to Your Company.

There is no need to show your ability before every one. Employ no more force than is necessary. Let there be no unnecessary expenditure either of knowledge or of power. The skilful **falconer**[1] only flies enough birds to serve for the chase. If there is too much display to-day there will be nothing to show to-morrow. Always have some novelty wherewith to **dazzle**[2]. To show something fresh each day keeps expectation alive and conceals the limits of capacity.

lix Finish off Well.

In the house of Fortune, if you enter by the gate of pleasure you must leave by that of sorrow and vice versa. You ought therefore to think of the finish, and attach more importance to a graceful exit than to applause on entrance. 'Tis the common lot of the unlucky to have a very fortunate **outset**[3] and a very tragic end. The important point is not the vulgar applause on entrance – that comes to nearly all – but the general feeling at exit. Few in life are felt to deserve an **encore**[4]. Fortune rarely accompanies any one to the door: warmly as she may welcome the coming, she speeds but coldly the parting guest.

60・判斷有方

有的人是天生的智者，帶著這個天生的優勢開始學習的時候，就已經成功了一半。隨著年齡和經驗的增長，他們的理智會逐漸成熟，使其獲得良好的判斷力。他們憎惡那些會誤導謹慎心智的奇思怪想，尤其在國家大事上更是如此，因為這些事情太重要了，一定要確保萬無一失。若以舟喻國，則他們就算不是引航員，也是掌舵者。

61・在崇高事業上做到出類拔萃

很少有人能做到出類拔萃。但是如果一個人沒有某些卓越的品格，他就稱不上是個偉人。平庸之輩絕難贏得掌聲。在高尚事業上做到出類拔萃可使我們超脫凡夫俗子，成為卓絕超群的人物。在卑微的職業上即使做得再出色也終會是無足輕重。成績來得越是輕鬆，也就越無榮耀可言。在高尚事業上出類拔萃能使你贏得人們的崇拜和好感。

---

1. moiety [`mɔɪətɪ] n. 二分之一，一部分，半族
2. whimsical [`hwɪmzɪkl] adj. 反覆無常的，古怪的
3. astray [ə`stre] adv. 迷途地，入歧途地
4. pilot [`paɪlət] n. 飛行員，領航員，引水員

lx A Sound Judgment.

S ome are born wise, and with this natural advantage enter upon their studies, with a **moiety**[1] already mastered. With age and experience their reason ripens, and thus they attain a sound judgment. They abhor everything **whimsical**[2] as leading prudence **astray**[3], especially in matters of state, where certainty is so necessary, owing to the importance of the affairs involved. Such men deserve to stand by the helm of state either as **pilots**[4] or as men at the wheel.

lxi To Excel in What Is Excellent.

A great rarity among excellences. You cannot have a great man without something preeminent. Mediocrities never win applause. Eminence in some distinguished post distinguishes one from the vulgar mob and ranks us with the elect. To be distinguished in a small post is to be great in little: the more comfort, the less glory. The highest eminence in great affairs has the royal characteristic of exciting admiration and winning goodwill.

62・善用利器

有人希望透過使用粗劣的工具來表現自己高超的智慧，這種自我滿足的做法是危險的。如果受到致命的打擊，那也是合情合理。身為王者的偉大絕不會因宰相有才能而減少。所有的榮耀都歸於主要領導者，失敗也是一樣。只有領導者才會贏得名聲。人們從來不談論說某人「這個人有好的幫手，那個人的幫手不好」，而是說某人「這是個好的藝術家，那個就不怎麼樣」。你必須精心選擇、考察、培養你的幫手，因為你要把創造你不朽聲譽的希望寄託於他們身上。

---

1. revert to 回復，歸還

lxii Use Good Instruments.

S ome would have the subtlety of their wits proven by the meanness of their instruments. 'Tis a dangerous satisfaction, and deserves a fatal punishment. The excellence of a minister never diminished the greatness of his lord. All the glory of exploits **reverts to**[1] the principal actor; also all the blame. Fame only does business with principals. She does not say, "This had good, that had bad servants," but, "This was a good artist, that a bad one." Let your assistants be selected and tested therefore, for you have to trust to them for an immortality of fame.

63・先下手為強

那你就能獲得雙倍的榮耀。假設其他條件均等時，先下手者必會占盡先機。許多人如果在他們所從事的行業中首開先例，那他們就可以獨領風騷。先下手者能像長子一樣贏得榮譽，後到者只能像次子一樣得一點微薄之利。無論後者做什麼，世人都會覺得他們只是學人說話的鸚鵡。智者也許會別出心裁，另闢蹊徑，但他們一路都會小心謹慎。正因為他們的標新立異，智者才會永垂青史。而有些人卻甘當二流人物之首，不做一流人物之次，即：寧為雞頭，不為牛尾。

---

1. eminent [`ɛmənənt] a. 出眾的，卓越的，顯赫的

lxiii To Be the First of the Kind
Is an Excellence,

a nd to be **eminent**[1] in it as well, a double one. To have the first move is a great advantage when the players are equal. Many a man would have been a veritable Phoenix if he had been the first of the sort. Those who come first are the heirs of Fame; the others get only a younger brother's allowance: whatever they do, they cannot persuade the world they are anything more than parrots. The skill of prodigies may find a new path to eminence, but prudence accompanies them all the way. By the novelty of their enterprises sages write their names in the golden book of heroes. Some prefer to be first in things of minor import than second in greater exploits.

64・避免憂愁

你就能收穫頗多,這不但為你減少了很多麻煩,還能為你帶來自在和快樂的生活。不到萬不得已,不要給別人帶來壞消息,更不要收到這類壞消息。有的人耳朵裏裝滿了甜蜜的奉承話;而有的人聽到的都是流言蜚語;還有人每天如果不聽到點煩心的事就活不下去,正如米斯利達特斯每天不服一劑毒藥就難以安心一樣。不管這個人和你的關係有多親密,你也不該為了討他一時的歡心而將自己陷入終生的痛苦中。有人雖曾為你出謀策劃,但他自己並不會因此擔任何風險,所以你也就無須為討好他而破壞自己的計畫。如果當你給予別人快樂意味著會給予自己痛苦時,那請你牢記這一教訓:與其讓你自己事後忍受無可救助的痛苦,不如讓別人現在就受一點痛苦!

---

1. 米斯利達特斯:龐圖斯國王,因怕敵人的毒害,天天服一點毒藥以便使身體產生抗毒能力。

lxiv Avoid Worry.

S uch prudence brings its own reward. It escapes much, and is thus the midwife of comfort and so of happiness. Neither give nor take bad news unless it can help. Some men's ears are stuffed with the sweets of flattery; others with the bitters of scandal, while some cannot live without a daily annoyance no more than **Mithridates**[1] could without poison. It is no rule of life to prepare for yourself lifelong trouble in order to give a temporary enjoyment to another, however near and dear. You never ought to spoil your own chances to please another who advises and keeps out of the affair, and in all cases where to oblige another involves disobliging yourself, 'tis a standing rule that it is better he should suffer now than you afterwards and in vain.

65 · 品味須高雅

高雅的品味如同聰明才智一樣，是可以培養出來的。淵博的知識可以提升你的審美能力，給你帶來快樂。你可以透過看某人品味的高下，來判斷他是不是擁有高尚的靈魂：因為只有偉大的事物才能滿足一顆偉大的靈魂。嘴張得大，咬下的東西才大；品味崇高者必從事崇高之事業。在品味高雅的人面前，即使最勇敢的人也會顫抖，最完美的人也會喪失自信。世間很少完美無瑕之物，因此，不要讓讚美之詞氾濫。品味可以從與別人的交談中習得，所以與那些品味高雅的人交友是莫大的榮幸。不要裝作對一切都不滿意，這是極端愚蠢的，虛偽造作的反感比唐吉訶德式的憤世嫉俗更加令人討厭。有些人寧願上帝創造一個不一樣的世界和完美的事物，來滿足他們不切實際的想像。

---

1. whet [hwɛt] vt. 刺激，促進（食慾、好奇心等）
2. Quixotry [ˋkwɪksətrɪ] n. 唐吉訶德式的憤世嫉俗

lxv Elevated Taste.

Y ou can train it like the intellect. Full knowledge **whets**[1] desire and increases enjoyment. You may know a noble spirit by the elevation of his taste: it must be a great thing that can satisfy a great mind. Big bites for big mouths, lofty things for lofty spirits. Before their judgment the bravest tremble, the most perfect lose confidence. Things of the first importance are few; let appreciation be rare. Taste can be imparted by intercourse: great good luck to associate with the highest taste. But do not affect to be dissatisfied with everything: 'tis the extreme of folly, and more odious if from affectation than if from **Quixotry**[2]. Some would have God create another world and other ideals to satisfy their fantastic imagination.

66・行事要善終

有人做事注重過程而不是結果，但是，對世人來說，如果最後失敗了，那麼之前不管多麼努力都是沒用的。勝利者無需解釋自己為什麼會獲勝，因為世人不會注意做事的具體方法，而只注重結果成功與否。只要你能達到目標，你就贏得了一切。不論你的手段多麼令人不滿意，結局好那一切就都好。因此，有時候，如果你需要不擇手段才能使事情大功告成的話，那麼不擇手段也是種生活的藝術。

---

1. rigour [ˈrɪgɚ] n. 嚴格
2. do away with 廢除，弄死

lxvi SeeThat Things End Well.

S ome regard more the **rigour**[1] of the game than the winning of it, but to the world the discredit of the final failure **does away with**[2] any recognition of the previous care. The victor need not explain. The world does not notice the details of the measures employed, but only the good or ill result. You lose nothing if you gain your end. A good end gilds everything, however unsatisfactory the means. Thus at times it is part of the art of life to transgress the rules of the art, if you cannot end well otherwise.

67 · 從事享譽讚揚的職業

大多數事情的好壞取決於別人是否滿意。別人的尊重對卓越的事物而言，正如春風對於嬌花，呼吸對於生命。有的職業會普遍受到世人的尊敬，但其他職業雖然更重要，卻無讚譽。前者是有目共睹，人人喜歡；而後者雖然更為稀少，更為可貴，卻顯得默默無聞，雖然可敬但無尊敬之聲。最知名的君王是那些獲得勝利的君王，所以阿拉貢諸王被尊為是戰士、征服者和偉人。一個有能力的人偏愛那些可享盛名的職業，因為那些職業人人都瞭解，人人都願意從事。如果他能贏得大家的讚揚，那他就能變得不朽。

---

1. zephyr [`zɛfɚ] n. 西風，[詩]和風，徐風
2. 也就是 "Esteem to excellence is just like the zephyr to flowers, they are both like the breath of life."
3. Aragon 西班牙北部地方
4. suffrage [`sʌfrɪdʒ] n. 投票，選舉權，參政權

lxvii Prefer Callings of Distinction

M ost things depend on the satisfaction of others. **Esteem is to excellence what the zephyr[1] is to flowers, the breath of life[2]**. There are some callings which gain universal esteem, while others more important are without credit. The former, pursued before the eyes of all, obtain the universal favour; the others, though they are rarer and more valuable, remain obscure and unperceived, honoured but not applauded. Among princes conquerors are the most celebrated, and therefore the kings of **Aragon**[3] earned such applause as warriors, conquerors, and great men. An able man will prefer callings of distincton which all men know of and utilise, and he thus becomes immortalised by universal **suffrage**[4].

68 · 運用智慧比運用
記憶去幫助別人更好

因為後者只需回憶，而前者則需你思考與斟酌。許多人在時機成熟時沒有做應該做的事，因為他們根本就沒有想到，在這種情況下，一個朋友的忠告也許就能讓他們看清利害得失。敏於審時度勢，這本身就是一項非常重要的才能。倘若你缺乏這種才能，你就會失掉許多成功的機運。如果你有審時度勢的能力，那就為別人指點迷津；如果你沒有，那就要向別人請教。為人指點迷津時須小心謹慎，但向別人請教時大可積極主動。這裏所說的只不過是這個暗示：如果此事與他人的利益息息相關，就要特別注意點到為止。你應該先投石問路，要是不夠的話再逐漸深入。如果對方想拒絕，你就要想怎麼讓他答應。這正是聰明才智的表現，**在大多數情況下，人們之所以失敗，是因為他們連試都沒有試過。**

---

1. omit [o`mɪt] vt. 忽略，忘記，遺漏

lxviii It Is Better to Help with Intelligence Than with Memory.

T he more as the latter needs only recollection, the former requires thought. Many persons **omit**[1] what is appropriate to the moment because it does not occur to them; a friend's advice on such occasions may enable them to see the advantages. 'Tis one of the greatest gifts of mind to be able to offer what is needed at the moment: for want of that many things fail to be performed. Share the light of your intelligence, when you have any, and ask for it when you have it not, the first cautiously, the last anxiously. Give no more than a hint: this finesse is especially needful when it touches the interest of him whose attention you awaken. You should give but a taste at first, and then pass on to more when that is not sufficient. If he thinks of No, go in search of Yes. Therein lies the cleverness, for most things are not obtained simply because they are not attempted.

69・不要屈服於平時的衝動

偉大的人從不會被別人的看法所影響。自省給人帶來智慧：你要瞭解自己的性格，順其自然，甚至反其道而行之，以便使人的修為與天性互相平衡。認識自我是自我進步的開端。有的人生性疏狂，行事總是任意妄為，任何風吹草動都會影響他們真實的意圖。由於受這種不穩情緒的擺佈，他們做起事來總是自相矛盾。慾望和知識往相反的方向拉扯，不但會使他們意志變得不堅定，也會使他們喪失所有的判斷力。

---

1. inclination [ɪnklə`neʃən] n. 意圖，傾向，愛好

lxix Do Not Give Way to Every Common Impulse.

H e is a great man who never allows himself to be influenced by the impressions of others. Self-reflection is the school of wisdom. To know one's disposition and to allow for it, even going to the other extreme so as to find the balance between nature and art. Self-knowledge is the beginning of self-improvement. There be some whose humours are so monstrous that they are always under the influence of one or other of them, and put them in place of their real **inclinations**[1]. They are torn asunder by such disharmony and their involved in contradictory obligations. Such excesses not only destroy firmness of will; all power of judgment gets lost, desire and knowledge pulling in opposite directions.

70・學會拒絕

一個人不應該在任何事情上或是對任何人都讓步，因此**學會拒絕與學會同意一樣重要**，對於有地位的人來說尤其如此。問題的關鍵在於如何拒絕。有些人的拒絕比別人的答應還要令人尊重，經過修飾的拒絕比生硬的許諾更讓人滿意。有些人總是把「不」字掛在嘴邊，因此把事情搞得很不愉快。他們總是一開始就拒絕，但後來還是會作出讓步，這對他們不會有什麼幫助，因為他們一開始的拒絕讓人很不高興。回絕別人不要回絕得太死，而要讓人們慢慢地接受失望，也不要一次就徹底回絕，那樣一來，人們就不會再指望你了。給人們留一點希望，不要拒絕得太生硬。雖然我們在行動上拒絕了別人，但是可以用禮貌和巧妙的言語加以補償。答應還是拒絕說起來很容易，但是應該三思而後行。

---

1. herald [`hɛrəld] n. 預兆
2. point-blank [`pɔɪnt`blæŋk] adj. 直截了當的，乾脆的

lxx Know How to Refuse.

One ought not to give way in everything nor to everybody. To know how to refuse is therefore as important as to know how to consent. This is especially the case with men of position. All depends on the how. Some men's No is thought more of than the Yes of others: for a gilded No is more satisfactory than a dry Yes. There are some who always have No on their lips, whereby they make everything distasteful. No always comes first with them, and when sometimes they give way after all, it does them no good on account of the unpleasing **herald**[1]. Your refusal need not be **point-blank**[2] : let the disappointment come by degrees. Nor let the refusal be final; that would be to destroy dependence; let some spice of hope remain to soften the rejection. Let politeness compensate and fine words supply the place of deeds. Yes and No are soon said, but give much to think over.

71・不要反覆不定

不要因為你的性情或情緒而令你的行為變得異常。一個有能力的人總是能使其最好的品格保持一致，他會讓人們覺得可靠。如果他改變了，那也是有充分的理由和經過了深思熟慮。一個人行為的反覆無常是最為忌諱的。有的人天天都在變化，他們的理解力每天都在變化，意志更是如此，因此他們的運氣也會跟著變化。昨天認為對的東西今天就變成錯的；昨天答應的事情今天就改口拒絕。他們自污其名，葬送了在別人眼中的信譽。

---

1. vacillate [ˋvæsḷˌet] v. 猶豫不定

lxxi Do Not Vacillate[1].

L et not your actions be abnormal either from disposition or affectation. An able man is always the same in his best qualities; he gets the credit of trustworthiness. If he changes, he does so for good reason or good consideration. In matters of conduct change is hateful. There are some who are different every day; their intelligence varies, still more their will, and with this their fortune. Yesterday's white is to-day's black: to-day's No was yesterday's Yes. They always give the lie to their own credit and destroy their credit with others.

72 · 行事果斷

執行出錯帶來的危害比行事猶豫不決所帶來的危害要小；流動的河流比被大壩圍起來的水的危害要小。有的人總是猶豫不決，常需別人指點幫忙，這並不是因為他們感到困惑，而是沒有行動力，因為他們都是明辨是非的人。看清困難所在需要技巧，找到解決困難的方法更需要技巧。有些人絕不會讓自己陷入困境，他們那冷靜的判斷和果敢的性格使他們勝任最重要的職位。他們的理智告訴他們如何找到問題的切入點，而他們的決心使得事情得以輕鬆完成。他們行事迅速，一旦完成某件事就開始準備做下一件事了。他們能很好地把握機會，所以一定能夠成功。

---

1. dam up　築壩攔水
2. be in straits　在困難中，在窘境中
3. drive home　使人理解
4. affiance [əˋfaɪəns] vt. 使訂婚

lxxii Be Resolute.

B ad execution of your designs does less harm than irresolution in forming them. Streams do less harm flowing than when **dammed up**[1]. There are some men so infirm of purpose that they always require direction from others, and this not on account of any perplexity, for they judge clearly, but from sheer incapacity for action. It needs some skill to find out difficulties, but more to find a way out of them. There are others who are never **in straits**[2] ; their clear judgment and determined character fit them for the highest callings: their intelligence tells them where to insert the thin end of the wedge, their resolution how to **drive it home**[3]. They soon get through anything: as soon as they have done with one sphere of action, they are ready for another. **Affianced**[4] to fortune, they make themselves sure of success.

73・退避有道

這是聰明人克服困難的妙招。他們會用一些機智的話語讓自己擺脫複雜的環境；裝作若無其事或是輕鬆一笑來使自己避免正面衝突。絕大多數偉大的領導者都深諳此道。如果你不得不拒絕，比較禮貌的方法是轉移話題。有時候，裝傻反而是大智的表現。

---

1. labyrinth [`læbə,rɪnθ] n. 難解的事物
2. contention [kən`tɛnʃən] n. 爭論，爭辯

lxxiii Utilise Slips.

T hat is how smart people get out of difficulties. They extricate themselves from the most intricate **labyrinth**[1] by some witty application of a bright remark. They get out of a serious **contention**[2] by an airy nothing or by raising a smile. Most of the great leaders are well grounded in this art. When you have to refuse, it is often the polite way to talk of something else. Sometimes it proves the highest understanding not to understand.

74 · 與人為善

人口越多的地方往往潛伏著越原始的野獸。那些對自己沒有自信的人的缺點就是難以讓人接近，他們所謂的榮譽感左右著他們對別人的態度。一個脾氣暴躁的人是不可能贏得別人的好感的。我們常常能看到那些不合群的怪胎，身邊一個朋友都沒有還要故作清高。如果他們的僕人不得不跟他們說話時，他們走近時提心吊膽，就像是準備要與虎相鬥一樣。這種人為了謀求高位曾對誰都卑躬屈膝；但一旦權力在握，便會對誰都顯得高高在上來補償自己。其實基於他現在的高位，他本應該成為大家爭相高攀的人物，但由於他的驕傲虛榮與刻薄無禮，卻使人人對其望而卻步、避而遠之。要懲罰這種人的一個文明方式就是不要理睬他們，不給他們交談的機會，從而讓他們沒有機會進步。

---

1. inaccessible [ˌɪnækˈsɛsəbl] adj. 達不到的，難以接近
2. make a point of 把…視為，說成必要的
3. impertinent [ɪmˈpɝtnənt] adj. 莽撞無禮的
4. ingratiate [ɪnˈgreʃɪˌet] vt. 使迎合，使討好
5. indemnify [ɪnˈdɛmnəˌfaɪ] v. 賠償
6. spleen [splin] n. 脾

lxxiv Do Not Be Unsociable.

The truest wild beasts live in the most populous places. To be **inaccessible**[1] is the fault of those who distrust themselves, whose honours change their manners. It is no way of earning people's goodwill by being ill-tempered with them. It is a sight to see one of those unsociable monsters who **make a point of**[2] being proudly **impertinent**[3] . Their dependants who have the misfortune to be obliged to speak with them, enter as if prepared for a fight with a tiger armed with patience and with fear. To obtain their post these persons must have **ingratiated**[4] themselves with every one, but having once obtained it they seek to **indemnify**[5] themselves by disobliging all. It is a condition of their position that they should be accessible to all, yet, from pride or **spleen**[6], they are so to none. 'Tis a civil way to punish such men by letting them alone, and depriving them of opportunities of improvement by granting them no opportunity of intercourse.

75・以英雄豪傑為師

但你應是努力趕上他而非模仿他。世界上有很多各種各樣功成名就的偉人。每個人都可以選擇本行業中的頂尖人物作為自己的楷模，但不要一味地模仿，而是要以此激勵自己前進。亞歷山大潸然淚下，不是因為阿基里斯已經長埋地下，而是因為想到自己的聲名還沒有像他一樣傳遍海內外。世間再沒有什麼比他人的盛名更能激起壯志雄心。他人的盛名就如催人奮進的號角，可增強嫉妒而使人昂然奮起，從而成就一番偉業。

76・別總是愛開玩笑

智慧往往是在嚴肅的事情上表現出來的，且比耍小聰明更容易讓人欣賞。總是喜歡開玩笑的人等到嚴肅的事情來臨時便會慌了神。他們就像是騙子一樣，人們覺得騙子總是說謊，而認為他們總是在開玩笑。因此，就算你正經說話的時候，別人也聽不出來，這和你什麼都沒說沒有什麼兩樣。如果一個人一直開玩笑很容易就讓人厭煩。許多人會被認為是幽默風趣，但卻不會有人覺得他們智慧明理。玩笑話只能逗一時之樂，嚴肅認真才是持久的。

---

1. emulate [ˋɛmjəˌlet] n. 彷效
2. calling [ˋkɔlɪŋ] n. 職業，行業
3. jest [dʒɛst] vi. 嘲笑，開玩笑

lxxv Choose an Heroic Ideal;

b ut rather to **emulate**[1] than to imitate. There are exemplars of greatness, living texts of honour. Let every one have before his mind the chief of his **calling**[2] not so much to follow him as to spur himself on. Alexander wept not on account of Achilles dead and buried, but over himself, because his fame had not yet spread throughout the world. Nothing arouses ambition so much in the heart as the trumpet-clang of another's fame. The same thing that sharpens envy, nourishes a generous spirit.

lxxvi Do Not Always Be Jesting[3].

W isdom is shown in serious matters, and is more appreciated than mere wit. He that is always ready for jests is never ready for serious things. They resemble liars in that men never believe either, always expecting a lie in one, a joke in the other. One never knows when you speak with judgment, which is the same as if you had none. A continual jest soon loses all zest. Many get the repute of being witty, but thereby lose the credit of being sensible. Jest has its little hour, seriousness should have all the rest.

77・調整自我，與人相宜

做一個謹慎的普魯吐斯，與學者相交時，談吐之間應顯露自我學識；與聖人相對時，行為舉止應彰顯高尚品德。這是讓每個人都喜歡你的妙法；他們會因為對你的好感而贊同你的一切。你應觀察對方的心情，然後根據每個人不同的情緒而調整自己的狀態，或親切友善，或嚴肅莊重。要順著對方的情緒走，察言觀色。這對有求於人的人更加重要。但是，這只有大智大慧的人才能做到。只有一個見多識廣、聰慧達能的人才能對此駕輕就熟。

78・做事的藝術

愚人總是破門而入，因為愚者多逞匹夫之勇。他們頭腦簡單，既不能預見危險，也不擔心因失敗而導致名譽掃地。但謹慎的人在進門前會深思熟慮。他們小心謹慎，先看看前面是不是有危險。儘管有時命運之神會網開一面，但小心駛得萬年船。如果你發覺前方有危險，就要小心前進，心存謹慎，摸索向前，這樣才能腳踏實地。當今之世，與人交往處處陷阱，故需步步為營。

---

1. Proteus [ˋprotjus] n. 希臘海神，多變的人
2. suffrage [ˋsʌfrɪdʒ] n. 投票，選舉權，參政權，[宗]代禱
3. genial [ˋdʒinjəl] adj. 親切的
4. precaution [prɪˋɔʃən] n. 預防，警惕，防範

lxxvii Be All Things to All Men –

a discreet **Proteus**[1], learned with the learned, saintly with the sainted. It is the great art to gain every one's **suffrages**[2] ; their goodwill gains general agreement. Notice men's moods and adapt yourself to each, **genial**[3] or serious as the case may be. Follow their lead, glossing over the changes as cunningly as possible. This is an indispensable art for dependent persons. But this savoir-faire calls for great cleverness. He only will find no difficulty who has a universal genius in his knowledge and universal ingenuity in his wit.

lxxviii The Art of Undertaking Things.

Fools rush in through the door; for folly is always bold. The same simplicity which robs them of all attention to **precautions**[4] deprives them of all sense of shame at failure. But prudence enters with more deliberation. Its forerunners are caution and care; they advance and discover whether you can also advance without danger. Every rush forward is freed from danger by caution, while fortune sometimes helps in such cases. Step cautiously where you suspect depth. Sagacity goes cautiously forward while precaution covers the ground. Nowadays there are unsuspected depths in human. intercourse, you must therefore cast the lead at every step.

79・和藹友善的性格

適度的和藹友善不是一種缺陷，而是種優點。一顆快樂的種子會四季常開。最偉大的人有時候也會顯得幽默風趣，這會讓他們受到眾人的喜歡。但在這種情況下他們也還是都會保持自己的威嚴，從不做失禮之事。還有些人開個玩笑就能幫自己擺脫困境。儘管有些事情在別人看來很嚴肅，但你也需談笑處之。你若能撫慰人心，才能吸引別人接近你。

80・慎聽明辨

我們所知之事，所見者少，依賴他人者多。耳朵聽到的有真相但更有謊言。眼見為實，耳聽為虛。真理之神從遠處翩翩而來，很少會有純潔無瑕的時候，因為傳播真理的人難免會夾雜自己的個人情緒；而人們對事物的喜惡，都會為事物加上自己的色彩。我們聽到的消息總是帶有說話者的個人色彩，因此，對於高唱讚歌者要小心提防，而對於批評者更需如此。**要注意說話人的意圖，你應該事先瞭解說話人的立場是什麼。要經常思考來辨別虛假或誇張的言論。**

---

1. decorum [dɪˋkorəm] n. 禮貌
2. placability [ˌplekəˋbɪlətɪ] n. 安撫，使平靜
3. magnet [ˋmægnɪt] n. 磁體，磁鐵
4. admixture [ədˋmɪkstʃɚ] n. 混合，混合物
5. assay [əˋse] v. 鑑定，分析

lxxix A Genial Disposition.

I f with moderation 'tis an accomplishment, not a defect. A grain of gaiety seasons all. The greatest men join in the fun at times, and it makes them liked by all. But they should always on such occasions preserve their dignity, nor go beyond the bounds of **decorum**[1] . Others, again, get themselves out of difficulty quickest by a joke. For there are things you must take in fun, though others perhaps mean them in earnest. You show a sense of **placability**[2], which acts as a **magnet**[3] on all hearts.

lxxx Take Care to Get Information.

W e live by information, not by sight. We exist by faith in others. The ear is the area-gate of truth but the front-door of lies. The truth is generally seen, rarely heard; seldom she comes in elemental purity, especially from afar; there is always some **admixture**[4] of the moods of those through whom she has passed. The passions tinge her with their colours wherever they touch her, sometimes favourably, sometimes the reverse. She always brings out the disposition, therefore receive her with caution from him that praises, with more caution from him that blames. Pay attention to the intention of the speaker; you should know beforehand on what footing he comes. Let reflection **assay**[5] falsity and exaggeration.

81 · 重鑄輝煌

在灰燼中重生是鳳凰特有的本領。不管能力多強，總會有衰竭的一天，到時候名聲也會隨之遠去。時間長了，人們對你的敬意就會減弱，再顯赫的成就一旦過時，就經常被新的平庸之術所超越。你的勇氣、才華、命運和其他一切都應該不斷自我更新，要為眾人帶來令人讚歎的新驚喜，就像太陽一樣每天都是新的。你也要像太陽一樣改變你照耀的方向。雖然你失去了過去的輝煌，但在新的舞臺上重放光彩會讓你贏得人們的掌聲。

82 · 不管好壞，都不要走極端

有個智者曾將所有的美德提煉概括為中庸之道。矯枉過正就會造成謬誤，正如柑橘汁液被榨乾之後僅存苦澀。即使欣喜之時亦要小心勿走極端，要知道濫用才華會才思枯竭。擠奶擠得過多，那擠出來的就不是奶而是血了。

---

1. dreg [drɛg] n. 渣滓，糟糠，沈澱物
2. golden mean 中庸之道

lxxxi Renew Your Brilliance.

❭ Tis the privilege of the Phoenix. Ability is wont to grow old, and with it fame. The staleness of custom weakens admiration, and a mediocrity that's new often eclipses the highest excellence grown old. Try therefore to be born again in valour, in genius, in fortune, in all. Display startling novelties, rise afresh like the sun every day. Change too the scene on which you shine, so that your loss may be felt in the old scenes of your triumph, while the novelty of your powers wins you applause in the new.

lxxxii Drain Nothing to the Dregs[1], Neither Good nor Ill.

A sage once reduced all virtue to the **golden mean**[2]. Push right to the extreme and it becomes wrong: press all the juice from an orange and it becomes bitter. Even in enjoyment never go to extremes. Thought too subtle is dull. If you milk a cow too much you draw blood, not milk.

83・容許自己犯小錯

有時一些無心的小錯更能展現你的才華。妒嫉的人通常會排斥別人，笑裏藏刀。完美的人錯就錯在什麼缺點都沒有，絕對的完美就是絕對的不完美。嫉妒會使人變成百眼巨人阿各斯，專門尋找瑕疵。指責如同閃電，總是襲擊最高的地方。即使是荷馬，也要不時地假裝承認在勇氣和智力上（但不是在謹慎性上）有敗筆之疏，來緩解別人的惡意，或至少不讓這種惡意傷人傷己。面對嫉妒的公牛時，你需將紅披風放在其利角上以便脫險求生。

---

1. venial [ˋvinjəl] adj. 可寬恕的
2. ostracism [ˋɑstrəsɪzəm] n. （古希臘）陶片放逐制，放逐，排斥
3. to perfection 完全地
4. Argus [ˋɑrgəs] n. 阿各斯，古希臘神話裡面的一位百眼巨人，可以觀察到所有方向的事物與動物，後世以此來比喻機警的守衛，機靈的護衛。

lxxxiii Allow Yourself Some Venial¹ Fault.

S ome such carelessness is often the greatest recommendation of talent. For envy exercises **ostracism**[2], most envenomed when most polite. It counts it **to perfection**[3] as a failing that it has no faults; for being perfect in all it condemns it in all. It becomes an **Argus**[4], all eyes for imperfection: 'tis its only consolation. Blame is like the lightning; it hits the highest. **Let Homer nod now and then and affect some negligence in valour or in intellect – not in prudence – so as to disarm malevolence, or at least to prevent its bursting with its own venom**[5]. You thus leave your cloak on the horns of Envy in order to save your immortal parts.

---

5. 典出賀拉斯的《詩藝》，意思是即使荷馬這樣的大詩人，也有寫得不盡如人意的地方。

84・學會利用對手

抓 東西勿抓其刃，因刃會傷身；但若抓其柄，則可護身。當面對你的敵人時，尤要善用此理。智者在對手身上學習到的東西比愚人在朋友身上學習到的東西更多。敵人的惡意往往會激起我們的鬥志去戰勝困難。許多偉人的成就都是他們的對手所造就的。奉承比憎恨更為險惡，奉承會掩飾你錯誤的一面，憎恨卻能讓你認識到錯誤並加以糾正。智者能將敵意轉化為監督自己的鏡子，這面鏡子比善意更忠實地反映了一切，從而幫助我們改掉缺點，解決問題。當我們與惡毒的對手競爭時，我們就會變得異常小心謹慎。

---

1. level [ˋlɛvl] vt. 夷平

lxxxiv Make Use of Your Enemies.

Y ou should learn to seize things not by the blade, which cuts, but by the handle, which saves you from harm: especially is this the rule with the doings of your enemies. A wise man gets more use from his enemies than a fool from his friends. Their ill-will often **levels**[1] mountains of difficulties which one would otherwise not face. Many have had their greatness made for them by their enemies. Flattery is more dangerous than hatred, because it covers the stains which the other causes to be wiped out. The wise will turn ill-will into a mirror more faithful than that of kindness. and remove or improve the faults referred to. Caution thrives well when rivalry and ill-will are next-door neighbours.

85·過猶不及

卓越的東西可以有很大的用處，而它的缺點是易被人濫用。所有的人都對它垂涎，而一旦得不到就惱羞成怒。百無一用是件壞事，而利於萬物也同樣糟糕。對處在這個階段的人來說，得就是失，最後他們會讓先前喜歡他們的人感到厭煩。而這種變盤會讓各種卓越的事物黯然失色，喪失了起初因獨一無二而獲得的讚譽，還被粗鄙之人蔑視。避免這種極端的方法就是要適度地展示你的才華。如果你願意，你可以全力追求完美，但展示之時則要把握好分寸。有道是火把愈亮，消耗愈多，持續愈短。越是真人不露相，人們就越會尊敬你。

---

1. manille [mə'nil] n. 一種以10點為最大牌的紙牌遊戲
2. covet [`kʌvɪt] v. 垂涎，覬覦
3. vex [vɛks] vt. 使煩惱，惱怒

lxxxv Do Not Play Manille[1].

I t is a fault of excellence that being so much in use it is liable to abuse. Because all **covet**[2] it, all are **vexed**[3] by it. It is a great misfortune to be of use to nobody; scarcely less to be of use to everybody. People who reach this stage lose by gaining, and at last bore those who desired them before. These Manilles wear away all kinds of excellence: losing the earlier esteem of the few, they obtain discredit among the vulgar. The remedy against this extreme is to moderate your brilliance. Be extraordinary in your excellence, if you like, but be ordinary in your display of it. The more light a torch gives, the more it burns away and the nearer 'tis to going out. Show yourself less and you will be rewarded by being esteemed more.

86 · 預防謠言

群眾像是一個多頭的怪物，它長著多雙充滿惡意的眼睛、多個會濫施誹謗的舌頭。一旦一個惡意的謠言傳播開來，它就會成為你良好名譽上的一個污點；如果它同綽號一樣附於你的身上，那你的名譽就岌岌可危。通常某些顯眼的缺點或是可笑的特徵會引得謠言四起。但有時候，謠言來自於公眾的不信任，再加上有些人出於嫉妒而惡意利用了這一點而憑空捏造出來。惡意的冷嘲熱諷比直接的指責更容易摧毀一個人的聲譽。要臭名遠播很容易，因為人們很容易相信別人做的壞事，而要證明自己的清白則很難。智者會根據情況盡力避免這種災難發生在自己身上，他會時時保持警覺，不讓流言蜚語有機可乘，要知道預防比治療容易百倍。

---

1. detraction [dɪ`trækʃən] n. 誹謗
2. wag [wæg] vt. 搖擺，饒舌
3. blemish [`blɛmɪʃ] n. 污點，缺點，瑕疵
4. mischance [mɪs`tʃæns] n. 不幸，災難
5. sedulous [`sɛdʒələs] adj. 孜孜不倦的

lxxxvi Prevent Scandal.

Many heads go to make the mob, and in each of them are eyes for malice to use and a tongue for **detraction**[1] to **wag**[2]. If a single ill report spread, it casts a **blemish**[3] on your fair fame, and if it clings to you with a nickname, your reputation is in danger. Generally it is some salient defect or ridiculous trait that gives rise to the rumours. At times these are malicious additions of private envy to general distrust. For there are wicked tongues that ruin a great reputation more easily by a witty sneer than by a direct accusation. It is easy to get into bad repute, because it is easy to believe evil of any one: it is not easy to clear yourself. The wise accordingly avoid these **mischances**[4], guarding against vulgar scandal with **sedulous**[5] vigilance. It is far easier to prevent than to **rectify**[6] .

---

6. rectify [ˋrɛktə͵faɪ] vt. 矯正，調整

87 · 文化和修養

人生來是野蠻的，只有後天的文化修養才能使其超越於動物之上。有文化才使我們成為真正的人，人性越強，他的文明程度也就越高。多虧有了文化，希臘人才能把世界上的其他人都稱為「野蠻人」。無知則等於粗野和愚魯，沒有什麼比知識更有助於教化了，但若缺乏優雅，知識也是粗而不精。除了我們的理智要高雅外，還有我們的欲望，尤其是我們的談吐，都要是高雅的。有些人不論是內在還是外在天生都是優雅的，包括他們的思想、言論和衣著（這是靈魂的外衣）以及他們的才華（這是靈魂的果實）。而另一方面，有些人則是如此粗俗，用他們那令人難以忍受的粗野與邋遢玷污了一切，甚至玷污了他們優秀的品格。

---

1. rind [raɪnd] n. 外皮
2. tarnish [`tɑrnɪʃ] v. 玷污，損害

lxxxvii Culture and Elegance.

M an is born a barbarian, and only raises himself above the beast by culture. Culture therefore makes the man; the more a man, the higher. Thanks to it, Greece could call the rest of the world barbarians. Ignorance is very raw; nothing contributes so much to culture as knowledge. But even knowledge is coarse if without elegance. Not alone must our intelligence be elegant, but our desires, and above all our conversation. Some men are naturally elegant in internal and external qualities, in their thoughts, in their address, in their dress, which is the rind[1] of the soul, and in their talents, which is its fruit. There are others, on the other hand, so gauche that everything about them, even their very excellences, is tarnished[2] by an intolerable and barbaric want of neatness.

88 · 行為舉止要豪爽大氣

　　一個偉大的人物不應該表現得小家子氣。他不應該對事物斤斤計較，尤其是那些令人不快的事物。儘管瞭解全局很重要，但沒有必要對事事都盤根究底。在這種情況下，一個人應該像紳士或勇士一樣得體。學會忽略細節是處事的一大要訣。對於親人和朋友間的大多數事情要視而不見，甚至是敵人間的事情也當如此。過猶不及，對令人討厭的事物更是如此。一直糾纏於那使你感到厭煩的事物也是種瘋狂的表現。一般說來，人們都聽從心靈和理性的聲音來行事。

---

1. pry [praɪ] v. 探查
2. superfluity [ˌsupəˋfluətɪ] n. 多餘，過剩
3. hover [ˋhʌvɚ] v. 徘徊

The Art of worldly wisdom ◀◀

lxxxviii Let Your Behaviour Ye Fine and Noble.

A great man ought not to be little in his behaviour. He ought never to **pry**[1] too minutely into things, least of all in unpleasant matters. For though it is important to know all, it is not necessary to know all about all. One ought to act in such cases with the generosity of a gentleman, conduct worthy of a gallant man. To overlook forms a large part of the work of ruling. Most things must be left unnoticed among relatives and friends, and even among enemies. All **superfluity**[2] is annoying, especially in things that annoy. To keep **hovering**[3] around the object or your annoyance is a kind of mania. Generally speaking, every man behaves according to his heart and his understanding.

89 · 認識你自己

你要認識自己的才華、能力、判斷力和想法。只有認識你自己，你才能做自己的主人。鏡子可以照出你的臉，卻不能照出你的靈魂，不妨讓細心的自我反思代替吧。當人們不再注重你的外在形象時，就應試著去提高和改善內在修養。要瞭解你的智力和處理事情的能力，考驗自己的勇氣，好在適當的時候表現出來。不管面對什麼，都要保持堅定的立場和冷靜的頭腦。

90 · 長壽的秘訣

要好好活著。有兩件事會加速生命的終結：愚蠢和墮落。有些人死是因為不知道如何維持生命；另外一些人則是因為不想維持生命。正如美德就是它自身的回報一樣，邪惡也是它自身的懲罰。在邪惡中度過一生的人，他的生命會加倍地縮短；而一個高尚的人將會獲得永生。你的身體能感覺到你靈魂的堅定力量，一個高尚的人生不但意願深遠，而且綿延長久。

---

1. substitute [`sʌbstəˌtjut] n. 代替物，代用品

lxxxix Know Yourself –

i n talents and capacity, in judgment and inclination. You cannot master yourself unless you know yourself. There are mirrors for the face but none for the mind. Let careful thought about yourself serve as a **substitute**[1]. When the outer image is forgotten, keep the inner one to improve and perfect. Learn the force of your intellect and capacity for affairs, test the force of your courage in order to apply it, and keep your foundations secure and your head clear for everything.

xc The Secret of Long Life.

L ead a good life. Two things bring life speedily to an end: folly and immorality. Some lose their life because they have not the intelligence to keep it, others because they have not the will. Just as virtue is its own reward, so is vice its own punishment. He who lives a fast life runs through life in a double sense. A virtuous life never dies. The firmness of the soul is communicated to the body, and a good life is long not only in intention but also in extension.

91・三思而後行

若你做事前就預感可能會失敗，那旁觀者就能確定你會失敗，尤其這旁觀者是你的對手時。當你激動的情緒使你的判斷猶豫不決、搖擺不定時，你必須冷靜下來，因為等你真正冷靜後，你會發現你之前的想法是多麼荒唐愚蠢。不確定時展開行動是極危險的，穩當的做法是這時不做任何事情。謹慎小心之人不會把寶押在可能性上，他們會始終保持理智。當一件事情在計畫醞釀之初就遭遇判斷力的譴責，那它怎麼可能會有好的結局呢？如果說經過內心審視而通過的辦法還難免出錯，對那些遭到理智的懷疑和非議的事情，我們又能期望會有什麼好的收穫呢？

---

1. set to work 開始工作
2. doer [`duɚ] n. 行為者，實幹家
3. scruple [`skrupl] n. 顧忌，顧慮
4. nem.con abbr. 全體一致地，無異議地

xci Never Set to Work[1] at Anything if You Have Any Doubts of Its Prudence.

A suspicion of failure in the mind of the **doer**[2] is proof positive of it in that of the onlooker, especially if he is a rival. If in the heat of action your judgment feels **scruples**[3], it will afterwards in cool reflection condemn it as a piece of folly. Action is dangerous where prudence is in doubt: better leave such things alone. Wisdom does not trust to probabilities; it always marches in the mid-day light of reason. How can an enterprise succeed which the judgment condemns as soon as conceived? And if resolutions passed **nem. con.**[4] by inner court often turn out unfortunately, what can we expect of those undertaken by a doubting reason and a vacillating judgment?

92 · 超凡的智慧

我是指在所有的事情中都應展現這種智慧，這是規範言行舉止的最高準則。當你的官職越高時，那這條準則就越有必要。一盎司的審慎明智抵得上許多聰明才智。穩定前進最為重要，雖然這不會為你贏得很多的掌聲。由智慧所帶來的名譽可以吹響最後成功的號角。你能使審慎之人對你的處事感到滿意就足夠了，因為他們的贊同幾乎就是成功的試金石。

93 · 成為多才多藝之人

一個人要是各方面都很優秀，那他就相當於許多人的結合體。他會讓生活時時刻刻充滿樂趣，並會將歡樂傳遞給他身邊的朋友們。多才多藝會使生活每天都充滿快樂。其實懂得如何欣賞、享受美好的事物亦是一種藝術，既然自然讓人成為整個自然世界的精華，那就用藝術去訓練人的品味和智慧，讓其成為真正的小宇宙。

---

1. transcendant:為法語詞，在英語中對應的詞為 transcendent [træn`sɛndənt] adj. 卓越的，出類拔萃的
2. numerous [`njumərəs] adj. 眾多的，許多的，無數的
3. ton [tʌn] n. 大量，許多
4. microcosm [`maɪkrə,kɑzəm] n. 小天地，小宇宙

xcii Transcendant[1] Wisdom.

I mean in everything. The first and highest rule of all deed and speech, the more necessary to be followed the higher and more **numerous**[2] our posts, is: an ounce of wisdom is worth more than **tons**[3] of cleverness. It is the only sure way, though it may not gain so much applause. The reputation of wisdom is the last triumph of fame. It is enough if you satisfy the wise, for their judgment is the touchstone of true success.

xciii Versatility.

A man of many excellences equals many men. By imparting his own enjoyment of life to his circle he enriches their life. Variety in excellences is the delight of life. It is a great art to profit by all that is good, and since Nature has made man in his highest development an abstract of herself, so let Art create in him a true **microcosm**[4] by training his taste and intellect.

94 · 掩飾自己的能力

聰明之人如果想要得到別人的尊重，那就不能讓其看穿你有多少知識和能力。可以讓人瞭解你，但不可讓人看穿你。沒有人看得出你才能的極限，也就沒有人會感到失望。沒有人有機會全盤瞭解你。讓別人猜測你的才能究竟有多大，哪怕是他們對你的才能產生懷疑，切記這都比全盤托出你的才能——無論你的才能多麼大——更能讓你贏得別人的尊敬和崇拜。

95 · 讓別人對你永遠抱有期望

要不斷地使他人對你抱有期望，讓他人對你的需要越來越多，讓他們由於你出色的業績而去盼望你能創造更大的業績。一開始不宜展示出你全部才能。你要學會隱藏你的才能和智慧，這會使得別人對你的期待之心永遠保持下去。

---

1. veneration [ˌvɛnəˈreʃən] n. 尊敬，崇拜
2. stir up 攪動，使揚起
3. herald [ˈhɛrəld] vt. 預示…的發生
4. dissipated [ˈdɪsəˌpetɪd] adj. 消散的

xciv Keep the Extent of Your Abilities Unknown.

T he wise man does not allow his knowledge and abilities to be sounded to the bottom, if he desires to be honoured by all. He allows you to know them but not to comprehend them. No one must know the extent of his abilities, lest he be disappointed. No one ever has an opportunity of fathoming him entirely. For guesses and doubts about the extent of his talents arouse more **veneration**[1] than accurate knowledge of them, be they ever so great.

xcv Keep Expectation Alive.

K eep **stirring it up**[2]. Let much promise more, and great deeds **herald**[3] greater. Do not rest your whole fortune on a single cast of the die. It requires great skill to moderate your forces so as to keep expectation from being **dissipated**[4].

96. 精準的辨別力

是理性的要素和謹慎的基石，有了它們，你就會較容易獲得成功。它是一種天賦，應該作為我們所能得到的最好的能力來祈禱。精準的辨別力是我們的護身鎧甲，沒有它，我們就有了缺陷，其他的品格就沒這麼重要，充其量也就是量的變化而達不到質的提升。人生大事的決策都有賴於它的指導和協助，因為一切事情都依賴理智。判斷力總有個自然趨向，那就是它總是朝向理性，總是接近真實。

97. 追求並保持你的聲譽

每個人都喜歡擁有聲譽，但聲譽得來不易，只有卓越不凡的才能才會帶來聲譽，而卓越的才能又難以輕易得到，不像平庸那樣易得。一旦我們擁有了聲譽，就會比較容易保持它。保持我們的聲譽需要承擔許多責任，做出許多成績。聲譽若來自於高貴的出身或高雅的行為，則更具一種威嚴，但只有名副其實的聲譽才能真正持久。

---

1. panoply [`pænəplɪ] n. 全副盔甲，華麗服飾
2. liking [`laɪkɪŋ] n. 愛好，嗜好
3. usufruct [`juzjʊˌfrʌkt] n. [律]用益權，使用權，行使用益權
4. sphere [sfɪr] n. 球體，領域

xcvi The Highest Discretion.

I t is the throne of reason, the foundation of prudence: by its means success is gained at little cost. It is a gift from above, and should be prayed for as the first and best quality. 'Tis the main piece of the **panoply**[1], and so important that its absence makes a man imperfect, whereas with other qualities it is merely a question of more or less. All the actions of life depend on its application; all require its assistance, for everything needs intelligence. Discretion consists in a natural tendency to the most rational course, combined with a **liking**[2] for the surest.

xcvii Obtain and Preserve a Reputation.

I t is the **usufruct**[3] of fame. It is expensive to obtain a reputation, for it only attaches to distinguished abilities, which are as rare as mediocrities are common. Once obtained, it is easily preserved. It confers many an obligation, but it does more. When it is owing to elevated powers or lofty **spheres**[4] of action, it rises to a kind of veneration and yields a sort of majesty. But it is only a well-founded reputation that lasts permanently.

98. 深藏不露

激情是心靈之窗，會顯露你的意圖，很多實用的技巧包括如何掩飾激情。顯露自己意圖者往往會是失敗者。對於別人的關注你更需小心謹慎：你要像烏賊噴墨一樣掩飾住你的意圖，甚至連你的興趣愛好也不要讓別人知道，以防被別人利用。不管是違逆抑或奉承對方，都儘量避免吧！

99. 真相與表相

世間萬物其表相與真相往往不一致，很少有人能透過表相看清真相，大多數人會只滿足於看到浮光掠影的表相。如果這種正確看起來虛偽又邪惡，那麼僅僅正確是不夠的。

---

1. cuttlefish [ˋkʌtl͵fɪʃ] n. [動]墨魚，烏賊
2. run counter to 違反，背道而馳

xcviii Write Your Intentions in Cypher.

T he passions are the gates of the soul. The most practical knowledge consists in disguising them. He that plays with cards exposed runs a risk of losing the stakes. The reserve of caution should combat the curiosity of inquirers: adopt the policy of the **cuttlefish**[1]. Do not even let your tastes be known, lest others utilise them either by **running counter to them**[2] or by flattering them.

xcix Reality and Appearance.

T hings pass for what they seem, not for what they are. Few see inside; many take to the outside. It is not enough to be right, if right seem false and ill.

100. 成為一個不抱愚蠢幻想的人，一個睿智的基督徒，一個真正的哲學家

不能只是看上去是，更不能假裝是。如今，哲學不受重視，然而它曾經是智者的主要旨趣。思考的藝術已經失去了它先前的良好聲譽。當初塞內加將其引入羅馬之時，曾一度使貴族們爭相效仿，如今卻被認為不合時宜。發現謊言一直被認為是深度思考的產物，也是高尚靈魂的真正樂趣所在。

---

1. courtier [`kortjɚ] n. 朝臣；奉承者，拍馬屁的人
2. affect [ə`fɛkt] vt. 假裝
3. out of place 不在適當的位置，不合適

c A Man Without Illusions,
a Wise Christian, a Philosophic Courtier¹.

B e all these, not merely seem to be them, still less **affect**² to be them. Philosophy is nowadays discredited, but yet it was always the chiefest concern of the wise. The art of thinking has lost all its former repute. Seneca introduced it at Rome: it went to court for some time, but now it is considered **out of place**³ there. And yet the discovery of deceit was always thought the true nourishment of a thoughtful mind, the true delight of a virtuous soul.

101. 世人總是喜歡彼此嘲笑，
殊不知他們都是傻子

世間萬物都有好與壞兩個方面，關鍵在於你怎樣去看待。你所追求喜歡的可能是別人所厭煩的。不要總是用自己的眼光去衡量、評價所有的事情。如果那樣做，只會顯得你無知與愚蠢。好事也並非意味著會讓某一個特定的人滿意：就如同每個人的趣味都各不相同。你所不喜歡的會有別的人去喜歡。不要因為別人喜歡這件事物，就改變自己的看法，要知道總會有其他人欣賞它。他們的欣賞會受旁人指責。讚揚的真正標準是得到知名人士和專業人士的認可。我們每個人不應該只限於一種判斷、一種品味和一種行為規範。

---

1. persecute [`pɜ·sɪˌkjut] vt. 厭煩，困擾，為難

ci One Half of the World Laughs at the Other, and Fools Are They All.

E verything is good or everything is bad according to the votes they gain. What one pursues another **persecutes**[1]. He is an insufferable ass that would regulate everything according to his ideas. Excellences do not depend on a single man's pleasure. So many men, so many tastes, all different. There is no defect which is not affected by some, nor need we lose heart if things please not some, for others will appreciate them. Nor need their applause turn our head, for there will surely be others to condemn. The real test of praise is the approbation of famous men and of experts in the matter. You should aim to be independent of any one vote, of any one fashion, of any one century.

102. 欲成大事，必要有胸襟

如果說智慧是個容器，你最重要的器官就是胃了，因為巨大的容量意味著巨大的消化能力。大富大貴不會讓一個有更大胃口的人覺得無福消受。同樣的東西，有人能吃飽，而有人則吃不飽。對於消化力差的人來說，大富大貴反而是很大的負擔，因為他們既天生不能擔大任，也不願後天居顯位。與人相處久了必然產生矛盾，富貴榮耀會沖昏他們的頭腦，使其不知所措，最終不能把握而失去。他們雖有機會身居顯位，但只會令其神智不清，好運連連只會令其神亂心迷，這所有的一切就是因為他們無胸懷度量。想功成名就就必須有容納萬物之胸襟度量，且需小心謹慎，避免做心胸狹隘之事。

---

1. surfeit [ˋsɝfɪt] n. 過食，過度

cii Be Able to Stomach Big Slices of Luck.

In the body of wisdom not the least important organ is a big stomach, for great capacity implies great parts. Big bits of luck do not embarrass one who can digest still bigger ones. What is a **surfeit**[1] for one may be hunger for another. Many are troubled as it were with weak digestion, owing to their small capacity being neither born nor trained for great employment. Their actions turn sour, and the humours that arise from their undeserved honours turn their head and they incur great risks in high place: they do not find their proper place, for luck finds no proper place in them. A man of talent therefore should show that he has more room for even greater enterprises, and above all avoid showing signs of a little heart.

103. 時刻維護尊嚴

世間之人不會都是王侯將相，但不論你身處哪個階層、擁有什麼樣的條件，你的言行舉止都應有王者風範。你要像國王一樣，擁有卓越非凡的表現和偉大崇高的思想。即使你在現實生活中不能為王，那你也應該在品格上達到王者的境界，你的正直品格會助你擁有王者之風。若你能成為這種品格的典範，就不必再羨慕他人的偉大。那些位高權重、接近王者之人應該學習王者的道德風範，而不只是追逐浮華的表面排場；應當追求高尚樸實之品性，而非奢靡浮華之心態。

---

1. deed [did] n. 行為，行動

ciii Let Each Keep up His Dignity.

L et each **deed**[1] of a man in its degree, though he be not a king, be worthy of a prince, and let his action be princely within due limits. Sublime in action, lofty in thought, in all things like a king, at least in merit if not in might. For true kingship lies in spotless rectitude, and he need not envy greatness who can serve as a model of it. Especially should those near the throne aim at true superiority, and prefer to share the true qualities of royalty rather than take parts in its mere ceremonies, yet without affecting its imperfections but sharing in its true dignity.

104. 把握不同工作的重點

工作所需條件不盡相同，這些工作的多樣性需要我們付出十分的精力和擁有非凡的判斷力。有些工作需要放手去做，而有些則需要更多技巧。最簡單的工作只要努力踏實就能做好，而最難的則需要聰明智慧。前者只需要一個人好的工作態度，而後者即使是付出一個人全部的注意力和熱忱也未必能完成。管理人是很困難的事情，若管理傻子或瘋子則更難，管理那些一無所知的人往往需要付出雙倍的努力。讓人無法忍受的是每天在固定的時間按著固定的模式去做那些無聊的大量重複工作。**那些本身很重要，又不單調，還能令我們總是保持新鮮感的工作才是更好的工作。**最受尊敬的工作是那些擁有獨立性和自主權的工作。最差的工作則是那些讓我們不停地操心憂慮的工作。

---

1. tax [tæks] vt. 使負重擔
2. discemment [dɪ`sɜnmənt] n. 識別力，眼力，洞察力
3. blockhead [`blɑk͵hɛd] n. 笨蛋，傻子
4. office [`ɔfɪs] n. 職位、職務
5. engross [ɪn`gros] vt. 使全神貫注

civ Try Your Hand at Office.

I t requires varied qualities, and to know which is needed **taxes**[1] attention and calls for masterly **discernment**[2]. Some demand courage, others tact. Those that merely require rectitude are the easiest, the most difficult those requiring cleverness. For the former all that is necessary is character; for the latter all one's attention and zeal may not suffice. 'Tis a troublesome business to rule men, still more fools or **blockheads**[3] : double sense is needed with those who have none. It is intolerable when an **office**[4] **engrosses**[5] a man with fixed hours and a settled routine. Those are better that leave a man free to follow his own devices, combining variety with importance, for the change refreshes the mind. The most in repute are those that have least or most distant dependence on others; the worst is that which worries us both here and hereafter.

105. 簡潔勝於繁瑣

若總是談論一個話題，則會令人感到沉悶、厭倦。簡潔處事令人輕鬆愉快，給人好感，且會有事半功倍之效。簡潔會在禮貌方面補償其失於草率的方面。好事若簡潔處之則會好處加倍。若混雜之事簡潔處理，亦不至於太壞。**少而精勝於多而繁**。眾所周知，話多之人在處理事情和做出正式的論述上很難有見地。有些人不善於為宇宙增添光彩，卻善於做絆腳石。他們像是無用之事，令人退避三舍。謹慎聰慧之人會避免因繁瑣的處事而令人生厭，特別是繁忙的重要人物，因為激怒這樣一個人會比惹惱其他所有的人更糟糕。談話高明之人即是言簡意賅之人。

---

1. be apt to 傾向於
2. flatter [`flætɚ] vt. 使高興，使滿意
3. curtness [`kɝtnɪs] n. 唐突，草率
4. farrago [fə`rɑgo] n. 混雜，混雜物
5. stumbling-stone = stumbling block 障礙物，絆腳石
6. centrepiece [`sɛntɚpis] n. 最重要的部分

cv Don't Be a Bore.

T he man of one business or of one topic is **apt to**[1] be heavy. Brevity **flatters**[2] and does better business; it gains by courtesy what it loses by **curtness**[3] . Good things, when short, are twice as good. The quintessence of the matter is more effective than a whole **farrago**[4] of details. It is a well-known truth that talkative folk rarely have much sense whether in dealing with the matter itself or its formal treatment. There are that serve more for **stumbling-stones**[5] than **centrepieces**[6], useless lumber in every one's way. The wise avoid being bores, especially to the great, who are fully occupied: it is worse to disturb one of them than all the rest. Well said is soon said.

187

106. 不可炫耀地位

炫耀高貴比炫耀個人魅力更容易遭人記恨。處處顯得自己像是偉人，只會讓人嫉妒，甚至讓人憎惡。往往你越是竭盡全力、挖空心思地去想得到他人的敬重，卻越得不到它，因為它取決於人們認為你是否值得崇拜。你有才能使其名副其實，方能得到讚譽，若是想巧取豪奪，那是萬萬不成的。身居高位需要具備相當的威權，因此有足夠的威權能使你有效率地履行你在該職位上的職責。不要強迫別人尊敬你，要試著做出成果讓別人主動來尊敬你。一個人老是強調地位的尊貴只能說明他不配擁有這份工作，他無法承受這份工作。如果你**想被看重，那讓別人看重你的才華吧**，而不是其他外在的東西。甚至國王都願意因為自己的個人品格而獲得敬重，而不是因為王位。

---

1. parade [pəˋred] v. 炫耀，誇耀
2. adventitious [ˌædvɛnˋtɪʃəs] adj. 偶然的，外來的

cvi Do Not Parade[1] Your Position.

T o outshine in dignity is more offensive than in personal attractions. To pose as a personage is to be hated: envy is surely enough. The more you seek esteem the less you obtain it, for it depends on the opinion of others. You cannot take it, but must earn and receive it from others. Great positions require an amount of authority sufficient to make them efficient: without it they cannot be adequately filled. Preserve therefore enough dignity to carry on the duties of the office. Do not enforce respect, but try and create it. Those who insist on the dignity of their office, show they have not deserved it, and that it is too much for them. If you wish to be valued, be valued for your talents, not for anything **adventitious**[2]. Even kings prefer to be honoured for their personal qualifications rather than for their station.

107. 勿要顯露自我得意之神態

人啊，既不要總是顯得對自己的一切都感到不滿意，這只是懦弱的表現；亦不要總是自鳴得意，這只是愚蠢的表現。自我感覺良好多數源於無知，無知讓我們逞一時之快，卻損害了我們的名聲。既然一個人無法達到如別人那般完美，他就開始對自己的平庸才智滿意起來。懷疑是一種智慧，它有其價值，能夠幫助我們避免禍端或者是讓我們在遇到挫折時因有心理準備而無所畏懼。世人皆是如此，荷馬也有打瞌睡的時候，亞歷山大也是因失敗才從自我欺騙中警醒過來。萬事依賴於當時的環境，促成一件事成功的因素可能會導致另一件事情的失敗。然而，對於一個無可救藥的蠢蛋來說，仍然保留著最空虛的自我滿足，還像鮮花一樣美麗綻放，並且還會繼續播撒許多滿足的種子。

---

1. superlative [sə`pɝlətɪv] adj. 最好的，最優秀的
2. distrust [dɪs`trʌst] n. 不信任
3. mishap [`mɪs,hæp] n. 災難
4. 這是一句諺語 Even Homer sometimes nods. 智者千慮，必有一失

cvii Show No Self-satisfaction.

Y ou must neither be discontented with yourself – and that were poor-spirited – nor self-satisfied – and that is folly. Self-satisfaction arises mostly from ignorance: it would be a happy ignorance not without its advantages if it did not injure our credit. Because a man cannot achieve the **superlative**[1] perfections of others, he contents himself with any mediocre talent of his own. **Distrust**[2] is wise, and even useful, either to evade **mishaps**[3] or to afford consolation when they come, for a misfortune cannot surprise a man who has already feared it. **Even Homer nods at times**[4], and Alexander fell from his lofty state and out of his illusions. Things depend on many circumstances: what constitutes triumph in one set may cause a defeat in another. In the midst of all incorrigible folly remains the same with empty self-satisfaction, blossoming, flowering, and running all to seed.

108. 藉他人智慧成就自我

交流是很好的方法。透過與聰明智慧者交流行為舉止、個人品味，你會從中受到潛移默化的影響。辦事優柔寡斷之人應與辦事雷厲風行之人交往，同理，其他氣質的人亦應與能夠互補之人多做交往。這樣，我們將會在不經意間融合二者之長。與別人和諧共處是一種偉大的藝術。讓對立相互交替將使宇宙變得更加美麗且不斷運轉。如果說這種交替可以讓自然世界變得更加和諧，那麼它對人們的精神世界會起更多作用。故你在選擇朋友或是僕人時，應該遵循此道。彼此迥異的兩極交往會創造一種更加有效的中庸之道。

---

1. intercourse [ˋɪntɚˌkors] n. 交往，交流
2. insensibly [ɪnˋsɛnsəblɪ] adv. 無意識地，無感覺地
3. sanguine [ˋsæŋgwɪn] adj. 樂觀的，充滿信心的
4. comrade [ˋkɑmræd] n. 朋友，同志，伙伴
5. lymphatic [lɪmˋfætɪk] adj. 遲鈍的，軟弱的

cviii The Path to Greatness Is Along with Others.

Intercourse[1] works well: manners and taste are shared, good sense and even talent grow **insensibly**[2] . Let the **sanguine**[3] man then make a **comrade**[4] of the **lymphatic**[5], and so with the other temperaments, so that without any forcing the golden mean is obtained. It is a great art to agree with others. The alternation of contraries beautifies and sustains the world: if it can cause harmony in the physical world, still more can it do so in the moral. Adopt this policy in the choice of friends and defendants; by joining extremes the more effective middle way is found.

109. 寬以待人

有的人脾氣暴躁，遇事易大動肝火，周圍的一切事情在他看來都存在缺點，但是他們這樣做並非是存在任何邪惡的動機，而是源於他們的天性。他們譴責一切，譴責已做的事，譴責那些將要做的事，這就暴露出比殘忍更可惡的性情。此種性情令人痛恨。這種人會過分誇大事情，將芝麻綠豆大的事情誇大成為西瓜，責難他人，並會因為一件事情而把人全盤否定。他們就像暴躁的工頭，能把天堂踐踏成牢房，在其盛怒之時，他們把一切都推到極端。相反，具有好性情的人懂得去原諒別人的過錯，認為這些過錯並非那些人的本意，至少認為只是那些人一時的不慎所造成的。

---

1. censorious [sɛn`sorɪəs] adj. 愛挑剔的
2. mote [mot] n. 塵埃，微粒
3. beam [bim] n. 光線，光束，橋樑
4. wherewith [hwɛr`wɪθ] adv. 那什麼，用那個，以其
5. force out 擠（出去），冲（出去）

cix Be Not Censorious[1].

T here are men of gloomy character who regard everything as faulty, not from any evil motive but because it is their nature to. They condemn all: these for what they have done, those for what they will do. This indicates a nature worse than cruel, vile indeed. **They accuse with such exaggeration that they make out of motes[2] beams[3] wherewith[4] to force out[5] the eyes[6].** They are always **taskmasters[7]** who could turn a paradise into a prison; if passion intervenes they drive matters to the extreme. A noble nature, on the contrary, always knows how to find an excuse for failings, if not in the intention, at least from oversight.

---

6. 英國作家威廉‧毛姆曾寫過一篇文章 On Motes and Beams，其中就講了人很容易原諒自己的缺點，卻抓住別人的缺點不放。

7. taskmaster [ˋtæskͺmæstɚ] n. 工頭

110. 知時而退

有句明智的格言說道：在被事物拋棄前先拋棄它們。末日來臨之前你應該及時奪取勝利，正如太陽即使在擁有燦爛的光輝時，有時也會悄悄地退隱於雲彩之後，這樣就會讓人們產生猜測，猜測其是否已經下山了呢。**要避免成為日落之境，在恰當的時候明智地選擇退出。**不要等到人們與你脊背相向，名聲不再時才選擇退出，此時你雖然身體還有知覺，但已失去了尊嚴。明智的騎士是不會等到馬在比賽中失敗時才會讓其退役的，那樣的話只會空留笑柄。絕代佳人應當知道在擁有美貌之際打碎鏡子，否則等容顏已老則悔之晚矣。

111. 擁有朋友

朋友是你另一個生命的所在。在朋友眼裏，他所有的朋友都聰明而善良，和他們相處時一切都變得如此的和諧與美好。人的價值在於朋友的祝願，而這有賴於贏得朋友的真心和讚譽。沒有所謂的奇蹟般的轉捩點，要獲得友誼只能做出友好的舉動。我們所擁有的大多數以及最好的品格都與他人密不可分。我們不是選擇與朋友相處，要不然就是選擇與敵人為伍。我們若每天都嘗試接觸一個新人，即使不能成為朋友，也可能成為你的支持與祝福者。經過不斷地接觸，有些人最終會成為你能傾吐心事的密友。

---

1. snatch [snætʃ] vi. 抓住　2. racer [ˋresɚ] n. 比賽者（包括人，動物，車輛等）
3. put to grass 使閒居，開除　4. derision [dɪˋrɪʒən] n. 嘲笑

cx Do Not Wait till You Are a Sinking Sun.

❱ Tis a maxim of the wise to leave things before things leave them. One should be able to **snatch**[1] a triumph at the end, just as the sun even at its brightest often retires behind a cloud so as not to be seen sinking, and to leave in doubt whether he has sunk or no. Wisely withdraw from the chance of mishaps, lest you have to do so from the reality. Do not wait till they turn you the cold shoulder and carry you to the grave, alive in feeling but dead in esteem. Wise trainers **put racers**[2] **to grass before**[3] they arouse **derision**[4] by falling on the course. A beauty should break her mirror early, lest she do so later with open eyes.

cxi Have Friends.

❱ Tis a second existence. Every friend is good and wise for his friend: among them all everything turns to good. Every one is as others wish him; that they may wish him well, he must win their hearts and so their tongues. There is no magic like a good turn, and the way to gain friendly feelings is to do friendly acts. The most and best of us depend on others; we have to live either among friends or among enemies. Seek some one every day to be a well-wisher if not a friend; by and by after trial some of these will become intimate.

112. 獲得他人的善意

即使處於最高層次的人在處理重要的問題時亦遵循此理。你可以透過獲得他人的友善而進一步獲得他的好評。有些人過於重視自己的才能而忽略了別人的善意。聰明智慧的人懂得，若有了別人的相助，自己無異於如虎添翼，會達到事半功倍之效。他人給你的善意與幫助會讓你的事情變得簡單容易，還會為你帶來你所缺乏的勇氣、誠實、智慧與謹慎。善意從來不會看到缺點，因為它沒想過要看。善意通常來自於一些共同的興趣與利益，比如性情、種族、家庭、國家或職業，或者來自於能力、責任、聲譽和功績。雖然獲得他人的善意很難，但是一旦我們贏得了它，那就能容易地保住它。雖然你能透過努力爭取到它，但你也必須知道如何運用它。

---

1. foresee [for`si] vt. 預見，預知
2. service road 便道

cxii Gain Good-will.

F or thus the first and highest cause **foresees**[1] and furthers the greatest objects. By gaining their good-will you gain men's good opinion. Some trust so much to merit that they neglect grace, but wise men know that **Service Road**[2] without a lift from favour is a long way indeed. Good-will facilitates and supplies everything: is supposes gifts or even supplies them, as courage, zeal, knowledge, or even discretion; whereas defects it will not see because it does not search for them. It arises from some common interest, either material, as disposition, nationality, relationship, fatherland, office; or formal, which is of a higher kind of communion, in capacity, obligation, reputation, or merit. The whole difficulty is to gain good-will; to keep it is easy. It has, however, to be sought for, and, when found, to be utilised.

113. 學會未雨綢繆

在 夏季即儲備過冬物資實乃聰明之舉，且更容易籌辦。鴻運當頭之際獲他人相助較易，且此時你會有眾多的朋友。但你要學會未雨綢繆，當你身陷逆境時，別人的幫助就會變得昂貴且難以獲得。在平時保持住擁有的好朋友和對你感恩戴德的人，有一天你會發現，這些人的價值不菲。卑鄙小人從來都不會有朋友，因為當他們處於好運之時，他們不屑於結交朋友；當霉運當頭時，別人也不屑於結交他們。

---

1. adversity [ədˋvɝsətɪ] n. 逆境，厄運，窘境

cxiii In Prosperity Prepare for Adversity.

I t is both wiser and easier to collect winter stores in summer. In prosperity favours are cheap and friends are many. 'Tis well therefore to keep them for more unlucky days, for **adversity**[1] costs dear and has no helpers. Retain a store of friendly and obliged persons; the day may come when their price will go up. Low minds never have friends; in luck they will not recognise them: in misfortune they will not be recognised by them.

114. 莫與人爭

競爭都會有損聲譽,你的競爭對手會絞盡腦汁來挑出你的缺點,讓你聲譽掃地。很少有不損聲譽的戰爭。處於敵對狀態之人則會挖空心思地去揭露我們想要隱藏的缺點。許多人在與他人成為對手之前一直都有著良好的聲譽。激烈的競爭會導致流言蜚語,甚至還會把埋藏已久的醜聞挖出來。**競爭由輕敵開始**,之後就是到處尋求幫助,甚至有點不擇手段。當辱罵這一武器不再有效時(它們大多數時候都是無效的),我們的對手為了報復也來辱罵我們,這樣做至少可以讓眾人淡忘我們曾經遭受的恥辱。善意之人總是心境平和。有良好聲譽及尊嚴之人即善意之人。

---

1. wage [wedʒ] v. 發動
2. skeleton [ˋskɛlətn] n. 骨架,骨骼
3. belittle [bɪˋlɪtl] vt. 輕視,使渺小,使…顯得渺小
4. beat away 打掉

cxiv Never Compete.

E very competition damages the credit: our rivals seize occasion to obscure us so as to out-shine us. Few **wage**[1] honourable war. Rivalry discloses faults which courtesy would hide. Many have lived in good repute while they had no rivals. The heat of conflict gives life, or even new life, to dead scandals, and digs up long-buried **skeletons**[2]. Competition begins with **belittling**[3], and seeks aid wherever it can, not only where it ought. And when the weapons of abuse do not effect their purpose, as often or mostly happens, our opponents use them for revenge, and use them at least for **beating away**[4] the dust of oblivion from anything to our discredit. Men of good-will are always at peace; men of good repute and dignity are men of good-will.

115. 習慣熟人的缺點

就如習慣一張醜陋的面孔一樣。當我們彼此互相依賴時，這是不可缺少的。有些很卑劣的人，我們雖無法與之相處，但卻又躲不開他們。聰明人必須習慣他們，正如我們看久了醜陋的面孔就會習慣一樣，和這種人處久了也就見怪不怪了。起初我們會感覺他們招人厭惡，漸漸地感覺也就不再像先前那樣強烈了。我們只需小心防範，儘量容忍寬容他們的缺點即可。

116. 只與有榮譽感的人打交道

你們之間可以彼此信任。他們的名譽便是他們行為的最好證明，即使是在被人誤解的時候，因為他們總是依照自己的原則行事。我們寧可與這類人爭論，也不要去戰勝那些卑劣的人。與卑劣之人共事很難，因為他們已經喪失了正直之心。在這些人之間不存在真正的友誼，他們的承諾不可信，儘管有時候他們也會顯得非常嚴肅認真，因為他們已經沒有了榮譽感。不要與這種人打交道，因為如果榮譽感都不能約束他的不良行為，那道德更沒有約束力了，因為榮譽感是正直的基石。

---

1. have regard to 注意到
2. hostage [ˋhɑstɪdʒ] n. 人質，抵押品
3. stringent [ˋstrɪndʒənt] adj. 嚴肅的

cxv Get Used to the Failings of Your Familiars,

a s you do to ugly faces. It is indispensable if they depend on us, or we on them. There are wretched characters with whom one cannot live, nor yet without them. Therefore clever folk get used to them, as to ugly faces, so that they are not obliged to do so suddenly under the pressure of necessity. At first they arouse disgust, but gradually they lose this influence, and reflection provides for disgust or puts up with it.

cxvi Only Act with Honourable Men.

Y ou can trust them and they you. Their honour is the best surety of their behaviour even in misunderstandings, for they always act **having regard to**[1] what they are. Hence 'tis better to have a dispute with honourable people than to have a victory over dishonourable ones. You cannot treat with the ruined, for they have no **hostages**[2] for rectitude. With them there is no true friendship, and their agreements are not binding, however **stringent**[3] they may appear, because they have no feeling of honour. Never have to do with such men, for if honour does not restrain a man, virtue will not, since honour is the throne of rectitude.

117. 莫要高談自我

否 則不是因虛榮而自誇，就是因自卑而自責，這樣的話不僅會讓你失去對自我的正確認識和判斷，同時也會為他人所不恥。在日常交談時你應盡力避免，在正式場合更是如此，因為在公眾場合任何不明智的表現都是很愚蠢的。同樣地，在某人面前談論他亦非明智之舉。因為你的言語舉止很可能被認為是曲意逢迎或口出不遜，從而讓你處於尷尬的境地。

118. 懂禮守節

這 使你深受大家的喜愛。禮節是文化的精髓，富有魅力，懂得禮節才會贏得別人的尊重；相反，粗魯言行只會令人厭煩，並對你產生敵意。若你因傲慢而粗魯，則會令人憎恨；若是缺乏修養所致，則定會遭人鄙視。禮節不怕周到而怕缺乏，其他事情亦是如此，少了禮節則不公正。若能對敵人仍以禮遇待之，則足以證明你有足夠的勇氣。以禮待人非難事，卻會讓你受益匪淺，敬人之人人亦敬之。**禮貌和尊敬有一大優點：即可施與他人，又於己無礙。**

---

1. little-minded 沒腦子的 2. beseem [bɪ`sim] v. 適合於 3. censure [`sɛnʃɚ] n. 責難 4. ingredient [ɪn`gridɪənt] n. 成分，因素 5. witchery [`wɪtʃərɪ] n. 巫術，魅力 6. abominable [ə`bɑmənəbl] adj. 討厭的，令人憎惡的
7. despicable [`dɛspɪkəbl] adj. 可鄙的，卑劣的

cxvii Never Talk of Yourself.

Y ou must either praise yourself, which is vain, or blame yourself, which is **little-minded**[1] :it ill **beseems**[2] him that speaks, and ill pleases him that hears. And if you should avoid this in ordinary conversation, how much more in official matters, and above all, in public speaking, where every appearance of unwisdom really is unwise. The same want of tact lies in speaking of a man in his presence, owing to the danger of going to one of two extremes: flattery or **censure**[3] .

cxviii Acquire the Reputation of Courtesy;

f or it is enough to make you liked. Politeness is the main **ingredient**[4]of culture, – a kind of **witchery**[5] that wins the regard of all as surely as discourtesy gains their disfavour and opposition; if this latter springs from pride, it is **abominable**[6] ; if from bad breeding, it is **despicable**[7]. Better too much courtesy than too little, provided it be not the same for all, which degenerates into injustice. Between opponents it is especially due as a proof of valour. It costs little and helps much: every one is honoured who gives honour. Politeness and honour have this advantage, that they remain with him who displays them to others.

119. 勿招人厭煩

要知道即使你不去招惹，別人的厭惡之心還會不招而至呢。人們常常對別人產生厭惡情緒，但卻又不知緣由何在。可能是因為厭惡之心比讚揚之心更易產生；對人報復的欲望會強於利己欲望的緣故吧。偏偏有些人總是想盡辦法招人生厭，可能是他們只想因此引起不快，抑或是樂於此道。但要切記，對你的厭惡之心一旦在他人心中產生，就很難抹去，正如惡名難改一樣。智慧之人令人敬畏，邪惡之人令人痛恨，傲慢之人令人不屑，取笑他人者則令人憎惡，古怪之人被人忽視。故欲得尊敬，先要敬人；欲得褒獎，先要褒獎他人。

---

1. cupidity [kju`pɪdətɪ] n. 貪心，貪婪
2. to be on bad terms with all 跟所有人都關係不好
3. malevolent [mə`lɛvələnt] adj. 有惡意的，壞心腸的
4. abhor [əb`hɔr] vt. 憎惡，痛恨
5. disdain [dɪs`den] n. 輕蔑

cxix Avoid Becoming Disliked.

There is no occasion to seek dislike: it comes without seeking quickly enough. There are many who hate of their own accord without knowing the why or the how. Their ill-will outruns our readiness to please. Their ill-nature is more prone to do others harm than their **cupidity**[1] is eager to gain advantage for themselves. Some manage **to be on bad terms with all**[2], because they always either produce or experience vexation of spirit. Once hate has taken root it is, like bad repute, difficult to eradicate. Wise men are feared, the **malevolent**[3] are **abhorred**[4], the arrogant are regarded with **disdain**[5], **buffoons**[6] with contempt, eccentrics with neglect. Therefore pay respect that you may be respected, and know that to be esteemed you must show esteem.

---

6. buffoon [bʌˈfun] n. 小丑

120. 生活要講究實際

知　識處於不斷更新之中，假裝無知是不明智的。人的思想與品味也在隨著時代的前進而改變，千萬不要讓你的思想落後過時，要讓你的品味與當代風格保持同步。大眾的品味總是正確的，若要出人頭地，需得先在品味上迎合大眾。明智之人不論是在思想的包裝還是在身體的包裝方面會努力調整自我去適應現實，即便過去看起來好得多也是如此。這一原則放諸四海而皆準，然為善應除外，因為善不分新舊，人人都需要時時行善。但在當今社會，為善似乎被認為過時而被忽略了，比如講真話與守諾言，這樣的誠實善良之人似乎只屬於過去的時代，但他們深受人愛戴。這種人雖然存在，但他們已經跟不上潮流，人們並不效仿他們。若是一個時代裏惡意盛行，善行難覓，那這個時代是何等的可悲啊！明智之人即使不能按照自己的意願生活，也要盡可能地發揮自身才能。**總想著命運沒有給你什麼，不如多想想命運之神給了你什麼！**

1. practically [ˈpræktɪklɪ] adv. 實際上，事實上，在實踐上
2. in（the）fashion 合乎時尚的，時髦的
3. for the time being 暫時
4. adornment [əˈdɔrnmənt] n. 裝飾，裝飾品

cxx Live Practically[1].

E ven knowledge has to be **in the fashion**[2], and where it is not it is wise to affect ignorance. Thought and taste change with the times. Do not be old-fashioned in your ways of thinking, and let your taste be in the modern style. In everything the taste of the many carries the votes; **for the time being**[3] one must follow it in the hope of leading it to higher things. In the **adornment**[4] of the body as of the mind adapt yourself to the present, even though the past appear better. But this rule does not apply to kindness, for goodness is for all time. It is neglected nowadays and seems out of date. Truth-speaking, keeping your word, and so too good people, seem to come from the good old times: yet they are liked for all that, but in such a way that even when they all exist they are not in the fashion and are not imitated. What a misfortune for our age that it regards virtue as a stranger and vice as a matter of course! If you are wise, live as you can, if you cannot live as you would. Think more highly of what fate has given you than of what it has denied.

121 · 勿庸人自擾

有人喜歡蜚短流長，而另外一些人則情願小題大做，庸人自擾。他們總喜歡高談闊論，事事都熱心關注，不是和別人爭論，就是把事情搞得很神秘。如果有些麻煩事可以避免，那就不要太慎重其事。對一些你本來應該拋開的事情耿耿於懷是荒謬可笑的。**若能超脫於物外而學會順其自然，則許多望之儼然之事將會化為輕風；若過分計較，則無足輕重之事反成壓肩之重擔。**當機立斷方能快刀斬亂麻，否則夜長夢多後患無窮。癒病之方有時反成致病之因。這無疑是人生的一條鐵律：做人要超脫豁達。

122 · 敏於言而踐於行

能夠讓你在眾多人中脫穎而出，深獲眾望。這個品格幾乎隨處可見，包括言語、外表，甚至是步伐。能夠征服人心實乃是偉大的勝利，但這絕非來自於愚蠢的推測或是傲慢的自誇，而是來自於因擁有美德和超凡才智而產生的威嚴。

---

1. preposterous [priˋpɑstərəs] adj. 荒謬的
2. gait [get] n. 步態，步法

cxxi Do Not Make a Business of What Is No Business.

A s some make gossip out of everything, so others business. They always talk big, take everything in earnest, and turn it into a dispute or a secret. Troublesome things must not be taken too seriously if they can be avoided. It is **preposterous**[1] to take to heart that which you should throw over your shoulders. Much that would be something has become nothing by being left alone, and what was nothing has become of consequence by being made much of. At the outset things can be easily settled, but not afterwards. Often the remedy causes the disease. 'Tis by no means the least of life's rules: to let things alone.

cxxii Distinction in Speech and Action.

B y this you gain a position in many places and carry esteem beforehand. It shows itself in everything, in talk, in look, even in **gait**[2]. It is a great victory to conquer men's hearts: it does not arise from any foolish presumption or pompous talk, but in a becoming tone of authority born of superior talent combined with true merit.

123 · 避免矯揉造作

越是有才能之人越不會刻意矯飾自己，矯揉造作會讓一切顯得粗俗不堪。這不但會讓他人厭倦，就連假裝者自己亦會感到不堪負荷，因為他活在眾人的目光之下，需要小心翼翼地掩飾自己。即使是最出眾的品格，若是矯揉造作也會黯然失色，因為這會讓它顯得驕傲做作、不自然，**自然的東西總是比虛假的東西要更受人歡迎。**人們總會肯定地以為，如果一個人假裝擁有某種美德，那一定是因為他自身缺乏這種美德。你越是努力做某件事，就越要顯得舉重若輕，這樣，別人看來就好像是你自然而然自發的行為一樣。但是你也不可對世間真情裝作默然而去突顯你不食人間煙火。**智慧之人永遠都顯得對自己的美德毫不自知，因為只有自己不去注意，你才能讓別人注意到它們。**如果除了他自己外，所有人都覺得他是個完美的人，那這個人就愈發偉大。他一生恪守此道而有口皆碑。

---

1. vulgar [`vʌlgɚ] a. 粗俗的，下流的
2. wearisome [`wɪrɪsəm] a. 令人厭倦的，使人疲倦的
3. spontaneously [spɑn`teniəsli] ad. 自然地，不由自主地

cxxiii Avoid Affectation.

T he more merit, the less affectation, which gives a **vulgar**[1] flavour to all. It is **wearisome**[2] to others and troublesome to the one affected, for he becomes a martyr to care and tortures himself with attention. The most eminent merits lose most by it, for they appear proud and artificial instead of being the product of nature, and the natural is always more pleasing than the artificial. One always feels sure that the man who affects a virtue has it not. The more pains you take with a thing, the more should you conceal them, so that it may appear to arise **spontaneously**[3] from your own natural character. Do not, however, in avoiding affectation fall into it by affecting to be unaffected. The sage never seems to know his own merits, for only by not noticing them can you call others' attention to them. He is twice great who has all the perfections in the opinion of all except of himself; he attains applause by two opposite paths.

124・成為眾望所歸之人

要贏得大多數人喜歡實屬不易，若你真能得到智者賞識，那真是無上快樂。雖然世態總是炎涼，但還是有些方法可以贏得人們的好感。最有把握的一個方法就是在自己的工作上、才能上都表現得出類拔萃，再加上討人喜歡的言行舉止，那就會是工作來找你，而不是你去找工作了。有些人可以給工作帶來榮耀，而有些人只能靠工作給自己帶來榮耀。若是因為繼任者的無能彰顯了前任的才能，那沒什麼可高興的，這並不意味前任是眾望所歸，而是繼任者不得人心。

125・勿只看他人短處

如果一個人只是專注於發現和宣揚他人的缺陷與惡名，那就表明他自己也是聲名狼藉之輩。有些人想用他人的過錯來掩飾自己的過錯，或至少幫自己的過錯開脫，或以此來尋求一種心理安慰，但只有傻瓜才會從中得到安慰。此種人無異於整座城池藏污納垢的陰溝，臭氣熏天。而專注於此道者，找到的缺點越多，自己也就越被沾染得臭氣熏天。人非聖賢，孰能無過，只是因為有些人名不見經傳，所以他的缺點才不為人所知。故要小心不要只看到別人的過錯，因為這樣會讓你變成一個討人厭的東西，一具沒有良心的行屍走肉。

---

1. sewer [`suɚ] n. 下水道　2. grub [grʌb] v. 尋找
3. registrar [`rɛdʒɪ,strɑr] n. 登記員

cxxiv Get Yourself Missed.

F ew reach such favour with the many; if with the wise 'tis the height of happiness. When one has finished one's work, coldness is the general rule. But there are ways of earning this reward of goodwill. The sure way is to excel in your office and talents: add to this agreeable manner and you reach the point where you become necessary to your office, not your office to you. Some do honour to their post, with others 'tis the other way. It is no great gain if a poor successor makes the predecessor seem good, for this does not imply that the one is missed, but that the other is wished away.

cxxv Do Not Be a Black List.

I t is a sign of having a tarnished name to concern oneself with the ill-fame of others. Some wish to hide their own stains with those of others, or at least wash them away: or they seek consolation therein – 'tis the consolation of fools. They must have bad breath who form the **sewers**[1] of scandal for the whole town. The more one **grubs**[2] about in such matters, the more one befouls oneself. There are few without stain somewhere or other, but it is of little known people that the failings are little known. Be careful then to avoid being a **registrar**[3] of faults. That is to be an abominable thing, a man that lives without a heart.

126・愚蠢的人不是蠢在犯錯，
而是犯了錯還不知道掩飾

人要學會掩飾欲望，更要掩飾缺點。有時候事情會變得一團糟，
但智者會試著掩飾自己的過錯，而愚蠢之人非但不掩藏，還到
處張揚他們所犯的錯誤。一個人名聲的好壞不只取決於你做了什麼，
更取決於你掩蓋了什麼。如果你不是一個潔身自愛之人，那你的言行
就必須謹慎。尤其是有地位之人，他們的過失就像是日蝕一樣格外引
人注目。即使是朋友之間，也很少彼此自曝其短，甚至可能的話，亦
勿對自己袒露心跡。還有一條人生箴言對你有很大幫助，那就是學會
忘記！

---

1. seal up 密封住
2. eclipse [ɪˋklɪps] n. 日（月）蝕

cxxvi Folly Consists Not in Committing Folly, but in Not Hiding It When Committed.

Y ou should keep your desires **sealed up**[1], still more your defects. All go wrong sometimes, but the wise try to hide the errors, but fools boast of them. Reputation depends more on what is hidden than on what is done; if a man does not live chastely, he must live cautiously. The errors of great men are like the **eclipses**[2] of the greater lights. Even in friendship it is rare to expose one's failings to one's friend. Nay, one should conceal them from oneself if one can. But here one can help with that other great rule of life: learn to forget.

127‧處事需從容灑脫

這樣更能彰顯你的才能，讓你妙語如珠，行動更有靈氣，使你別具風範。各種美德裝飾了我們的天性，而從容灑脫將這些美德修飾得更加完善。這種風範會對你的思想產生影響。這種優雅一般是與生俱來的，而非後天所能習得，就連各種訓練也往往難以獲得。這種從容灑脫的氣質並非安逸悠閒，它讓人顯得從容自然，氣定神閒，而又能戰勝困難，為完美畫上濃墨重彩的一筆。若是缺少處事之優雅風度，縱有花容月貌也只是具空殼而無生機，熱情對之亦會失去優雅大方之態。從容灑脫會使人超然物外，即使英勇無敵，謹言慎行，甚至帝王之尊與之相比都相形見絀。此乃成功之佳途，擺脫困境之妙方。

128‧高尚的品格

高尚的品格是紳士所必須具備的主要品格，它會激發你去追求其他的高貴品格。高尚的品格會使你品味高雅，品德高尚，思路開闊，情感細膩，飽受尊敬。擁有此品格，無論你在何處，都會引人注目，有時還能抹平出其不意的厄運。即使在行動上不能有所表現，它還是會作用於思想。雅量、慷慨以及各種英雄的品格均源於此。

---

1. finishing touch 最後一筆
2. dispatch [dɪˋspætʃ] vt. 辦完（全部事情）
3. highmindedness 古英語（＝ high mindedness）

cxxvii Grace in Everything.

❯ Tis the life of talents, the breath of speech, the soul of action, and the ornament of ornament. Perfections are the adornment of our nature, but this is the adornment of perfection itself. It shows itself even in the thoughts. 'Tis most a gift of nature and owes least to education; it even triumphs over training. It is more than ease, approaches the free and easy, gets over embarrassment, and adds the **finishing touch**[1] to perfection. Without it beauty is lifeless, graciousness ungraceful: it surpasses valour, discretion, prudence, even majesty it-self. 'Tis a short way to **dispatch**[2] and an easy escape from embarrassment.

cxxviii Highmindedness[3].

One of the principal qualifications for a gentleman, for it spurs on to all kinds of nobility. It improves the taste, ennobles the heart, elevates the mind, refines the feelings, and intensifies dignity. It raises him in whom it is found, and at times remedies the bad turns of Fortune, which only raises by striking. It can find full scope in the will when it cannot be exercised in act. Magnanimity, generosity, and all heroic qualities recognise in it their source.

129·永遠不要抱怨

抱 怨常常只會讓你失去名譽，我們應當學會自力更生，而不應企圖獲得他人的憐憫。我們所抱怨的事會引導聽者把同樣的事再加到我們身上，把屈辱揭示給別人，就會為聽者以同樣的方式羞辱我們提供了藉口。如果我們對過去的錯誤怨天尤人，那只會讓我們以後接著犯錯，我們想得到他人的幫助或撫慰，最終卻只會得到他人的漠不關心或是蔑視。比較明智的做法是誇讚他人給予你的恩惠，這樣他人就不得不繼續施惠與你。當你告訴他人那些不在場的人是怎樣對你好時，你就是在要求那些在場的人向他們看齊，這樣你會得到同樣好處。精明的人從來都不會把自己的失敗或缺點暴露在世人面前，而只會表現出那些增加友誼，減少敵意的優點。

1. politic [`pɑlə,tɪk] adj. 明智的，深謀遠慮的
2. recount [,ri`kaʊnt] vt. 敘述
3. enmity [`ɛnmətɪ] n. 敵意，憎恨

cxxix Never Complain.

T o complain always brings discredit. Better be a model of self-reliance opposed to the passion of others than an object of their compassion. For it opens the way for the hearer to what we are complaining of, and to disclose one insult forms an excuse for another. By complaining of past offences we give occasion for future ones, and in seeking aid or counsel we only obtain indifference or contempt. It is much more **politic**[1] to praise one man's favours, so that others may feel obliged to follow suit. To **recount**[2] the favours we owe the absent is to demand similar ones from the present, and thus we sell our credit with the one to the other. The shrewd will therefore never publish to the world his failures or his defects, but only those marks of consideration which serve to keep friendship alive and **enmity**[3] silent.

130·做事要踏實、亦要學會展現

事物為人所瞭解並非是依據它們實際是什麼，而是依據它們所展現出來的樣子。你要肯做，且讓別人看到你的勞動成果，這樣才會事半功倍。看不到的東西等同於不存在。就連正義的東西，如果看起來是非正義的，那它也不會得到人們的重視。能夠做到審慎觀察者少，而為事物表相所蒙蔽者多。欺詐盛行，觀其表相而下結論，許多事情往往名不符實。好的外表往往會讓人以為其內在也完美。

131·擁有胸襟與氣度

靈魂擁有某種重要的品格，這種高尚的品格能促使人做出英勇的行為，使人的整個性格顯得高雅脫俗。這種氣質並非人皆有之，只有氣度宏大的人才能得到。其首要的特點就是即使對敵人也毫不吝嗇讚美之辭，在行動上對敵人更加寬大仁慈。當復仇之機到來時，這胸襟就愈顯得光輝燦爛，他不僅會選擇放棄報復敵人，相反還會善加利用，化報復為出乎意料的寬宏大量。這是政治權術的高超境界，治國之道亦在於此。這樣的人從不炫耀自己的勝利，亦從不裝腔作勢，即便其成功憑本事得來，他也會懂得深藏不露。

---

1. rule the roast 做主人，當家
2. distinction [dɪ`stɪŋkʃən] n. 優秀，卓越
3. presuppose [ˌprisə`poz] vt. 以⋯為先決條件，意味著
4. pretence [prɪ`tɛns] n. 自吹

cxxx Do and Be Seen Doing.

T hings do not pass for what they are but for what they seem. To be of use and to know how to show yourself of use, is to be twice as useful. What is not seen is as if it was not. Even the Right does not receive proper consideration if it does not seem right. The observant are far fewer in number than those who are deceived by appearances. Deceit **rules the roast**[1], and things are judged by their jackets, and many things are other than they seem. A good exterior is the best recommendation of the inner perfection.

cxxxi Nobility of Feeling.

T here is a certain **distinction**[2] of the soul, a highmindedness prompting to gallant acts, that gives an air of grace to the whole character. It is not found often, for it **presupposes**[3] great magnanimity. Its chief characteristic is to speak well of an enemy, and to act even better towards him. It shines brightest when a chance comes of revenge: not alone does it let the occasion pass, but it improves it by using a complete victory in order to display unexpected generosity. 'Tis a fine stroke of policy, nay, the very acme of statecraft. It makes no **pretence**[4] to victory, for it pretends to nothing, and while obtaining its deserts it conceals its merits.

132 · 遇事反覆思量

才能保證萬無一失，尤其在你對事情還沒有把握之際，這會讓你有時間來堅定自己的決心或是改進自己的計畫。它會讓你的判斷更有依據。在送禮物的時候，倘若能考慮周全，要比匆促的脫手會更令人珍惜，因為越是讓人期待的禮物才越讓人珍惜。如果你不得不拒絕他人，你需要仔細斟酌，用什麼方式，在什麼時間拒絕才會比較讓人容易接受。隨著時間的流逝，最初的熱望會慢慢削弱，在這個時候被拒絕才不會顯得那麼冷酷。尤其是別人催促著你給予答覆時，你最好虛應一下，這樣的話可以分散一下他的注意力。

---

1. corroborate [kəˋrɑbə,ret] vt. 確證，證實
2. palatable [ˋpælətəbl] adj. 合意的，受歡迎的
3. press for 迫切要求
4. feint [fent] n. 佯攻，虛晃一招
5. disarm [dɪsˋɑrm] vt. 消除（敵意，疑慮等）

cxxxii Revise Your Judgments.

T o appeal to an inner Court of Revision makes things safe. Especially when the course of action is not clear, you gain time either to confirm or improve your decision. It affords new grounds for strengthening or **corroborating**[1] your judgment. And if it is a matter of giving, the gift is the more valued from its being evidently well considered than for being promptly bestowed: long expected is highest prized. And if you have to deny, you gain time to decide how and when to mature the No that it may be made **palatable**[2] . Besides, after the first heat of desire is passed the repulse of refusal is felt less keenly in cold blood. But especially when men **press for**[3] a reply is it best to defer it, for as often as not that is only a **feint**[4] to **disarm**[5] attention.

133・勿要眾人皆醉我獨醒

政治家們如是說：倘若所有人都瘋了，那獨自清醒的人就會被視為傻瓜。**學會隨波逐流是非常重要的。**大智大慧通常表現為無知或是大智若愚。人不可能脫離群體而生活，而群體裏面的大多數都是愚昧無知之徒。「離群獨居的不是神就是野獸」。不過我要說：甯與世人共醒，而不獨醉。不過，也有人為了變得特立獨行而去追逐空幻之物。

---

1. aphorism [ˈæfəˌrɪzəm] n. 格言，警語，諺語
2. chimera [kaɪˈmɪərə] n. [希神]獅頭羊身蛇尾的吐火怪物，引申為空幻之物

cxxxiii Better Mad with the Rest of the World Than Wise Alone.

S o say politicians. If all are so, one is no worse off than the rest, whereas solitary wisdom passes for folly. So important is it to sail with the stream. The greatest wisdom often consists in ignorance, or the pretence of it. One has to live with others, and others are mostly ignorant. "To live entirely alone one must be very like a god or quite like a wild beast," but I would turn the **aphorism**[1] by saying: Better be wise with the many than a fool all alone. There be some too who seek to be original by seeking **chimeras**[2].

134・要儲存雙倍的資源

這樣你的生活將會變得更加豐富多彩。一個人不能只依賴於某一種事物或侷限於一種資源，無論它們如何重要。每一種東西都應當加倍儲存，特別是可以讓你成功，獲得別人的恩惠或尊重的東西。有道是月有陰晴圓缺，世事無常，那些有賴於人類的意志而存在的事物更是如此。因此，聖人應當防範這些無常之變化，儲存雙倍的有用良品是一個重要的生活法則。正如大自然使我們最重要和最容易遇到危險的四肢都成雙成對一樣，我們也必須用我們的智慧來加倍儲存我們所賴以成功的資源。

---

1. mutability [ˌmjutəˋbɪlətɪ] n. 易變性
2. brittle [ˋbrɪtl̩] adj. 易碎的，脆弱的
3. duplicate [ˋdjupləkɪt] n. 複製品，副本

cxxxiv Double Your Resources.

Y ou thereby double your life. One must not depend on one thing or trust to only one resource, however pre-eminent. Everything should be kept double, especially the causes of success, of favour, or of esteem. The moon's **mutability**[1] transcends everything and gives a limit to all existence, especially of things dependent on human will, the most **brittle**[2] of all things. To guard against this inconstancy should be the sage's care, and for this the chief rule of life is to keep a double store of good and useful qualities. Thus as Nature gives us in **duplicate**[3] the most important of our limbs and those most exposed to risk, so Art should deal with the qualities on which we depend for success.

135・不要與人唱反調

這只會證明你的愚蠢或暴躁，所以謹慎之人都應努力設法避免。對任何事情都抱有異議固然可以顯示你的聰明，但是固執己見會讓你像個傻瓜。這些人往往會將愉快的閒談演變成為一場舌戰，而這樣的舌戰會讓你在朋友面前而不是在討厭的人面前表現得像個敵人。美味佳餚中的沙子更為磨牙，閒談之際的反駁甚為掃興。將野獸與溫順的動物綁在一起是既愚蠢又殘忍的做法。

136・抓住事物的主要矛盾

這樣才能夠把握事情的脈絡。許多人在對枝微末節的思考和討論中迷失了方向，而沒有意識到真正的問題在哪裏。他們反覆糾纏於某一個細節，把自己和別人都搞得筋疲力盡，卻還是沒有把握住事情的主要矛盾。這是因為他們頭腦混亂，根本就沒有清理頭緒。他們把時間和耐心都浪費在那些無關緊要的事情上，反而沒有時間與耐性來處理那些重要的事務了。

---

1. peevish [`pivɪʃ] adj. 易怒的，暴躁的
2. strenuously [`strɛnjʊəslɪ] adv. 奮發地，費力地
3. grit [grɪt] n. 沙粒
4. grate [gret] vt. 使某人感到煩躁
5. yoke [jok] v. 把…套在一起

cxxxv Do Not Nourish the Spirit of Contradiction.

I t only proves you foolish or **peevish**[1], and prudence should guard against this **strenuously**[2] . To find difficulties in everything may prove you clever, but such wrangling writes you down a fool. Such folk make a mimic war out of the most pleasant conversation, and in this way act as enemies towards their associates rather than towards those with whom they do not consort. **Grit**[3] **grates**[4] most in delicacies, and so does contradiction in amusement. They are both foolish and cruel who **yoke**[5] together the wild beast and the tame.

cxxxvi Post Yourself in the Centre of Things.

S o you feel the pulse of affairs. Many lose their way either in the **ramifications**[6] of useless discussion or in the **brushwood**[7] of wearisome **verbosity**[8] without ever realising the real matter at issue. They go over a single point a hundred times, wearying themselves and others, and yet never touch the all-important centre of affairs. This comes from a confusion of mind from which they cannot extricate themselves. They waste time and patience on matters they should leave alone, and cannot spare them afterwards for what they have left alone.

---

6. ramification [ˌræməfəˈkeʃən] n. 分枝，支流
7. brushwood [ˈbrʌʃˌwʊd] n. 折斷的小樹枝
8. verbosity [vɚˈbɑsətɪ] n. 冗長

137・聖人應自足

曾有一個聖人，其自身所帶的即為其全部所有。若是有一位學富五車之士能夠告訴我們關於羅馬和世界的其他地方的情況，那你就讓他自己做自己的朋友，然後他就能夠獨自生活了。假如沒有人比他更聰明或更有品味，那他還會需要誰呢？這樣的人完全可以自立更生，就像神仙一樣活著，這是人生最大的快樂和最高的境界。能夠獨自生存的人肯定不是野蠻人，反而像是一位聖者，也更像是一位逍遙自在的神仙。

---

1. 希臘哲學家麥格拉人斯蒂爾芬在一場大火中失掉了妻子、兒女和所有的財產，他從廢墟裡站起來，說道：「我所有的財富都在身上了」。
2. 指羅馬政治家兼士兵的老者坎托，西塞羅曾稱頌他的能力和善於交友。

cxxxvii The Sage Should Be Self-sufficing.

He that was all in all to himself carried all with him when he carried himself[1]. If **a universal friend**[2] can represent to us Rome and the rest of the world, let a man be his own universal friend, and then he is in a position to live alone. Whom could such a man want if there is no clearer intellect or finer taste than his own? He would then depend on himself alone, which is the highest happiness and like the Supreme Being. He that can live alone resembles the brute beast in nothing, the sage in much and God in everything.

138·學會順其自然的處事藝術

無論公事還是私事，越是風急浪湧，你越是應該順其自然。工作生活中難免都會遇到狂風暴雨，此時明智的做法是退入一個安全的港灣，待其自然消退。所謂的解藥經常會加重病情，在這種情況下，你最好是順其自然，讓時間來治癒一切。高明的醫生知道何時不開藥方，因為有時候不開藥方對疾病的康復反而會更有效。平息眾怒的好方法莫過於什麼都不做，讓他們自己平靜下來。**現在的退讓是為了今後的征服**。清澈之水攪之即渾，但若是靜止不動，則自動變清。撥亂之道，莫善於待其自正。

---

1. suasion [`sweʒən] n. 說服，勸告

cxxxviii The Art of Letting Things Alone.

The more so the wilder the waves of public or of private life. There are hurricanes in human affairs, tempests of passion, when it is wise to retire to a harbour and ride at anchor. Remedies often make diseases worse: in such cases one has to leave them to their natural course and the moral **suasion**[1] of time. It takes a wise doctor to know when not to prescribe, and at times the greater skill consists in not applying remedies. The proper way to still the storms of the vulgar is to hold your hand and let them calm down of themselves. To give way now is to conquer by and by. A fountain gets muddy with but little stirring up, and does not get clear by our meddling with it but by our leaving it alone. The best remedy for disturbances is to let them run their course, for so they quiet down.

139 · 時運不濟時需冷靜

在這種時候，沒有什麼事是順心的，無論你做什麼事情，運氣總是不好。只要試過兩次就應該知道你今天走不走運了。世間萬事都在變化，甚至人的思想也在變化，因此沒有人會永遠聰明，甚至想要寫封好信也是需要運氣的。完美往往只是在特定時候才會出現，就連美麗也有其時。有時甚至智者都會失敗，要不是因為他們想得太多，就是因為他們想得太少。只有在正確的時候才能把事情做好。為什麼有的人事事都不如意；而有的人不怎麼費力氣就事事順心，這是因為他們萬事俱備，思路清晰，鴻運當頭。在這種時候，你必須抓住時機，充分利用這個機會。但是，一個謹慎的人不會因為一件好事或是壞事就斷定今天的運氣是好還是壞，因為這可能只是僥倖，或者只是短暫的霉運。

---

1. ascendant [əˋsɛndənt] n. 有支配力，占有優勢
in the ascendant 方興未艾，正在走紅

cxxxix Recognise Unlucky Days.

They exist: nothing goes well on them; even though the game may be changed the ill-luck remains. Two tries should be enough to tell if one is in luck today or not. Everything is in process of change, even the mind, and no one is always wise: chance has something to say, even how to write a good letter. All perfection turns on the time; even beauty has its hours. Even wisdom fails at times by doing too much or too little. To turn out well a thing must be done on its own day. This is why with some everything turns out ill, with others all goes well, even with less trouble. They find everything ready, their wit prompt, their presiding genius favourable, their lucky star **in the ascendant**[1]. At such times one must seize the occasion and not throw away the slightest chance. But a shrewd person will not decide on the day's luck by a single piece of good or bad fortune, for the one may be only a lucky chance and the other only a slight annoyance.

140・要能馬上發現事物好的一面

這是品味高雅之人的長處所在。就像是蜜蜂搜尋釀蜜的花粉，毒蛇尋找造毒的苦物一樣，品味亦是如此。有人追求美好之精萃，而有人偏偏去追求醜惡之糟粕。**世間萬物均有其用，特別是書籍，它們是我們的精神食糧。**但是，許多人卻會在千般優點中抓住其中一個缺點不放，加以責難，就像是收集垃圾一樣專門找他人的缺點。他們這樣把別人的各種缺點列了滿滿一張表，但這只會顯出他們品味的低下，而不會讓他們顯得聰明。他們的生活是可悲的，他們只與苦澀相交、與垃圾為伍。而那些能在千般缺點中偶然發現其亮點的人則要幸運得多。

1. comb [kom] n. 蜂巢
2. serpent [`sɝpənt] n. 大毒蛇
3. gall [gɔl] n. 膽汁
4. scavenger [`skævɪndʒɚ] n. 在廢棄物中尋找（可食或可用的東西）
5. batten [`bætn] v. 變肥

cxl Find the Good in a Thing at Once.

❭ Tis the advantage of good taste. The bee goes to the honey for her **comb**[1], the **serpent**[2] to the **gall**[3] for its venom. So with taste: some seek the good, others the ill. There is nothing that has no good in it, especially in books, as giving food for thought. But many have such a scent that amid a thousand excellences they fix upon a single defect, and single it out for blame as if they were **scavengers**[4] of men's minds and hearts. So they draw up a balance sheet of defects which does more credit to their bad taste than to their intelligence. They lead a sad life, nourishing themselves on bitters and **battening**[5] on garbage. They have the luckier taste who midst a thousand defects seize upon a single beauty they may have hit upon by chance.

141・莫要只聽自己的聲音

如果你不能取悅他人，那光取悅自己是沒有用的，因為自滿往往會招人蔑視。把注意力都放在自己身上就意味著你不夠關注他人。自說自話，剛愎自用之人往往不會有什麼好下場。如果說孤身一人時自言自語是愚蠢的話，那在別人在場時還是只聽得到自己的聲音，就是加倍愚蠢。偉人有個弱點，就是講話的時候經常會問他人「我說得對吧？」或者「是不是？」讓聽他們說話的人抓狂。他們每說一句話都期待得到他人的贊同或奉承，卻讓聽者越來越沒有耐心。自大之人說話的時候也需要得到他人的認可，只有得到他人的支持他們才會繼續說下去，所以他們每句話都需要有傻瓜高呼「說得好！」來支持。

---

1. recurrent [rɪ`kɚənt] adj. 一再發生的，反覆出現的
2. totter [`tɑtɚ] vi. 蹣跚，踉蹌
3. stilt [stɪlt] n. 支撐物

cxli Do Not Listen to Yourself.

I t is no use pleasing yourself if you do not please others, and as a rule general contempt is the punishment for self-satisfaction. The attention you pay to yourself you probably owe to others. To speak and at the same time listen to yourself cannot turn out well. If to talk to oneself when alone is folly, it must be doubly unwise to listen to oneself in the presence of others. It is a weakness of the great to talk with a **recurrent**[1] "as I was saying" and "eh?" which bewilders their hearers. At every sentence they look for applause or flattery, taxing the patience of the wise. So too the pompous speak with an echo, and as their talk can only **totter**[2] on with the aid of **stilts**[3], at every word they need the support of a stupid "bravo!"

142・不要因為對手站在了正確的一方，就頑固地站在錯誤的一方

若是這樣，一開始你就輸了，一定很快就會輸得落荒而逃。壞的武器是不可能取得勝利的。狡猾的對手懂得先下手為強，而要是你落後了，卻選擇了錯誤的一方，就會顯得很愚蠢。**行動上的執拗比嘴硬更危險**，因為行動更危險。固執倔強之人常常會因好反駁而失理，好爭辯而失益。不管是一眼就看清是非，還是後來改進，聰明之人從不會衝動行事，而是會站在正義的一邊。如果你的對手很愚蠢，那在此種情況下他就會轉而選擇相反的錯誤的一方。把對手導入歧途的唯一方法就是自己選擇正途，因為他會蠢到自動放棄正途，同時因為頑固而受到懲罰。

---

1. astute [ə`stjut] adj. 機敏的，狡猾的
2. lag [læg] vi. 落後，滯後

cxlii Never from Obstinacy Take the Wrong Side Because Your Opponent Has Anticipated You in Taking the Right One.

Y ou begin the fight already beaten and must soon take to flight in disgrace. With bad weapons one can never win. It was **astute**[1] in the opponent to seize the better side first: it would be folly to come **lagging**[2] after with the worst. Such obstinacy is more dangerous in actions than in words, for action encounters more risk than talk. 'Tis the common failing of the obstinate that they lose the true by contradicting it, and the useful by quarrelling with it. The sage never places himself on the side of passion, but espouses the cause of right, either discovering it first or improving it later. If the enemy is a fool, he will in such a case turn round to follow the opposite and worse way. Thus the only way to drive him from the better course is to take it yourself, for his folly will cause him to desert it, and his obstinacy be punished for so doing.

143 · 莫要為免俗而玩詭辯之術

陷入庸俗與詭辯這兩個極端做法都會有損我們的聲譽。凡是與理性相違背的事情都是愚蠢的。詭辯也是一種欺騙，一開始可能會因其刺激、新奇而令人讚賞，但隨後如果揭穿其偽裝，發現它只是空空如也，它就會遭人們唾棄。這只是一種變戲法的把戲而已，如果被用在政治上，可能會給整個國家帶來七國之災。不能或不敢透過正途成就大業之人，就會走悖理逆情的詭辯之路，但這只有傻瓜才會欣賞，而智者則會洞悉一切。詭辯建立在有失偏頗的判斷力的基礎上，就算其根據不完全錯誤，那也肯定是不確定的，這是拿人生中的大事在冒險。

---

1. trite [traɪt] adj. 陳腐的
2. piquancy [ˋpikənsɪ] n. 有趣，激動人心
3. jugglery [ˋdʒʌglərɪ] n. 戲法，雜耍，魔術

cxliii Never Become Paradoxical in Order to Avoid the Trite[1].

B oth extremes damage our reputation. Every undertaking which differs from the reasonable approaches foolishness. The paradox is a cheat: it wins applause at first by its novelty and **piquancy**[2], but afterwards it becomes discredited when the deceit is foreseen and its emptiness becomes apparent. It is a species of **jugglery**[3], and in matters political would be the ruin of states. Those who cannot or dare not reach great deeds on the direct road of excellence go round by way of Paradox, admired by fools but making wise men true prophets. It argues an unbalanced judgment, and if it is not altogether based on the false, it is certainly founded on the uncertain, and risks the weightier matters of life.

144・他人開始，自己收穫

這 是達成目標的有效手段。即便是在神聖的問題上，基督教的牧師們也會強調這條神聖的錦囊妙計。這種掩飾非常重要，因為那些被預見到的好處會影響對方的意志。有的人看來是在按部就班地忙他自己的事，可是事實上卻是在為別人作嫁。**不要不做任何偽裝就貿然前進，尤其是當環境很險惡的時候。**在和那些一開始總是說「不」的人交往的時候，為了避免被拒絕，掩飾就很有用了，因為這樣當你巧妙地說出自己的意圖時，他們就不會覺得說「是」有什麼困難了。這則箴言與箴言13有關三思而後行的箴言道理相通，是包含了精妙、細微的技巧的處世哲學。

---

1. dissimulation [dɪ,sɪmjəˋleʃən] n. 掩飾，隱藏
2. ward off 避開，擋住
3. manoeuvre [məˋnuvɚ] n. 花招，策略

cxliv Begin with Another's to End with Your Own.

❯ Tis a politic means to your end. Even in heavenly matters Christian teachers lay stress on this holy cunning. It is a weighty piece of **dissimulation**[1], for the foreseen advantages serve as a lure to influence the other's will. His affair seems to be in train when it is really only leading the way for another's. One should never advance unless under cover, especially where the ground is dangerous. Likewise with persons who always say No at first, it is useful to **ward off**[2] this blow, because the difficulty of conceding much more does not occur to them when your version is presented to them. This advice belongs to the rule about second thoughts [xiii], which covers the most subtle **manoeuvres**[3] of life.

145・不要暴露你受傷的手指

不然它會受到四面八方的攻擊，也不要抱怨，因為惡人總是會打擊我們的弱點。生氣是沒有用的，成為別人的笑柄只會讓你更生氣。不懷好意的人總是想利用你的痛處激怒你，不擇手段地往你傷口上撒鹽。智者從不會坦承自己受傷的經歷，或是公開自己的或是家族的醜事，因為即使是命運女神有時也喜歡踩你的痛處。這往往會使本來就受傷的軀體更加痛苦。如果你想不再痛苦，就不要公開痛苦的根源；如果你想繼續快樂，就不要公開你快樂的源泉。

---

1. butt [bʌt] n. 笑柄
2. irritate [`ɪrə,tet] vt. 激怒，使急躁
3. dart [dɑrt] n. 投擲
4. hereditary [hə`rɛdə,tɛrɪ] adj. 世襲的，遺傳的
5. mortification [,mɔrtəfə`keʃən] n. 羞辱

cxlv Do Not Show Your Wounded Finger,

For everything will knock up against it; nor complain about it, for malice always aims where weakness can be injured. It is no use to be vexed: being the **butt**[1] of the talk will only vex you the more. Ill-will searches for wounds to **irritate**[2], aims **darts**[3] to try the temper, and tries a thousand ways to sting to the quick. The wise never own to being hit, or disclose any evil, whether personal or **hereditary**[4] . For even Fate sometimes likes to wound us where we are most tender. It always mortifies wounded flesh. Never therefore disclose the source of **mortification**[5] or of joy, if you wish the one to cease, the other to endure.

146・透過現象，看本質

事物往往不是它們所表現出來的樣子，無智慧之人只見表面，甚至當你把實質展示給他的時候，他還是不會幡然醒悟。謊言總是一馬當先，愚癡之人會被它牽著鼻子走，而真相則往往姍姍來遲，隨著時間的流逝而慢慢顯現出來。因此，智者會把自然之母賜予的一半才能留著以聆聽真相。欺詐是膚淺的，只有膚淺之人才會輕易相信它。謹慎辨別真相需退隱靜觀，只有聖人和智者才能做到。

---

1. disabuse[ˌdɪsəˈbjuz] vt. 使省悟，使消除錯誤觀念
2. kernel [ˈkɝnl] n. （事物、問題的）核心，要點
3. irreparable [ɪˈrɛpərəbl] adj. 不能挽回的
4. limp [lɪmp] vi. 跛行
5. recess [rɪˈsɛs] n. 隱秘處，幽深處

cxlvi Look into the Interior of Things.

Things are generally other than they seem, and ignorance that never looks beneath the rind becomes **disabused**[1] when you show the **kernel**[2]. Lies always come first, dragging fools along by their **irreparable**[3] vulgarity. Truth always lags last, **limping**[4] along on the arm of Time. The wise therefore reserve for it the other half of that power which the common mother has wisely given in duplicate. Deceit is very superficial, and the superficial therefore easily fall into it. Prudence lives retired within its **recesses**[5], visited only by sages and wise men.

147 · 不要難於接近

世間沒有人是完美的，所有人時不時地都需要別人的忠告。從不傾聽他人建議的人是無可救藥的傻瓜。即使是卓越超凡的智者也應留心聽取他人善意的忠告；即便是統治者也需要學會聽取他人的意見。而有些人之所以不可救藥只是因為他們拒人於千里之外，沒有人敢在他們失足時拉他們一把。身居高位之人應將友誼之門打開，他們也許能因此獲得幫助。朋友應該可以隨時對我們提出忠告，甚至責備我們，而彼此不會覺得難堪。是我們對他的滿意和對他堅定的信任賦予了他這項權力。我們不必尊重或相信每一個人，但是在我們的內心深處，我們需要一位能推心置腹的知己作鏡子，來糾正自己的錯誤，讓我們對其心存感激。

---

1. incorrigible [ɪnˋkɔrɪdʒəbl] adj. 無藥可救的，不能被糾正的
2. fall to ruin 毀滅，滅亡
3. extricate [ˋɛkstrɪˌket] vt. 解救，救出
4. upbraid [ʌpˋbred] v. 責備
5. confidant [ˌkɑnfɪˋdænt] n. 心腹朋友，知己

cxlvii Do Not Be Inaccessible.

None is so perfect that he does not need at times the advice of others. He is an incorrigible ass who will never listen to any one. Even the most surpassing intellect should find a place for friendly counsel. Sovereignty itself must learn to lean. There are some that are **incorrigible**[1] simply because they are inaccessible: they **fall to ruin**[2] because none dares to **extricate**[3] them. The highest should have the door open for friendship; it may prove the gate of help. A friend must be free to advise, and even to **upbraid**[4], without feeling embarrassed. Our satisfaction in him and our trust in his steadfast faith give him that power. One need not pay respect or give credit to every one, but in the innermost of his precaution man has a true mirror of a **confidant**[5] to whom he owes the correction of his errors, and has to thank for it.

148. 掌握談話的藝術

談話能夠體現出談話之人的真實品性。雖然談話是我們生活中最普通的一件事，但卻沒有任何事情比其更需小心謹慎的了。我們的成敗得失盡在於此。書信是深思熟慮並訴諸筆端的交談，尚且需小心謹慎為之，而談話需要即時展現你的智慧，則豈不更需小心謹慎嗎？那些深諳交際的智者能夠透過他人的談話而把握其靈魂的跳動。先賢說：「聽其言，即知其人。」有些人認為，談話的藝術就在於沒有藝術，猶如穿衣，整潔舒適即可，不需要過多的掩飾。這適用於朋友間的閒談。但是，如果你是在跟地位比你高的人談話，就應該要謹慎作答以示尊重。說話要得體，需要考慮對方的想法和語氣。不要挑他人的語病，那樣別人會覺得你過於學究；也不要仔細檢視別人的想法，這樣別人會迴避你，或至少不會輕易表露他們的想法。在交談中，審慎的言辭比滔滔的口才更為重要。

---

1. 指蘇格拉底：古希臘哲學家，柏拉圖的老師。因「瀆神違教」之罪入獄，被判死刑。

2. gaudy [`gɔdɪ] adj. 華而不實的

3. interlocutor [ˌɪntɚˋlɑkjətɚ] n. 對話者，對談者

4. pedant [`pɛdnt] n. 學究式人物

5. taxgatherer [ˌtæksˋgæðrɚ] n. [古]稅務員（= tax collector）

cxlviii Have the Art of Conversation.

T hat is where the real personality shows itself. No act in life requires more attention, though it be the commonest thing in life. You must either lose or gain by it. If it needs care to write a letter which is but a deliberate and written conversation, how much more the ordinary kind in which there is occasion for a prompt display of intelligence? Experts feel the pulse of the soul in the tongue, wherefore **the sage**[1] said, "Speak, that I may know thee." Some hold that the art of conversation is to be without art – that it should be neat, not **gaudy**[2], like the garments. This holds good for talk between friends. But when held with persons to whom one would show respect, it should be more dignified to answer to the dignity of the person addressed. To be appropriate it should adapt itself to the mind and tone of the **interlocutor**[3]. And do not be a critic of words, or you will be taken for a **pedant**[4] ; nor a **taxgatherer**[5] of ideas, or men will avoid you, or at least sell their thoughts dear. in conversation discretion is more important than eloquence.

149・學會委過於人

懂得找一個擋箭牌保護自己不受惡意的傷害是領導者的重要才能。這不是像那些不懷好意者想的那樣是無能的表現，而是駕馭他人的明智策略和高超的處世之道。世間萬事不會盡如人意，你也不可能讓所有的人都對你滿意。即使要以放下我們的驕傲為代價，也不妨找一隻代罪羔羊，讓他成為替代我們受罪的靶子。

150・推銷有方

僅有內在的價值是遠遠不夠的，因為並非每個人都會去探究其內在價值，做到慧眼識英雄。大部分人都隨波逐流，看到他人動，自己也跟著動。因此宣傳推銷某物是項高超的技巧，有時，我們可以大力讚揚，從而引起別人對它的欲望；有時亦可以為其賦予美名，提高其價值，但切記不要顯得矯飾造作。還有一條計策是宣稱此貨只賣內行的人，每個人都相信自己是專家高手，即使不是，他們的虛榮心也會激起他們購買的欲望。絕不要說貨物簡單、平凡，這會讓它們變得貶值，而不會暢銷。人人都爭先追求與眾不同的東西，只有與眾不同的東西才最符合人的品味和心智。

---

1. resort [rɪ`zɔrt] n. 憑藉，手段　2. detestation [ˌditɛs`teʃən] n. 憎惡，嫌惡　3. scapegoat [`skep.got] n. 替罪羊　4. intrinsic [ɪn`trɪnsɪk] adj. （指價值、性質）固有的，內在的，本質的　5. at a premium 以高價，以超出一般的價格　6. profess [prə`fɛs] v. 聲稱，公開表明　7. connoisseur [ˌkɑnə`sɝ] n. 鑑賞家，鑑定家，內行　8. appetising [`æpɪtaɪzɪŋ] adj. 美味可口的，促進食慾的

cxlix Know How to Put off Ills on Others.

To have a shield against ill-will is a great piece of skill in a ruler. It is not the **resort**[1] of incapacity, as ill-wishers imagine, but is due to the higher policy of having some one to receive the censure of the disaffected and the punishment of universal **detestation**[2]. Everything cannot turn out well, nor can every one be satisfied: it is well therefore, even at the cost of our pride, to have such a **scapegoat**[3], such a target for unlucky undertakings.

cl Know to Get Your Price for Things.

Their **intrinsic**[4] value is not sufficient; for all do not bite at the kernel or look into the interior. Most go with the crowd, and go because they see others go. It is a great stroke of art to bring things into repute; at times by praising them, for praise arouses desire; at times by giving them a striking name, which is very useful for putting things **at a premium**[5], provided it is done without affectation. Again, it is generally an inducement to **profess**[6] to supply only **connoisseurs**[7], for all think themselves such, and if not, the sense of want arouses the desire. Never call things easy or common: that makes them depreciated rather than made accessible. All rush after the unusual, which is more **appetising**[8] both for the taste and for the intelligence.

151‧放寬眼界，深謀遠慮

今日需考慮明日之事，甚至為未來做更多打算。智者的高明遠見是做到有備無患。凡事富有遠見，提前做好準備，則會避免遭受厄運，也不至於陷入窘境，無路可退。不可等到陷入困難之際才想到運用才智。當困難來臨之時則需三思而行。枕頭是個無聲的預言家，與其等到火燒眉毛了才輾轉難眠，不如提前把事情解決，高枕無憂。有些人行而後思：所思考的是如何尋找失敗的藉口，而不是怎樣達到成功的結果。更有甚者，事前事後均不思考。人生行事就在於不斷去思索如何才能避免迷失腳步，誤入歧途。若能做到三思而後行，並且有先見之明，人生的道路就會好走許多。

---

1. up to the chin 直到下巴，深陷
2. mire [maɪr] n. 處於（陷於）困境中
3. sibyl [ˋsɪbɪl] n. 女預言家，女先知
4. rumination [ˌruməˋneʃən] n. 沈思，長時間思考

cli Think Beforehand.

Today for tomorrow, and even for many days hence. The greatest foresight consists in determining beforehand the time of trouble. For the provident there are no mischances and for the careful no narrow escapes. We must not put off thought till we are **up to the chin**[1] in **mire**[2]. Mature reflection can get over the most formidable difficulty. The pillow is a silent **Sibyl**[3], and it is better to sleep on things beforehand than lie awake about them afterwards. Many act first and then think afterwards – that is, they think less of consequences than of excuses: others think neither before nor after. The whole of life should be one course of thought how not to miss the right path. **Rumination**[4] and foresight enable one to determine the line of life.

152・勿與令你黯然失色之人為伍

　　一個人越是優秀，你越是不能與他為伍。因為人越是優秀完美，就越會受他人的崇拜，這樣的人總是遙遙領先，你若和他在一起，就很難超越他，只能望其項背。即使你偶爾有機會引人注目，那些機會也只是他挑剩下的。月亮獨掛天庭之時可與眾星爭輝，而驕陽一出，則其頓時光彩黯然，甚至蹤跡全無。**不要去接近那些會令你黯然失色之人**，而應當去接近那些能夠映襯出你才華與能力的人。馬歇爾詩中聰明的法布拉之所以在那些其貌不揚又不修邊幅的女僕當中顯得美麗不凡、光彩照人，也正是如此。勿要自尋煩惱，亦不要做貶損自己而徒增他人光耀之事。年輕創業時須多與優秀的人結交，而事業有成之後則當與凡人為伴。

---

1. Martial　馬歇爾，古羅馬的諷刺詩人
2. imperil [ɪmˋpɛrɪl] vt. 使處於危險，危害

clii Never Have a Companion Who Casts You in the Shade.

T he more he does so, the less desirable a companion he is. The more he excels in quality the more in repute: he will always play first fiddle and you second. If you get any consideration, it is only his leavings. The moon shines bright alone among the stars: when the sun rises she becomes either invisible or imperceptible. Never join one that eclipses you, but rather one who sets you in a brighter light. By this means the cunning Fabula in **Martial**[1] was able to appear beautiful and brilliant, owing to the ugliness and disorder of her companions. But one should as little **imperil**[2] oneself by an evil companion as pay honour to another at the cost of one's own credit. When you are on the way to fortune associate with the eminent; when arrived, with the mediocre.

153・不要填補前人留下的巨大空缺

若一定要這樣做，則需確定自己的才華能夠超越前人。僅僅做到和前人平分秋色都需要雙倍於前人的才華。要讓人們寧選你而不要你的繼任者需頗費心思；而要想不為前人光彩所湮沒則需有更高超的功夫。填補一個巨大的空缺極為不易，人們常常厚古薄今，只和前人不相上下是不夠的，先行者已占盡優勢，你必須有超凡的才能，方能取代前人盛名。

154・勿輕易相信，勿輕易喜歡

思想成熟的明顯標誌就是不會輕信他人。這個世上的謊言太多，因此讓信任成為稀有之物吧。人們在匆忙之時做出的判斷往往會令人陷入窘迫，招致他人鄙視。但亦不可公然質疑他人的可信度，這樣會顯得無禮，因為你將他人當成了說謊者或是上當受騙者。這樣做的壞處不僅如此，不信任他人同時意味著你自己也存有偽詐之心。這種人會受雙重煎熬：既不敢相信他人，同時也不為他人所信。謹慎的傾聽者會較遲做出判斷，這樣可讓他人說出所有的資訊。還有一種類似的行為，那就是輕易地喜歡。人們的話可能是謊言，人們的行動也可能是偽裝的。這種謊言和偽裝在現實生活中更具危害性。

---

1. appeal to 喚起…

cliii Beware of Entering Where There Is a Great Gap to be Filled.

B ut if you do it be sure to surpass your predecessor; merely to equal him requires twice his worth. As it is a fine stroke to arrange that our successor shall cause us to be wished back, so it is policy to see that our predecessor does not eclipse us. To fill a great gap is difficult, for the past always seems best, and to equal the predecessor is not enough, since he has the right of first possession. You must therefore possess additional claims to oust the other from his hold on public opinion.

cliv Do Not Believe, or Like, Lightly.

M aturity of mind is best shown in slow belief. Lying is the usual thing; then let belief be unusual. He that is lightly led away, soon falls into contempt. At the same time there is no necessity to betray your doubts in the good faith of others, for this adds insult to discourtesy, since you make out your informant to be either deceiver or deceived. Nor is this the only evil: want of belief is the mark of the liar, who suffers from two failings: he neither believes nor is believed. Suspension of judgment is prudent in a hearer: the speaker can **appeal to**[1] his original source of information. There is a similar kind of imprudence in liking too easily, for lies may be told by deeds as well as in words, and this deceit is more dangerous for practical life.

155・控制情緒

盡可能讓謹慎的思考與反省來控制情緒,明慎之人不難做到此點。控制情緒第一步要做到的就是意識到這一點。這樣,你就開始了控制自我情緒的鬥爭,我們要將自己的情緒控制在一個恰到好處的範圍之內。這種高明的防範是控制怒氣的關鍵技巧。要懂得制怒之法,且止息於當止之時:奔跑時再想停下來就會很難。這充分證明了狂怒時保持頭腦清醒是很難的。情緒激動的人往往會做出喪失理智的行為。一旦對發怒有了這種警醒,發怒就很難使你失去控制了,也不會損害你良好的辨別力。駕馭情緒的方法是以明思慎辨來控制它,那麼你將會成為馬背上第一個清醒的人,也許還是最後一個。

---

1. at the double 飛快地,迅速地
2. excess [ɪk`sɛs] n. 過度,超額
3. digression [daɪ`grɛʃən] n. 離題,脫軌
4. synthesis [`sɪnθəsɪs] n. 綜合,合成
5. 西班牙有句諺語:「馬背上無智者」。

clv The Art of Getting into a Passion.

I f possible, oppose vulgar importunity with prudent reflection; it will not be difficult for a really prudent man. The first step towards getting into a passion is to announce that you are in a passion. By this means you begin the conflict with command over your temper, for one has to regulate one's passion to the exact point that is necessary and no further. This is the art of arts in falling into and getting out of a rage. You should know how and when best to come to a stop: it is most difficult to halt while running **at the double**[1]. It is a great proof of wisdom to remain clear-sighted during paroxysms of rage. Every **excess**[2] of passion is a **digression**[3] from rational conduct. But by this masterly policy reason will never be transgressed, nor pass the bounds of its own **synthesis**[4]. To keep control of passion one must hold firm the reins of attention: he who can do so will be the first man "**wise on horseback**,"[5] and probably the last.

156・擇友

選擇朋友需周密考察,幾經逆境和順境的考驗而始終不渝,其情感和領悟力也都值得信賴,才能成為朋友。擇友是人生中的大事,但世人對此很少用心。只有少數人是用聰明智慧來選擇朋友,而大多數人則是純靠機緣巧遇來交朋友。人們通常會根據你所交的朋友來判斷你的為人:智者永遠不與愚者為伍。樂與某人為伍,並不表示他們是知己。有時我們只是覺得和他們在一起很開心,但並不表示欣賞他們的才智。有的友誼不夠純潔,只是為了娛樂;有些友誼真摯,能拓展思維,催人上進。一個人的知己極少,大多數只是迫於環境的泛泛之交。一位朋友的真知灼見比其他人的祝福可貴得多。交友要精心挑選,而不是隨意結交。聰明的朋友能為你驅憂除患,而愚蠢的朋友只會集憂致患。此外,若想讓友誼地久天長,不要總希望你的朋友運氣太好。

1. matriculation [məˌtrɪkjəˈleʃən] n. (在大學)註冊入學
2. fecundity [fɪˈkʌndətɪ] n. 多產,旺盛
3. ward off 避開,擋住

clvi Select Your Friends.

O nly after passing the **matriculation**[1] of experience and the examination of fortune will they be graduates not alone in affection but in discernment. Though this is the most important thing in life, it is the one least cared for. Intelligence brings friends to some, chance to most. Yet a man is judged by his friends, for there was never agreement between wise men and fools. At the same time, to find pleasure in a man's society is no proof of near friendship: it may come from the pleasantness of his company more than from trust in his capacity. There are some friendships legitimate, others illicit; the latter for pleasure, the former for their **fecundity**[2] of ideas and motives. Few are the friends of a man's self, most those of his circumstances. The insight of a true friend is more useful than the goodwill of others: therefore gain them by choice, not by chance. A wise friend **wards off**[3] worries, a foolish one brings them about. But do not wish them too much luck, or you may lose them.

157 · 不要識錯人

識錯人是個很嚴重的錯誤，也很容易犯。就像買東西，與其買到的東西品質很差，不如價格稍微高點但品質好的。沒有一件事比識人更需要仔細明察了。辨貨與識人不同，需要能洞察他人內心的真實想法，分辨其性情，這是一門高深的學問。識人，就如精讀一本書一樣，需讀深讀透，能夠將其研究透徹。

---

1. profound [prə`faʊnd] a. 淵博的，深奧的

clvii Do not Make Mistakes
About Character.

That is the worst and yet easiest error. Better be cheated in the price than in the quality of goods. In dealing with men, more than with other things, it is necessary to look within. To know men is different from knowing things. It is **profound**[1] philosophy to sound the depths of feeling and distinguish traits of character. Men must be studied as deeply as books.

158・善用朋友

這 是需要判斷力的技巧。有的朋友需遠交，而有的則需近交。不善言談的朋友可能擅長寫信，故可成為筆友。距離能淨化近在身邊無法容忍的缺陷，也即是我們所說的距離產生的美感。交友需要講求實效，而非只圖快樂。**世間任何美好事物所包含的三大特質：和諧、善良和真誠，友誼兼而有之。朋友就是一切。良友難覓，若不懂得如何選擇則更難求。留住老朋友比去結交更多的新朋友更為重要。交友需尋友誼長存之友。時間久了自會成老友。最好的朋友是那些歷久彌新，能彼此分享生活感受的人。沒有朋友的人生如同沒有綠草的荒原。好的友誼會使你歡樂加倍，憂患減半。它是應對厄運、失意的良藥，是滋潤心靈的美酒。**

1. correspondent [ˌkɔrɪˋspɑndənt] n. 通信者
2. soaking [sokɪŋ] n. 浸泡，浸透
3. testing [ˋtɛstɪŋ] n. 考驗
4. ventilation [ˌvɛnt!ˋeʃən] n. 通風，流通的空氣

clviii Make Use of Your Friends.

T his requires all the art of discretion. Some are good afar off, some when near. Many are no good at conversation but excellent as **correspondents**[1], for distance removes some failings which are unbearable in close proximity to them. Friends are for use even more than for pleasure, for they have the three qualities of the Good, or, as some say, of Being in general: unity, goodness, and truth. For a friend is all in all. Few are worthy to be good friends, and even these become fewer because men do not know how to pick them out. To keep is more important than to make friends. Select those that will wear well; if they are new at first, it is some consolation they will become old. Absolutely the best are those well salted, though they may require **soaking**[2] in the **testing**[3]. There is no desert like living without friends. Friendship multiplies the good of life and divides the evil. 'Tis the sole remedy against misfortune, the very **ventilation**[4] of the soul.

159·忍受愚蠢

智者常常會沒有耐性，因為隨著他們的學識增加，他們對愚蠢的忍耐度會降低。知識淵博之人很難被取悅。愛比克泰德告訴我們，生活最重要的準則在於學會容忍，他將其視為智慧的一半真諦。容忍種種愚蠢需要極大耐心。有時最令我們痛苦，不得不容忍的人恰恰會是我們最依賴的人，這有助於我們鍛煉自我控制能力。耐心能讓我們心如止水，這種心態尤為可貴，是世間至福。若不懂得如何容忍他人，那就只能孤獨終老，即使是孤獨一人，也還要能忍受自己。

160·言語謹慎

與對手談話時需要審慎小心；與他人交談時，為了言語得體，也需要小心謹慎。話出口容易，一言既出，如覆水難收。說話應該像寫遺囑一樣，言詞愈少，紛爭才會愈少。在細微事情上注意鍛煉自己的言談，遇大事時才能應付自如。深藏不露可增加神秘感。口風不緊的人言出而事敗。

---

1. Epictetus 愛比克泰德，公元前一世紀時的希臘斯多噶派哲學家、教師。
2. boon [bun] n. 恩惠
3. litigation [`lɪtə`geʃən] n. 訴訟，起訴

clix Put up with Fools.

T he wise are always impatient, for he that increases knowledge increase impatience of folly. Much knowledge is difficult to satisfy. The first great rule of life, according to **Epictetus**[1], is to put up with things: he makes that the moiety of wisdom. To put up with all the varieties of folly would need much patience. We often have to put up with most from those on whom we most depend: a useful lesson in self-control. Out of patience comes forth peace, the priceless **boon**[2] which is the happiness of the world. But let him that bath no power of patience retire within himself, though even there he will have to put up with himself.

clx Be Careful in Speaking.

W ith your rivals from prudence; with others for the sake of appearance. There is always time to add a word, never to withdraw one. Talk as if you were making your will: the fewer words the less **litigation**[3]. In trivial matters exercise yourself for the more weighty matters of speech. Profound secrecy has some of the lustre of the divine. He who speaks lightly soon falls or fails.

161．明察自己的缺陷

即使最優秀的人也有缺陷，這些缺陷與人形影不離，且通常與人的才智相關。智力超群的人往往是缺陷最多的，或者至少是越引人注目的。並不是一個人自己沒有察覺這些缺陷，而是他對這些缺陷情有獨鐘，這樣就造成了雙重不幸，即往往對可以避免的錯誤懷有不理智的情感。這些缺陷猶如美麗臉蛋上的斑點，令他人生厭，而臉蛋的主人卻將其視作美人痣。能夠消除這些缺陷是很了不起的，是戰勝自我的一種優秀表現。知道人們在觀察一個人的時候往往都善於看他的缺點，而不會欽佩他的才華，人們緊盯著缺點，盡可能地抹黑他們，以使其他才智黯然失色。

---

1. conspicuous [kənˋspɪkjʊəs] a. 引人注目的，明顯的

clxi Know Your Pet Faults.

T he most perfect of men has them, and is either wedded to them or
has illicit relations with them. They are often faults of intellect, and
the greater this is, the greater they are, or at least the more **conspicuous**[1].
It is not so much that their possessor does not know them: he loves them,
which is a double evil: irrational affection for avoidable faults. They are
spots on perfection; they displease the onlooker as much as they please the
possessor. 'Tis a gallant thing to get clear of them, and so give play to one's
other qualities. For all men hit upon such a failing, and on going over your
qualifications they make a long stay at this blot, and blacken it as deeply as
possible in order to cast your other talents into the shade.

162 · 戰勝他人的嫉妒與惡意

對嫉妒與惡意表現出鄙棄的態度是不夠的；相反地以大度來應
對，能取得更好的效果。世間最讓人敬佩的莫過於以美言加
諸於曾經惡言中傷你的人，最顯英雄氣概的報復莫如以德行與才智征
服並折磨那些嫉妒你的人。你的每一次成功都會折磨一次與你為敵的
人；你的每一次輝煌都能沉重打擊你的對手。嫉妒者不會猝死，而是
對手每贏得一次掌聲，他就死一次。對手不朽的名聲丈量著嫉妒者的
痛苦，前者享用不竭的榮譽讓後者飽受無邊的痛苦。成功的號角一方
面歌頌成功者的輝煌，另一方面也宣告了嫉妒者煎熬的開始。

---

1. detractor [dɪˋtræktɚ] n. 誹謗者，惡意批評者
2. vengeance [ˋvɛndʒəns] n. 復仇，報仇
3. oft [ɔft] adv. 常常，再三
4. clarion [ˋklærɪən] n. 號角

clxii How to Triumph over Rivals and Detractors[1].

I t is not enough to despise them, though this is often wise: a gallant bearing is the thing. One cannot praise a man too much who speaks well of them who speak ill of him. There is no more heroic **vengeance**[2] than that of talents and services which at once conquer and torment the envious. Every success is a further twist of the cord round the neck of the ill-affected, and an enemy's glory is the rival's hell. The envious die not once, but as **oft**[3] as the envied wins applause. The immortality of his fame is the measure of the other's torture: the one lives in endless honour, the other in endless pain. The **clarion**[4] of Fame announces immortality to the one and death to the other, the slow death of envy long drawn out.

163 · 不要因同情他人
而陷入他人的不幸

有人認為不幸的事，而他人卻可能認為是幸運。正是不幸的人眾多，所以才會有人自稱幸運。不幸之人往往會贏得人們的同情心，人們總是懷著同情心去安慰那些不幸的人，雖然這些安慰沒有什麼實際意義。你有時會發現過去發達時遭人忌恨之人，突然變成了眾人憐憫的對象。人們對他過往的仇恨變成了現在的憐憫。命運之神如何出牌需要很精明的頭腦才能察覺。有一些人專門與不幸之人結交。一旦有人走霉運，他們便聚集其身邊；而當初這些人得勢之時，他們卻避而遠之。或許這種做法能體現他們心靈的高貴，但絕對不是明智的作法。

---

1. abhor [əb`hɔr] vt. 憎惡，痛恨
2. on the wing 在飛行中，在進行中
3. afoot [ə`fʊt] adv. 在準備中，在進行中
4. shuffle the cards 進行角色大調動，改變方針

clxiii Never, from Sympathy with the Unfortunate, Involve Yourself in His Fate.

O ne man's misfortune is another man's luck, for one cannot be lucky without many being unlucky. It is a peculiarity of the unfortunate to arouse people's goodwill who desire to compensate them for the blows of fortune with their useless favour, and it happens that one who was **abhorred**[1] by all in prosperity is adored by all in adversity. Vengeance **on the wing**[2] is exchanged for compassion **afoot**[3]. Yet 'tis to be noticed how fate **shuffles the cards**[4]. There are men who always consort with the unlucky, and he that yesterday flew high and happy stands today miserable at their side. That argues nobility of soul, but not worldly wisdom.

164 · 投石問路

瞭解這件事情是否能夠被人接受,特別是當你對其能否被認可持懷疑態度時,這樣才可保證行事順利,而且可以讓你明智果斷地決定要不要繼續做下去。聰明人善於透過試探別人的想法來判斷自己眼前所處的形勢。這種做法在請教別人、向人索取和做決定時都至關重要。

165 · 戰而有道

人們都可能會迫不得已捲入戰爭,但絕對不會暗中使用陰招。人需要保持自己的本性,不受他人的脅迫或影響。在人生的鬥爭中,要想征服對手且獲得讚賞,不僅要靠力量,還要靠道義。卑鄙的征服不會帶來榮耀與讚賞,只會讓你名譽掃地。在單純的征服面前,榮譽永遠佔上風。善良的人從來都不會使用禁用的武器,例如不利用朋友之間的友誼作為手段來達到報仇的目的:不可把他人對你的信任作為復仇的工具。任何背信棄義的手段都會毀掉你的聲譽。品性高貴之人在任何情況下都不會做出背信忘義之事。人應當隨時隨地皆可問心無愧地對世人宣稱,即使世人已經將慷慨磊落與誠信忠實的美德拋棄,你也一定要把它們牢記在心。

---

1. gallantry [ˈgæləntrɪ] n. 勇敢

clxiv Throw Straws in the Air,

t o find how things will be received, especially those whose reception or success is doubtful. One can thus be assured of its turning out well, and an opportunity is afforded for going on in earnest or withdrawing entirely. By trying men's intentions in this way, the wise man knows on what ground he stands. This is the great rule of foresight in asking, in desiring, and in ruling.

clxv Wage War Honourably.

Y ou may be obliged to wage war, but not to use poisoned arrows. Every one must needs act as he is, not as others would make him to be. **Gallantry**[1] in the battle of life wins all men's praise: one should fight so as to conquer, not alone by force but by the way it is used. A mean victory brings no glory, but rather disgrace. Honour always has the upper hand. An honourable man never uses forbidden weapons, such as using a friendship that's ended for the purposes of a hatred just begun: a confidence must never be used for a vengeance. The slightest taint of treason tarnishes the good name. In men of honour the smallest trace of meanness repels: the noble and the ignoble should be miles apart. Be able to boast that if gallantry, generosity, and fidelity were lost in the world men would be able to find them again in your own breast.

166・明辨能言與善行之人

這很重要，就像你在朋友、眾人和工作這些有很多不同形態的事物中要有的辨別力一樣。即使無惡行，有惡言已經足夠惡劣，但無惡言而有惡行則更為不堪。人不能以言語果腹，有道是言語如風，亦不能靠禮儀充饑，因為禮儀也只是文雅的欺騙。以鏡捉鳥是完全的虛幻，只有那些虛榮的人才會滿足於空泛的言辭。**言語要有價值，必須以行動來做保證。**只長葉卻不結果之樹通常是無心無髓之樹，我們需分辨清楚，其只能遮蔭而已，除此之外別無用處。

167・自立自強

危難之時，**勇敢的心是最好的夥伴。**如果心靈過於脆弱，就只能依靠其附近的器官來支撐。再大的困難在堅強不屈的人面前也會變得微不足道。人千萬不能向厄運低頭，否則厄運之神會變本加厲，更加囂張。身陷困境之時，很多人都不能自拔，而且不知道如何面對，因此倍感痛苦。那些有自知之明的人則能深思熟慮，克服自身的弱點。明智之人能夠征服一切，乃至星辰。

---

1. dine off （在進餐時）吃…　2. take their wages 拿工資
3. windy [ˈwɪndɪ] adj. 誇誇其談的，空話連篇的　4. pawn-ticket 當票
5. pith [pɪθ] n. （植物的）木髓，骨髓，重要部分　6. die away 漸息，漸弱

clxvi Distinguish the Man of Words from the Man of Deeds.

D iscrimination here is as important as in the case of friends, persons, and employments, which have all many varieties. Bad words even without bad deeds are bad enough: good words with bad deeds are worse. One cannot **dine off**[1] words, which are wind, nor off politeness, which is but polite deceit. To catch birds with a mirror is the ideal snare. It is the vain alone who **take their wages**[2] in **windy**[3] words. Words should be the pledges of work, and, like **pawn-tickets**[4], have their market price. Trees that bear leaves but not fruit have usually no **pith**[5]. Know them for what they are, of no use except for shade.

clxvii Know How to Take Your Own Part.

I n great crises there is no better companion than a bold heart, and if it becomes weak it must be strengthened from the neighbouring parts. Worries **die away**[6] before a man who asserts himself. One must not surrender to misfortune, or else it would become intolerable. Many men do not help themselves in their troubles, and double their weight by not knowing how to bear them. He that knows himself knows how to strengthen his weakness, and the wise man conquers everything, even the stars in their courses.

168・莫成為愚蠢的怪物

像虛榮、僭妄、自負、不可信賴、反覆無常、執拗、空想、裝模作樣、異想天開、過於好奇、荒謬詭異、加入派系和片面看問題的人，都是偏執的怪物。精神上的畸形比生理上的殘缺更令人生厭，因為它違反了美的原則。有誰能夠幫助糾正這種混亂的思維呢？缺乏自制之人必然聽不進他人的忠告與指正。這些人不在乎別人的嘲諷，總是盲目地去相信那些毫無根據的事，去追逐虛假的喝采。

169・小心謹慎，避免
萬一失手勝過百發百中

沒有人會直視太陽，然而卻爭相觀看日蝕。人們一般不會關注你做了什麼對的事情，而是往往喜歡找出你做錯了什麼。有道是好事不出門，壞事傳千里。許多人都是去世之後才揚名立萬的。一個人所有的輝煌和成就都難以掩蓋一個小小的過失。切記，要盡力避免犯錯誤，要知道，有些不懷好意的目光只盯著你犯下的每一個錯誤，從來都看不到你的成就。

---

1. egotistical [ˌigəˈtɪstɪkl] adj. 自大的，自負的　2. whimsical [ˈhwɪmzɪkl] adj. 異想天開的，古怪的　3. sectarian [sɛkˈtɛrɪən] adj. 教派的，宗派的　4. monstrosity [mɑnsˈtrɑsətɪ] n. 畸形　5. impertinence [ɪmˈpɜtnəns] n. 不適宜，魯莽，無禮　6. obnoxious [əbˈnɑkʃəs] adj. 不愉快的，討厭的　7. contravene [ˌkɑntrəˈvin] vt. 違反，違背　8. wanting [ˈwɑntɪŋ] adj. 某物不足，缺少某物

clxviii Do Not Indulge
in the Eccentricities of Folly.

L ike vain, presumptuous, **egotistical**[1], untrustworthy, capricious, obstinate, fanciful, theatrical, **whimsical**[2], inquisitive, paradoxical, **sectarian**[3] people and all kinds of one-sided persons: they are all **monstrosities**[4] of **impertinence**[5]. All deformity of mind is more **obnoxious**[6] than that of the body, because it **contravenes**[7] a higher beauty. Yet who can assist such a complete confusion of mind? Where self-control is **wanting**[8], there is no room for others' guidance. Instead of paying attention to other people's real derision, men of this kind blind themselves with the unfounded assumption of their imaginary applause.

clxix Be More Careful Not to Miss
Once Than to Hit a Hundred Times.

N o one looks at the blazing sun; all gaze when he is eclipsed. The common talk does not reckon what goes right but what goes wrong. Evil report carries farther than any applause. Many men are not known to the world till they have left it. All the exploits of a man taken together are not enough to wipe out a single small blemish. Avoid therefore falling into error, seeing that ill-will notices every error and no success.

170・一切事物均需有所保留

這樣你才不會江郎才盡。任何時候，才不可露盡，力不可使完。即使是知識也應該有所保留，這樣，你才會有更多的策略，永遠給自己保存一些應變策略以應付危急時刻。適當保留比全力以赴更為重要，因為保留對於勇氣和名聲來說是很重要的。謹慎之人總是能夠穩穩的駕馭航行。從這一點來說，「一半多於全部」這個似是而非的論點是有道理的。

171・不輕易使用他人欠你的人情

至關重要的朋友要留在關鍵的時候再用，莫要把重要朋友的友誼濫用在細微的事情上。備用錨要留在最危急的時候用。倘若你輕易用掉重要的關係，那日後你還有什麼可用呢？沒有什麼比能夠使你得到保護的情義或友誼最為珍貴。他們能成事，也能敗事；他們能使你多智亨通，也能讓你黔驢技窮。雖然自然和名望比較青睞智者，但也常會招來命運之神的嫉妒。所以說一定要重視貴人的寵信，其他的東西不值一提。

---

1. rearguard [`rɪrgɑrd] n. 後衛
2. hold good 仍然有效
3. sheet anchor 備用錨
4. goods and chattels 有形動產，家具雜貨

clxx In All Things Keep Something in Reserve.

❭ Tis a sure means of keeping up your importance. A man should not employ all his capacity and power at once and on every occasion. Even in knowledge there should be a **rearguard**[1], so that your resources are doubled. One must always have something to resort to when there is fear of a defeat. The reserve is of more importance than the attacking force: for it is distinguished for valour and reputation. Prudence always sets to work with assurance of safety: in this matter the piquant paradox **holds good**[2] that the half is more than the whole.

clxxi Waste Not Influence.

The great as friends are for great occasions. One should not make use of great confidence for little things: for that is to waste a favour. The **sheet anchor**[3] should be reserved for the last extremity. If you use up the great for little ends what remains afterwards? Nothing is more valuable than a protector, and nothing costs more nowadays than a favour. It can make or unmake a whole world. It can even give sense and take it away. As Nature and Fame are favourable to the wise, so Luck is generally envious of them. It is therefore more important to keep the favour of the mighty than **goods and chattels**[4].

172・絕不要與一無所有者爭鬥

這種鬥爭是不公平的。競爭的一方一無所有，可以肆無忌憚，甚至無廉恥之心。他們不會害怕失去什麼，敢於為所欲為，孤注一擲。而你絕不可拿你珍貴的名聲與這種人鬥，要知道**好名聲得之不易**，失之容易，切勿因此小事而使你的名譽毀於一旦。有榮譽感和責任心的人深知名譽的重要性，所以他們會權衡利弊，謹慎從事，循序漸進，以便有充足的時間趁勢而退，以保全名譽。貿然涉險本身就是一種失策，縱然獲勝，也難彌補損失。

---

1. slight [slaɪt] n. 輕蔑，忽視，怠慢，侮辱
2. circumspection [ˋsɝkəmˋspɛkʃən] n. 細心，慎重

clxxii Never Contend with a Man Who Has Nothing to Lose;

For thereby you enter into an unequal conflict. The other enters without anxiety; having lost everything, including shame, he has no further loss to fear. He therefore resorts to all kinds of insolence. One should never expose a valuable reputation to so terrible a risk, lest what has cost years to gain may be lost in a moment, since a single **slight**[1] may wipe out much sweat. A man of honour and responsibility has a reputation, because he has much to lose. He balances his own and the other's reputation: he only enters into the contest with the greatest caution, and then goes to work with such **circumspection**[2] that he gives time to prudence to retire in time and bring his reputation under cover. For even by victory he cannot gain what he has lost by exposing himself to the chances of loss.

173・與人交往不要太脆弱

有些人太脆弱，總是想像自己受到了侵害和壓制。他們的感情十分敏感，甚至超過了瞳孔，不論是開個玩笑還是一本正經談話，一點細小的事都能冒犯他們，更不用說大的刺激了。和這種人交往的時候需要十分小心，時刻注意他們的情感，觀察他們的行為，絲毫的怠慢都會引起他們的不悅。這種人大多很自我，是自我情緒的奴隸，甚至為此棄置其他一切重要的事情。他們是細節的盲目崇拜者。相反，真正有愛的人應該是堅定而持久的，所以說聲名狼藉者有一半都很固執。

---

1. consort with 陪伴 2. demeanour [dɪ`minɚ] n. 行為，舉止
3. cast aside 消除，廢除 4. punctilio [pʌŋk`tɪlɪ,o] n. 細節，拘泥形式
5. arrant [`ærənt] adj. 聲名狼藉的，極惡的
6. adamant [`ædəmənt] adj. 固執的

clxxiii Do Not Be Glass in Intercourse, still Less in Friendship.

S ome break very easily, and thereby show their want of consistency. They attribute to themselves imaginary offences and to others oppressive intentions. Their feelings are even more sensitive than the eye itself, and must not be touched in jest or in earnest. Motes offend them: they need not wait for beams. Those who **consort with**[1] them must treat them with the greatest delicacy, have regard to their sensitiveness, and watch their **demeanour**[2], since the slightest slight arouses their annoyance. They are mostly very egoistic, slaves of their moods, for the sake of which they **cast everything aside**[3] : they are the worshippers of **punctilio**[4]. On the other hand, the disposition of the true lover is firm and enduring, so that it may be said that the **Arrant**[5] is half **adamant**[6].

174 · 人生莫匆忙

當你懂得如何有條不紊地處理事物時，你就會懂得如何從中享受快樂。有許多人只有等到好運逝去時方才醒悟。他們匆匆略過快樂，來不及享受，等他們發現已經跳過時卻想著回去。他們行色匆匆，加快速度去追逐自己的欲望。他們總想在一日之中吞掉一生消受的養分。他們總是想著成功在望，妄想將未來的歲月一併吞掉，從而把享受置於身後。但結果往往是凡事過於倉促，欲求速戰速決，換來的卻是欲速則不達。即便對知識的渴求也應好好把握，才不至於囫圇吞棗，一知半解。人生漫長，快樂卻往往短暫。行動宜速，享受宜緩，這樣你才能體會到工作之後的快樂而不是歡愉之後的落寞。

---

1. devour [dɪˋvaʊr] vt. （尤指動物）吞吃，狼吞虎嚥
2. in advance of 在…前面，超過

clxxiv Do Not Live in a Hurry.

To know how to separate things is to know how to enjoy them. Many finish their fortune sooner than their life: they run through pleasures without enjoying them, and would like to go back when they find they have over-leaped the mark. Postilions of life, they increase the ordinary pace of life by the hurry of their own calling. They **devour**[1] more in one day than they can digest in a whole life-time; they live **in advance of**[2] pleasures, eat up the years beforehand, and by their hurry get through everything too soon. Even in the search for knowledge there should be moderation, lest we learn things better left unknown. We have more days to live through than pleasures. Be slow in enjoyment, quick at work, for men see work ended with pleasure, pleasure ended with regret.

175 · 做人要厚道

倘若你是個實在厚道之人,就不會欣賞那些不實虛偽之人。聲名顯赫若不以實在厚道為根基,實在是可悲。在生活中,表面上貌似實在之人往往多於真正實在厚道的人。虛偽會導致欺騙,虛偽之人在妄想的驅使下產生出邪念。有些人喜歡謊言,因為謊言可以承諾很多,而真相給予人們的卻很少。但妄想必然導致惡果,因為他們缺乏牢固的根基。**惟有實在厚道才能給你帶來真實的名望;惟有內涵才會使你受益匪淺。**一次欺詐會帶來許多次欺詐,環環相扣,不久整個大廈就像空中樓閣一樣,因為缺少根基而不會長久。承諾太多,難以讓人相信,就像是證明太多,卻往往有如虛幻泡影。

---

1. impregnate [ɪmˋprɛgˌnet] vt. 使懷孕
2. imposition [ˌɪmpəˋzɪʃən] n. 無理要求

clxxv A Solid Man.

O ne who is finds no satisfaction in those that are not. 'Tis a pitiable eminence that is not well founded. Not all are men that seem to be so. Some are sources of deceit; **impregnated**[1] by chimeras they give birth to **impositions**[2]. Others are like them so far that they take more pleasure in a lie, because it promises much, than in the truth, because it performs little. But in the end these caprices come to a bad end, for they have no solid foundation. Only Truth can give true reputation: only reality can be of real profit. One deceit needs many others, and so the whole house is built in the air and must soon come to the ground. Unfounded things never reach old age. They promise too much to be much trusted, just as that cannot be true which proves too much.

176・自知或從智者處知

生活在這個世界上需要有足夠的理解力,不僅是你自己的理解力,也包括從他人那裏獲得的理解力。很多人都沒有意識到他們自己的無知,更有甚者不懂裝懂。愚蠢之病無藥可醫。無知者因無自知之明,故不知去尋找自己所欠缺的東西。如果他們有自知之明,知道去彌補自己能力的話,有些人本來可以是智者。充滿智慧之人本就很少,但向他們求教之人更是寥寥可數。求教高明之人無損你的偉大,亦不會讓人懷疑你的能力與才華。恰恰相反,它可以證明你善於聽取別人的意見。只有適當徵求他人的意見,聽取忠告,你才不會失敗。

---

1. oracle [ˈɔrək!] n. 聖賢,哲人

clxxvi Have Knowledge,
or Know Those that Have Knowledge.

W ithout intelligence, either one's own or another's, true life is impossible. But many do not know that they do not know, and many think they know when they know nothing. Failings of the intelligence are incorrigible, since those who do not know, do not know themselves, and cannot therefore seek what they lack. Many would be wise if they did not think themselves wise. Thus it happens that though the **oracles**[1] of wisdom are rare, they are rarely used. To seek advice does not lessen greatness or argue incapacity. On the contrary, to ask advice proves you well advised. Take counsel with reason it you do not wish to court defeat.

177 · 切莫與人過於親近

亦不要讓他人過於親近你，否則，你將失去影響力賦予你的所有優勢，使你喪失掉名譽與聲望。天上之繁星從不與我們貼近，故能永保輝煌。神聖需要尊嚴與禮節，親近易滋生輕慢。最常用之物與最常交往之人往往最不受珍惜，因接觸愈多，缺點越明顯；而緘默則可將缺陷掩飾。切勿與任何人過於親密，因為親密永遠不悅人心意：不要與你的上司過熟，否則危險將至；不要過於親近你的下屬，否則有失尊嚴；最不可與烏合之眾為伍，因為他們蠻橫而愚蠢。他們看不出你是出自善意，卻認為是你應盡之責。過分親近與粗俗一般無二。

1. decorum [dɪˋkorəm] n. 端莊，得體，有禮
2. trench on 接近，近似

clxxvii Avoid Familiarities in Intercourse.

N either use them nor permit them. He that is familiar, loses any superiority his Influence gives him, and so loses respect. The stars keep their brilliance by not making themselves common. The Divine demands **decorum**[1]. Every familiarity breeds contempt. In human affairs, the more a man shows, the less he has, for in open communication you communicate the failings that reserve might keep under cover. Familiarity is never desirable; with superiors because it is dangerous, with inferiors because it is unbecoming, least of all with the common herd, who become insolent from sheer folly: they mistake favour shown them for need felt of them. Familiarity **trenches on**[2] vulgarity.

178 · 信任自己內心的聲音

相信你的內心，尤其是當它堅強而有力，值得信賴之時，切勿與其背道而馳。它常能為你預測各種重要的事情，是你的天生先知。許多人因為恐懼自己的內心而招致毀滅，但是只是恐懼而不補救，那又有何益？許多人天生就對自己的內心忠貞不渝，因此其內心總給他們啟發，警鐘長鳴，挽救他們於困境之中。追逐邪惡是不明智的，除非你想去征服它們。

179 · 深沉含蓄乃才能之標誌

無秘密之心如同一封攤開在眾人面前的信一般。要有潛藏隱秘的城府才能深藏不露，大窟小洞均可讓重要事情沉澱深藏。含蓄緘默來自於自我控制，能夠保持緘默方為真正的勝利。你必須為你洩露的每一個秘密交付贖金。明慎處世的關鍵在於內心之平和與節制。當有人想摸透你的心思，反覆盤問，旁敲側擊，試圖讓你洩露內心的秘密時，為了免於這些危險，審慎之人會更加沉默。所做的不需直言，所說的不必照做。

---

1. things of moment　重大的，重要的事情
2. ransom [ˋrænsəm] n. 贖金，贖取
3. worm out　鑽出，爬出

clxxviii Trust Your Heart,

e specially when it has been proved. Never deny it a hearing. It is a kind of house oracle that often foretells the most important. Many have perished because they feared their own heart, but of what use is it to fear it without finding a better remedy? Many are endowed by Nature with a heart so true that it always warns them of misfortune and wards off its effects. It is unwise to seek evils, unless you seek to conquer them.

clxxix Reticence Is the Seal of Capacity.

A breast without a secret is an open letter. Where there is a solid foundation secrets can be kept profound: there are spacious cellars where **things of moment**[1] may be hid. Reticence springs from self-control, and to control oneself in this is a true triumph. You must pay **ransom**[2] to each you tell. The security of wisdom consists in temperance in the inner man. The risk that reticence runs lies in the cross-questioning of others, in the use of contradiction to **worm out**[3] secrets, in the darts of irony: to avoid these the prudent become more reticent than before. What must be done need not be said, and what must be said need not be done.

180・不要被敵人誤導

愚人從不聽從智者的告誡，因他不知道遵循合理的方法以從中獲益。智者更不會因循他人之見，因為他總是隱藏起自己的真實想法，而執行另一套方案。凡事都應該從兩方面體察權衡事物，儘量保持不偏不倚。不要去考慮「很可能」發生什麼，而要多想想什麼「有可能」發生。

181・真情不宜全盤托出

沒有什麼比吐露真情更需要謹慎的了，這如同從心臟裏放血。隱藏真相和說出真相一樣需要很大技巧。一句簡單的謊言可能會毀掉你整個誠實的名聲。欺騙被視為背叛，而說謊之人更糟糕地被認定為叛徒。但是並非所有真相都可以講出來，有時為了保全自己要學會閉口不言，有時為了保全他人亦要學會保持沉默。

---

1. lancet [ˈlænsɪt] n. （外科用）柳葉刀，小刀

clxxx Never Guide the Enemy to What He Has to Do.

T he fool never does what the wise judge wise, because he does not follow up the suitable means. He that is discreet follows still less a plan laid out, or even carried out, by another. One has to discuss matters from both points of view – turn it over on both sides. Judgments vary; let him that has not decided attend rather to what is possible than what is probable.

clxxxi The Truth, But Not the Whole Truth.

N othing demands more caution than the truth: 'tis the **lancet**[1] of the heart. It requires as much to tell the truth as to conceal it. A single lie destroys a whole reputation for integrity. The deceit is regarded as treason and the deceiver as a traitor, which is worse. Yet not all truths can be spoken: some for our own sake, others for the sake of others.

182・做事勇敢

是處事謹慎的一個要點。改變你對他人的看法，不要過分抬高他人以致對其心懷畏懼；亦不要讓你的想像被自己的心智所擺佈。許多人貌似偉大，一旦與之相交熟悉之後才知並非如此，與之相交越深，越讓人失望，使你很難提高對他的評價。無人能超越人性的侷限，每個人都有弱點，不是存在於大腦就是存在於內心。社會地位往往賦予人表面上的權威，但這種權威很少與人自身的才德相符。那些位高權重之人，命運往往使其才德不稱其職位以示懲罰。人的想像力往往在所見所知之前，誇大事物使其名不副實，想像思考的不是現實存在的東西而是它希望存在的東西。理性則憑藉經驗明辨事理，糾正過度的想像力。如果說君子不宜懦弱膽怯，那愚人不應魯莽大膽。如果說自信可以為愚魯之人增威，那對有勇有謀之人則不啻於如虎添翼！

---

1. disillusionize [ˌdɪsɪ`luʒənd] v. 使幻滅，使覺醒
2. o'ersteps 是古英語中 oversteps 的縮寫。
3. redress [rɪ`drɛs] vt. 修正，改正，矯正
4. attentive [ə`tɛntɪv] adj. 注意的，專心的，留意的
5. timorous [`tɪmərəs] adj. 膽小的

clxxxii A Grain of Boldness in Everything.

❭ Tis an important piece of prudence. You must moderate your opinion of others so that you may not think so high of them as to fear them. The imagination should never yield to the heart. Many appear great till you know them personally, and then dealing with them does more to **disillusionize**[1] than to raise esteem. No one **o'ersteps**[2] the narrow bounds of humanity: all have their weaknesses either in heart or head. Dignity gives apparent authority, which is rarely accompanied by personal power: for Fortune often **redresses**[3] the height of office by the inferiority of the holder. The imagination always jumps too soon, and paints things in brighter colours than the real: it thinks things not as they are but as it wishes them to be. **Attentive**[4] experience disillusionised in the past soon corrects all that. Yet if wisdom should not be **timorous**[5], neither should folly be rash. And if self-reliance helps the ignorant, how much more the brave and wise?

183 · 勿要固執己見

愚 蠢之人十分堅信自己是正確的，同樣固執己見的人都很愚蠢。他們觀點越是錯誤，越是執迷不悟。即便你真的站在有理的一方，也不妨做一些讓步。人們最終將會承認你是正確的，並會由此敬佩你的寬容和大度。固執給你帶來的損失遠遠大於你擊敗他人之所得，這時你所維護的並不是真理，而是粗暴無理了。有的人腦袋似頑石，固執己見，不可救藥。如果妄想與固執相結合那就是愚蠢至極。人的意志需要堅定不移，但並不是在做判斷時過於固執己見。當然，總有一些例外，即判斷一旦改變，在行動上就絕不可游移不定，否則你會導致雙重失敗。

---

1. erroneous [ɪ`ronɪəs] adj. 錯誤的，不正確的
2. caprice [kə`pris] n. 反覆無常，任性
3. wearisome [`wɪrɪsəm] adj. 使疲倦的，使厭倦的
4. steadfastness [`stɛd,fæstnɪs] n. 堅定，穩當
5. execution [,ɛksɪ`kjuʃən] n. 實行，執行

clxxxiii Do Not Hold Your Views Too Firmly.

Every fool is fully convinced, and every one fully persuaded is a fool: the more **erroneous**[1] his judgment the more firmly he holds it. Even in cases of obvious certainty, it is fine to yield: our reasons for holding the view cannot escape notice, our courtesy in yielding must be the more recognised. Our obstinacy loses more than our victory yields: that is not to champion truth but rather rudeness. There be some heads of iron most difficult to turn: add **caprice**[2] to obstinacy and the sum is a **wearisome**[3] fool. **Steadfastness**[4] should be for the will, not for the mind. Yet there are exceptions where one would fail twice, owning oneself wrong both in judgment and in the **execution**[5] of it.

184・不要拘泥於繁文縟節

就算是國王，過分拘泥於繁文縟節也會有怪癖之嫌。過分拘泥於形式或細節往往令人厭惡，有些國度舉國上下均受其累。他們用繁文縟節的針法織就蠢人的衣服，這些愚人崇拜自身的尊嚴，而其顯示的體面不過是雞腸鳥肚，根本就不夠格，任何細微的事情似乎都會損傷他們的尊嚴。希望得到尊重誠然不錯，但如果過分注重儀式則不太明智。當然，一個完全不拘泥於繁文縟節之人，若其想取得成功，那是需要超凡才能的。禮節不應過分誇大，亦不應鄙棄。在這種小事上顯得了不起的人不會是真正的偉人。

185・切莫孤注一擲

因為若失敗，損失難以彌補。一個人總有失意的經歷，尤其是剛開始的時候。你所處的環境不會總是有利的，因此才有了這句諺語，「人人皆有得意時」。**要學會總是給自己預留再試的機會，這樣無論第一次成功與否，都會對第二次有益**。你總能找到更好的辦法和更多的資源可以利用。諸事有賴於種種情勢，能一次成功之事畢竟不常有。

---

1. ceremonious [ˌsɛrəˈmonjəs] adj. 講究儀式的，隆重的
2. punctilious [pʌŋkˈtɪlɪəs] adj. 拘泥細節的，謹小慎微的
3. garb [gɑrb] n. 服裝
4. weave [wiv] vt. 編織
5. worshipper [ˈwɝʃɪpɚ] n. 崇拜者

clxxxiv Do Not Be Ceremonious¹.

E ven in a king affectation in this was renowned for its eccentricity. To be **punctilious**² is to be a bore, yet whole nations have this peculiarity. The **garb**³ of folly is **woven**⁴ out of such things. Such folk are **worshippers**⁵ of their own dignity, yet show how little it is justified since they fear that the least thing can destroy it. It is right to demand respect, but not to be considered a master of ceremonies. Yet it is true that a man to do without ceremonies must possess supreme qualities. Neither affect nor despise etiquette: he cannot be great who is great at such little things.

clxxxv Never Stake Your Credit on a Single Cast;

f or if it miscarries the damage is irreparable. It may easy happen that a man should fail once, especially at first: circumstances are not always favourable: **hence**⁶ they say, "Every dog has his day." Always connect your second attempt with your first: whether it succeed or fail, the first will redeem the second. Always have resort to better means and appeal to more resources. Things depend on all sorts of chances. That is why the satisfaction of success is so rare.

6. hence [hɛns] adv. 因此，從此

186・識別位高權重者的缺點

醜惡即使以綾羅綢緞裝飾自己，誠實也能識別它。惡習有時可能頭戴金冠，但終究不能掩其本質。奴性即使以其主人的高官厚祿喬裝打扮，仍不減其醜惡。邪惡可能身處高位，但它永遠卑下。芸芸眾生只看到英雄身有瑕疵，卻不懂得他們之所以成為英雄並非那些瑕疵。居高位者外表華麗，卻掩蓋著醜陋。人們追捧這些居高位者，甚至連醜陋也一併模仿。殊不知那些掩蓋在偉大光環下的醜陋，一旦偉大消失，則令人望而生厭。

---

1. brocade [brə`ked] n. 織錦，錦緞
2. perchance [pə`tʃæns] adv. 偶然，碰巧
3. vaunt [vɔnt] v. 大肆吹噓，過分誇耀
4. specious [`spiʃəs] adj. 華而不實的，似是而非的
5. viciousness [`vɪʃəsnɪs] n. 惡意，邪惡

clxxxvi Recognise Faults, However High Placed.

Integrity cannot mistake vice even when clothed in **brocade**[1] or **perchance**[2] crowned with gold, but will not be able to hide its character for all that. Slavery does not lose its vileness, however it **vaunt**[3] the nobility of its lord and master. Viccs may stand in high place, but are low for all that. Men can see that many a great man has great faults, yet they do not see that he is not great because of them. The example of the great is so **specious**[4] that it even glosses over **viciousness**[5], till it may so affect those who flatter it that they do not notice that what they gloss over in the great they **abominate**[6] in the lower classes.

---

6. abominate [ə`bɑmə‚net] vt. 痛恨，憎惡

187 · 令眾人愉快之事，親自為之；令眾人不快之事，他人代勞

這樣你會贏得好感，把惡感轉嫁給他人。偉大而高貴之人總是認為施比受更會令人愉悅，這是其慷慨本性所帶來的殊榮。他們不會隨便讓人受到苦難，因為他們會因此而產生愧疚與懊悔。當你身居高位，需要透過對下屬的獎懲來開展工作之時，若是獎賞，則宜親自為之；若是懲罰，則由他人代勞。你需要找一個代罪羔羊，讓別人的不滿、厭惡、誹謗等矛頭都指向他。烏合之眾的怨恨猶如患狂犬病之瘋狗，他們不知痛從何處而來，只知亂咬嘴上之緊箍。緊箍無過，只不過是代人受罪而已。

---

1. remorse [rɪ`mɔrs] n. 懊悔，悔恨
2. grant [grænt] vt. 給予，授予
3. inflict [ɪn`flɪkt] v. 使遭受（不愉快的事），使承受
4. slander [`slændɚ] n. 誹謗
5. culprit [`kʌlprɪt] n. 問題的起因

clxxxvii Do Pleasant Things Yourself, Unpleasant Things Through Others.

B y the one course you gain goodwill, by the other you avoid hatred. A great man takes more pleasure in doing a favour than in receiving one: it is the privilege of his generous nature. One cannot easily cause pain to another without suffering pain either from sympathy or from **remorse**[1]. In high place one can only work by means of rewards and punishment, so **grant**[2] the first yourself, **inflict**[3] the other through others. Have some one against whom the weapons of discontent, hatred, and **slander**[4] may be directed. For the rage of the mob is like that of a dog: missing the cause of its pain it turns to bite the whip itself, and though this is not the real **culprit**[5], it has to pay the penalty.

315

188・發掘美好的事物來加以讚美

這樣做可提升你的品味，讓你高尚的品味為人所稱道。做一個讚美者可以顯示出我們知道什麼是卓越的事物，並且知道何時在同伴面前誇獎該事物。讚美可提供話題和效仿的範本，激勵人們去做好事情。同時，我們也以一種高雅的方式向傑出人士表達了崇敬之情。但有些人恰恰相反，他們總能找出事物的缺陷來加以批評，貶損不在場的人來奉承那些在場的人。這種伎倆往往使那些淺薄的人陷入他們的圈套，因為他們看不出其中的狡猾之處，即明責不在場的人，暗刺在場的人。許多人慣於薄古頌今，即慣於稱頌今日的平庸，輕視昨日的顯赫，但慎思之人往往一眼就會識破這些小伎倆，既不因他人惡意誇大而沮喪，亦不因他人阿諛獻媚而狂妄。他十分清楚，那些人其實是在做同樣的事情，只是針對不同的人採取了不同的手段罷了。

---

1. homage [ˋhɑmɪdʒ] n. 敬意

clxxxviii Be the Bearer of Praise.

T his increases our credit for good taste, since it shows that we have learnt elsewhere to know what is excellent, and hence how to prize it in the present company. It gives material for conversation and for imitation, and encourages praiseworthy exertions. We do **homage**[1] besides in a very delicate way to the excellences before us. Others do the opposite; they accompany their talk with a sneer, and fancy they flatter those present by belittling the absent. This may serve them with superficial people, who do not notice how cunning it is to speak ill of every one to every one else. Many pursue the plan of valuing more highly the mediocrities of the day than the most distinguished exploits of the past. Let the cautious penetrate through these subtleties, and let him not be dismayed by the exaggerations of the one or made over-confident by the flatteries of the other; knowing that both act in the same way by different methods, adapting their talk to the company they are in.

189. 學會利用他人的欲望

人的欲望越大,越容易被控制。哲學家們說匱乏根本不存在,政治家們說匱乏無處不在,後者的觀點是對的。有的人把別人的欲望當作階梯,拼命攀登以達到自己的目的。他們利用這種機會,指出滿足這種欲望多麼困難,藉此吊起別人的胃口。欲望帶來的刺激比擁有的滿足更有用。事情越困難,阻力越大,欲望越強烈。其精妙之處在於:滿足他人的欲望,但同時需維持人們對你的依賴。

---

1. turn of the screw （為達到某種目的所施加的）壓力
2. privation [praɪ`veʃən] n. 缺乏,匱乏
3. want [wɑnt] n. 需要,短缺
4. tantalise [`tæntl͵aɪz] vt. 逗弄,使乾著急
5. inertia [ɪn`ɝʃə] n. 慣性,慣量

clxxxix Utilise Another's Wants.

T he greater his wants the greater the **turn of the screw**[1]. Philosophers say **privation**[2] is non-existent, statesmen say it is all-embracing, and they are right. Many make ladders to attain their ends out of **wants**[3] of others. They make use of the opportunity and **tantalise**[4] the appetite by pointing out the difficulty of satisfaction. The energy of desire promises more than the **inertia**[5] of possession. The passion of desire increases with every increase of opposition. It is a subtle point to satisfy the desire and yet preserve the dependence.

190. 在萬物中尋找慰藉

即 使是毫無用處之物往往也能帶給你慰藉,它們永恆持久。世間萬物均有其有利的一面。俗話說:傻人有傻福,醜女有俊夫。往往是**事物的價值越小,其壽命就越長**。令人惱火的破鏡子偏偏不會徹底破碎,且耐用得讓人產生厭煩。大多數結局是天妒英才,無用之徒卻長壽。才華橫溢者總是帶有悲傷,而無足輕重之人卻活得悠然自在,不是看上去如此,就是事實是如此。運氣和死亡似乎串通一氣,將不幸遺忘在一旁。

---

1. compensation [ˌkɑmpənˈseʃən] n. 補償,賠償
2. come to grief 失敗,受損,被毀

cxc Find Consolation in All Things.

E ven the useless may find it in being immortal. No trouble without compensation[1]. Fools are held to be lucky, and the good-luck of the ugly is proverbial. Be worth little and you will live long: it is the cracked glass that never gets broken, but worries one with its durability. It seems that Fortune envies the great, so it equalises things by giving long life to the useless, a short one to the important. Those who bear the burden **come soon to grief**[2], while those who are of no importance live on and on: in one case it appears so, in the other it is so. The unlucky thinks he has been forgotten by both Death and Fortune.

191・不要被恭維迷惑

那是一種欺騙人的手段。有些人無需迷藥便能施展迷魂術，比如僅僅是一個得體優雅的脫帽禮，他們就讓那些愛慕虛榮的傻瓜們鬼迷心竅。他們開辦了一個優雅銀行，支付手段為花言巧語。許諾是為傻瓜設下的陷阱，因為什麼都許諾反而是什麼都沒有許諾。真正的謙恭禮貌是履行職責，而偽裝和無用都是欺騙。假裝謙恭並非真正尊敬別人，而只是獲得權力的手段。諂媚的人並非拜倒於對方高尚的人品，而是向他們的財富與權力低頭；恭維並非因為對方的品性與德行，而是為了從他那裏得到某些好處。

192・心境平和，延年益壽

自己過自由自在的生活，也容許他人過自由自在的生活。心平氣和者不僅活得長而且成為自己的主宰。做人就應當多聽、多看、慎言。白日與世無爭，夜晚便能安枕而眠。這樣既活得長壽，又活得快樂，從而相當於活了兩次，這就是心平氣和所帶來的好處。不去計較無關緊要的瑣事，那你便會應有盡有。最傻莫過於錙銖必較。事不關己卻偏為之傷神，事關自己卻漠不關心，這兩者同樣愚蠢。

---

1. Thessaly ['θesəli] 塞薩利，希臘東部一地區，構成一行政區
2. spurious [`spjʊrɪəs] adj. 偽造的，假造的，欺騙的
3. obeisance [o`besns] n. 敬禮
4. perversity [pɚ`vɝsətɪ] n. 反常，執迷不悟

cxci Do Not Take Payment in Politenes;

For it is a kind of fraud. Some do not need the herbs of **Thessaly**[1] for their magic, for they can enchant fools by the grace of their salute. Theirs is the Bank of Elegance, and they pay with the wind of fine words. To promise everything is to promise nothing: promises are the pitfalls of fools. The true courtesy is performance of duty: the **spurious**[2] and especially the useless is deceit. It is not respect but rather a means to power. **Obeisance**[3] is paid not to the man but to his means, and compliments are offered not to the qualities that are recognised but to the advantages that are desired.

cxcii Peaceful Life, a Long Life.

To live, let live. Peacemakers not only live: they rule life. Hear, see, and be silent. A day without dispute brings sleep without dreams. Long life and a pleasant one is life enough for two: that is the fruit of peace. He has all that makes nothing of what is nothing to him. There is no greater **perversity**[4] than to take everything to heart. There is equal folly in troubling our heart about what does not concern us and in not taking to heart what does.

193・防備那些利用他人達到自己目的的人

做事謹慎，提高警惕，這是防欺詐的唯一辦法。需留意他人的真實意圖，有人善於利用別人做自己的事，此時你若看不透他們的意圖，終會被人利用。你辛辛苦苦從火中取了栗子，還傷了手，卻讓別人坐享其成。

---

1. 這句話隱含了「火中取栗」的典故，最早出於公元前3世紀的《伊索寓言》：狡猾的猴子哄騙頭腦簡單的貓，讓貓替它從爐火中取出烤熟的栗子來。饞嘴的貓兒應命去做，爪子上的毛都被火燒掉了，結果它辛辛苦苦取出的栗子卻被猴子悄悄吃光了，自己什麼也沒吃到。

cxciii Watch him that Begins with Another's to End with His Own.

W atchfulness is the only guard against cunning. Be intent on his intentions. Many succeed in making others do their own affairs, and unless you possess the key to their motives you may at any moment be forced to **take their chestnuts out of the fire to the damage of your own fingers**[1].

194・理性對待自己以及
自己面臨的事情

初涉社會之人更應如此。人人自視甚高，而且最平庸的人自視最高。人人都夢想走好運，發大財，自以為是個天才，原以為會大展鴻圖，實現人生抱負，但到頭來是不遂人願。現實是對虛妄想像的折磨。明智之人總是會懷抱最好的願望，但卻做最壞的打算，只有這樣才能平靜地接受任何結果。目標訂得高遠並沒有錯，但絕不能是遙不可及，從而導致自己一開始就錯失機會。在你剛開始一項工作時，需要調整好你的期望值，因為在你親自經歷之前，你的理想肯定是很高的。我們需用謹慎明智來預防和治療各種愚行，給自己一個正確的認識，就能夠很好地調節理想和現實之間的差距。

---

1. extravagant [ɪk`strævəgənt] adj. 奢侈的，過分的
2. well-spring 水源，源頭
3. equanimity [ˌikwə`nɪmətɪ] n. 鎮定
4. panacea [ˌpænə`sɪə] n. 萬全之策

cxciv Have Reasonable Views of Yourself and of Your Affairs,

e specially in the beginning of life. Every one has a high opinion of himself, especially those who have least ground for it. Every one dreams of his good-luck and thinks himself a wonder. Hope gives rise to **extravagant**[1] promises which experience does not fulfil. Such idle imaginations merely serve as a **well-spring**[2] of annoyance when disillusion comes with the true reality. The wise man anticipates such errors: he may always hope for the best. but he always expects the worst, so as to receive what comes with **equanimity**[3]. True, It is wise to aim high so as to hit your mark, but not so high that you miss your mission at the very beginning of life. This correction of the ideas is necessary, because before experience comes expectation is sure to soar too high. The best **panacea**[4] against folly is prudence. If a man knows the true sphere of his activity and position, he can reconcile his ideals with reality.

195・學會欣賞他人

每個人都有其過人之處，沒有人優秀到無人可以超越。**學會欣賞每個人會讓你受益無窮**。智者尊重每一個人，他能看到每個人的優點，知道人有所專長非常不容易。愚蠢之人喜歡貶低每個人，他們往往不會看出別人的優點，只會挑剔缺點。

196・知道自己的貴人

不能找到自己貴人的人最無助。若是你倒楣的話，只能說明你還未發現你的貴人。有人能攀龍附鳳，得貴人相助，但他們卻並不知其所以然，以為僅是運氣的眷顧，他們只是順應這份運氣，不需花費太多心力。有的人會受到智者垂青。有些人在一個國家比在另一個國家會更順利；或者在一個城市會比另一個城市更加出名。即使一個人資質未變，他在某個職位或地位上也會比在其他情況下更好運。幸運女神總是喜歡隨心所欲地洗牌，是故每一個人都需要瞭解自己的運氣，就如同知道自己的才能一樣，輸贏成敗全在於此。要知道如何追隨你的幸運星，不要將其與其他的星辰相混淆，即使它的鄰居北極星以雷鳴般的聲音召喚你也不要理睬它，否則就會迷失方向。

---

1. excel [ɪk`sɛl] v. 勝過他人　2. potentate [`potn,tet] n. 當權者
3. welcome [`wɛlkəm] adj. 受歡迎的　4. polestar [`pol,stɑr] n. 北極星

cxcv Know How to Appreciate.

T here is none who cannot teach somebody something, and there is none so excellent but he is **excelled**[1]. To know how to make use of every one is useful knowledge. Wise men appreciate all men, for they see the good in each and know how hard it is to make anything good. Fools depreciate all men, not recognising the good and selecting the bad.

cxcvi Know Your Ruling Star.

N one so helpless as not to have one; if he is unlucky, that is because he does not know it. Some stand high in the favour of princes and **potentates**[2] without knowing why or wherefore, except that good luck itself has granted them favour on easy terms, merely requiring them to aid it with a little exertion. Others find favour with the wise. One man is better received by one nation than by another, or is more **welcome**[3] in one city than in another. He finds more luck in one office or position than another, and all this though his qualifications are equal or even identical. Luck shuffles the cards how and when she will. Let each man know his luck as well as his talents, for on this depends whether he loses or wins. Follow your guiding star and help it without mistaking any other for it, for that would be to miss the North, though its neighbour (the **polestar**[4]) calls us to it with a voice of thunder.

197・不要與蠢人共事

所謂蠢人就是那種不會識別蠢人的人,更蠢之人就是即使看出一個人是蠢人但也不會擺脫他,與其保持距離的人。與蠢人交往,哪怕是泛泛之交,也會招致危險。倘若對他們推心置腹,危害無疑更大。即便開始之時,愚蠢之人會因自己的謹慎或他人的告誡而暫時安分一些,但終究還會說蠢話、做蠢事,而且會因為克制太久導致日後更為過分。要知道聲名狼藉之徒不會幫助你提高聲譽,只會玷污你的名聲。蠢人總是不走運,這是他們的所作所為必須付出的代價。他們還有一樣東西不算太糟糕,那就是:儘管他們對智者來說沒什麼用處,但是確實可以為智者充當反面教材。

---

1. at length 最後,最終
2. in stock 有庫存,有現貨
3. Nemesis [ˋnɛməsɪs] n. [希臘]復仇女神。報應,不可避免的懲罰
4. signpost [ˋsaɪnˏpost] n. 路標

cxcvii Do Not Carry Fools on Your Back.

H e that does not know a fool when he sees him is one himself: still more he that knows him but will not keep clear of him. They are dangerous company and ruinous confidants. Even though their own caution and others' care keeps them in bounds for a time, still **at length**[1] they are sure to do or to say some foolishness which is all the greater for being kept so long **in stock**[2]. They cannot help another's credit who have none of their own. They are most unlucky, which is the **Nemesis**[3] of fools, and they have to pay for one thing or the other. There is only one thing which is not so bad about them, and this is that though they can be of no use to the wise, they can be of much use to them as **signposts**[4] or as warnings.

198・人挪活，樹挪死

有些國家的人，尤其是那些身居高位者，只有在離開他的祖國之後才能令其價值得到人們的重視。其祖國對待他們這些出類拔萃的卓越子民就如同後母一般，嫉妒氾濫橫行，它使世人只記得他人起初的渺小，看不到後來他所取得的偉大成就。因此即使是一針一線從舊世界移到新世界也會增值，正如一個來自遠方的彩色玻璃球可讓人們唾棄鑽石一樣。每件異物往往備受重視，可能部分因為它來自遠方，而部分因為人們在它臻於完美時才得一見，從而倍加推崇。有些人在自己所處的小角落中遭受鄙夷，而走出原來的地方卻成為了世界的奇蹟，備受同胞和現居住地人民的尊敬。後者是因為他們來自遠方，能夠獲得前者的讚譽是因為只能從遠處遙望他們。如果人們知道了聖壇上的雕像只是樹林中的一棵樹幹，那人們的崇拜之心就會消失殆盡。

---

1. transplant [træns`plænt] v. 搬遷，遷移
2. outvie [`aut`vaɪ] vt. 競爭勝過
3. 暗指歐洲人在新大陸探險時發生的事情。

cxcviii Know How to Transplant[1] Yourself.

There are nations with whom one must cross their borders to make one's value felt, especially in great posts. Their native land is always a stepmother to great talents: envy flourishes there on its native soil, and they remember one's small beginnings rather than the greatness one has reached. A needle is appreciated that comes from one end of the world to the other, **and a piece of painted glass might outvie[2] the diamond in value if it comes from afar[3]**. Everything foreign is respected, partly because it comes from afar, partly because it is ready made and perfect. We have seen persons once the laughing-stock of their village and now the wonder of the whole world, honoured by their fellow-countrymen and by the foreigners [among whom they dwell]; by the latter because they come from afar, by the former because they are seen from afar. The statue on the altar is never reverenced by him who knew it as a trunk in the garden.

199・以德行贏得尊重

若加之勤奮努力，則會更快達到目的。只有正直是不夠的，不顧顏面的一味追求很丟人，靠這種方式得到的東西必然是被玷污的，這樣就破壞了名譽。正確的途徑是兼有二者，選擇中庸之道，具備美德，同時亦懂得如何表現自己。

200・為自己保留願望

這樣你就不會樂極生悲。身體需要呼吸，精神要有渴望。如果你擁有了一切，那麼一切終將幻滅，從而讓你失望與不滿。即使學習知識也是該保留一些，從而存留好奇與希望。過度的幸福是災難。幫助他人也需要講求技巧，絕對不能令他們完全滿足。當他們再無所求時，你就得處處當心。當欲望不再時，恐懼因之而生。

---

1. presumption [prɪˋzʌmpʃən] n. 放肆，冒昧，自以為是
2. besprinkle [bɪˋsprɪŋkl] vt. 酒，佈滿

cxcix To Find a Proper Place by Merit, Not by Presumption[1].

The true road to respect is through merit, and if industry accompany merit the path becomes shorter. Integrity alone is not sufficient, push and insistence is degrading, for things arrive by that means so **besprinkled**[2] with dust that the discredit destroys reputation. The true way is the middle one, half-way between deserving a place and pushing oneself into it.

cc Leave Something to Wish for,

So as not to be miserable from very happiness. The body must respire and the soul aspire. If one possessed all, all would be disillusion and discontent. Even in knowledge there should be always something left to know in order to arouse curiosity and excite hope. Surfeits of happiness are fatal. In giving assistance it is a piece of policy not to satisfy entirely. If there is nothing left to desire, there is everything to fear, an unhappy state of happiness. When desire dies, fear is born.

201·看起來愚笨之人都是蠢人，看起來聰明之人一半是蠢人

蠢人是伴隨著世界的產生而來的。即使智慧尚有存餘，在神明眼中還是愚蠢。那些自認為自己聰明，他人愚蠢之人其實是最愚蠢的。若是想成為智者，看似賢明是不夠的，自覺聰明則更差。自認不知便為有知，不見人之所見即為無知。世界上儘管充滿了蠢人，卻無一人會自認為愚蠢，甚至他們會懷疑世上多半是蠢人這一事實。

202·言行共同造就完美

人應當說話得體，行事磊落。前者顯示睿智的頭腦，後者顯示慈悲的心靈，二者皆源自於高貴的靈魂。語言是行為的影子，語言為陰，行動為陽。用行為獲得稱讚比用言語讚美他人更為重要。有道是言易行難。行為是生命的本質，言語只是修飾。卓越的行為可以延續永生，再驚人的語言也會消逝。行為是思考的產物。如果思考是明智的，那麼行為就會是有效的。

---

1. least of all 最不
2. frippery [ˈfrɪpərɪ] n. 俗麗無用的裝飾品，多而無用的東西

cci They Are All Fools Who Seem So Besides Half the Rest.

F olly arose with the world, and if there be any wisdom it is folly compared with the divine. But the greatest fool is he who thinks he is not one and all others are. To be wise it is not enough to seem wise, **least of all**[1] to oneself. He knows who does not think that he knows, and he does not see who does not see that others see. Though all the world is full of fools, there is none that thinks himself one, or even suspects the fact.

ccii Words and Deeds Make the Perfect Man.

O ne should speak well and act honourably: the one is an excellence of the head, the other of the heart, and both arise from nobility of soul. Words are the shadows of deeds; the former are feminine, the latter masculine. It is more important to be renowned than to convey renown. Speech is easy, action hard. Actions are the stuff of life, words its **frippery**[2]. Eminent deeds endure, striking words pass away. Actions are the fruit of thought; if this is wise, they are effective.

203・結識同時代的偉人

世間偉人不多。整個世界只有一隻鳳凰，百年才能有一個偉大的將領、一個完美的演說家和一個真正的哲學家，數百年才得見一個賢明的君主。平庸之輩比比皆是，故很少受到敬重。各個領域的傑出人物屈指可數，因為他們追求的是盡善盡美，所以等級越高，越難達到。很多人都想成為凱撒和亞歷山大，以「偉大」自居，但卻是虛有其名，沒有功績，那個名號只不過是大話而已。塞內加式的人物歷來不多，名垂青史的畢竟只有阿佩利斯一人而已。

204・舉輕若重，舉重若輕

舉輕若重可以避免過分自信，舉重若輕可以避免自暴自棄。不想做某事，你只當它已經做成就好。另一方面，勤奮且有耐心可以幫助你征服看似不可能的事情。想要成就大事，不必考慮太多，只須行動起來，不要為困難空耗心力。

---

1. illustrious [ɪˋlʌstrɪəs] adj. 傑出的
2. Apelles 阿佩利斯。公元前4世紀希臘畫家，曾給馬其頓的腓力二世及亞歷山大大帝充當宮廷畫師。在當時很受歡迎，其畫像無一傳世。
3. brood over 深思，沈思

cciii Know the Great Men of Your Age.

They are not many. There is one Phonix in the whole world, one great general, one perfect orator, one true philosopher in a century, a really **illustrious**[1] king in several. Mediocrities are as numerous as they are worthless: eminent greatness is rare in every respect, since it needs complete perfection, and the higher the species the more difficult is the highest rank in it. Many have claimed the title "Great," like Caesar and Alexander, but in vain, for without great deeds the title is a mere breath of air. There have been few Senecas, and fame records but one **Apelles**[2].

cciv Attempt Easy Tasks as if They Were Difficult, and Difficult as if They Were Easy.

In the one case that confidence may not fall asleep, in the other that it may not be dismayed. For a thing to remain undone nothing more is needed than to think it done. On the other hand, patient industry overcomes impossibilities. Great undertakings are not to be **brooded over**[3], lest their difficulty when seen causes despair.

205・善用不屑

想要得到你喜歡的一樣東西，最好方法就是對它們假裝不屑一顧，毫不在意。世間之物，當你苦苦尋覓之時卻不見其蹤影，而稍後，你不必費力，它們卻奔湧而來，正所謂踏破鐵鞋無覓處，得來全不費工夫。塵世萬物是天國的影子，其行止亦如影子。當你苦苦追趕它們之時，它們就逃走；而當你逃離它們之際，它們卻追逐你而來。此外，藐視還是最巧妙的報復方式。有這麼一句智慧的箴言：就是永遠不要用筆來為自己辯解，這會留下痕跡，不但達不到懲罰敵人的目的，反而會給敵人以可乘之機，使他們揚名天下。卑鄙小人常用的伎倆就是狡猾地對抗偉人，試圖間接地由此得到他們沿正途根本得不到的榮耀。假如傑出人物對他們採取漠視態度，就沒人會知道這些人了。沒有任何報復比漠視更能把那些小人埋葬在他們愚昧的塵土之下。那些膽大妄為之人企圖火燒當代與歷史傳頌的奇人偉事來成就自己的不朽。平息流言蜚語的最有效方法就是置之不理。若是應戰，只會給自己帶來傷害；若是對它們反唇相譏，也只會使自己榮譽受損，讓對手得意洋洋。儘管污點不能完全損毀我們的名譽，但至少可以掩蓋它的光環。

---

1. mundane [`mʌnden] adj. 世俗的，人間的
2. notoriety [ˌnotə`raɪətɪ] n. 惡名，聲名狼藉
3. roundabout [`raʊndəˌbaʊt] adj. 迂迴的，繞圈子的
4. audacious [ɔ`deʃəs] adj. 魯莽的，膽大妄為的
5. reprove [rɪ`pruv] v. 責備

ccv Know How to Play the Card of Contempt.

I t is a shrewd way of getting things you want, by affecting to depreciate them: generally they are not to be had when sought for, but fall into one's hands when one is not looking for them. As all **mundane**[1] things are but shadows of the things eternal, they share with shadows this quality, that they flee from him who follows them and follow him that flees from them. Contempt is besides the most subtle form of revenge. It is a fixed rule with the wise never to defend themselves with the pen. For such defence always leaves a stain, and does more to glorify one's opponent than to punish his offence. It is a trick of the worthless to stand forth as opponents of great men, so as to win **notoriety**[2] by a **roundabout**[3] way, which they would never do by the straight road of merit. There are many we would not have heard of if their eminent opponents had not taken notice of them. There is no revenge like oblivion, through which they are buried in the dust of their unworthiness. **Audacious**[4] persons hope to make themselves eternally famous by setting fire to one of the wonders of the world and of the ages. The art of **reproving**[5] scandal is to take no notice of it, to combat it damages our own case; even if credited it causes discredit, and is a source of satisfaction to our opponent, for this shadow of a stain dulls the lustre of our fame even if it cannot altogether deaden it.

206・須知庸俗之輩無處不在

甚至在科林斯和最顯赫的家族也未能倖免。每個人都會在自己周圍見到這些庸俗之輩。比庸俗的本性更糟糕的是庸俗的行為。他們反射出庸俗的氣質，就如同鏡子的碎片，更具傷害。他們言語庸俗並且常常妄加批評。他們是無知之徒，守護愚蠢的教父，醜聞昔日的主人。對他們的言語你可以置之不理，更不必去理會他們的感受。重要的是認識粗俗以避開他們，避免與他們同流合污或成為他們的攻擊目標。任何愚蠢都是庸俗，而粗俗之眾又都是由蠢人組成。

---

1. 指科林斯灣內伯羅奔尼撒半島東北希臘南部的一個城市，在公元前6、7世紀是一個富裕的海上強國，以文化和教育揚名。
2. pernicious [pɚˋnɪʃəs] adj. 有害的
3. impertinently [ɪmˋpɝtnəntlɪ] adv. 莽撞無禮地，不禮貌地
4. disciple [dɪˋsaɪpl] n. 信徒，弟子，門徒

ccvi Know that There Are Vulgar Natures Everywhere,

e ven in **Corinth**[1] itself, even in the highest families. Every one may try the experiment within his own gates. But there is also such a thing as vulgar opposition to vulgarity, which is worse. This special kind shares all the qualities of the common kind, just as bits of a broken glass: but this kind is still more **pernicious**[2] ; it speaks folly, blames **impertinently**[3], is a **disciple**[4] of ignorance, a patron of folly, and past master of scandal; you need not notice what it says, still less what it thinks. It is important to know vulgarity in order to avoid it, whether it is subjective or objective. For all folly is vulgarity, and the vulgar consist of fools.

207・力求自制

對 偶然事件要有高度的警惕性。突如其來的激情、衝動容易使人
無法保持謹慎和理智,這正是你有可能栽跟斗的地方。人在
一瞬間狂怒或歡喜要比在心平氣和的狀態下更容易失控,**切記,即使
一秒中的放縱也可能會讓你終生悔恨。**工於心計的人會狡猾地利用這
種時機為謹慎的人們設下陷阱,去摸清你的底細並試探你的心思。為
了偵察到秘密,他們必須深入到最偉大的靈魂深處。那你應如何對付
呢?自制就是最好的對策,特別是對於突發的緊急事情更應如此。為
防止衝動,需三思而行,控制自己的衝動就如同駕馭烈馬,馬背上的
智者比平時的智者還要聰明。能夠預見危險的人才會謹慎行事,衝動
之下的言語往往是言者無心,但聽者有意。

---

1. wrath [ræθ] n. 憤怒
2. counterplot [`kaʊntɚˌplɑt] n. 對抗另一計謀的計謀,對抗策略
3. take the bit between the teeth 不服控制
4. 西班牙有句諺語:「馬背上無智者」,所以能在馬背上做智者自然需要雙倍的
聰明。

ccvii Be Moderate.

O ne has to consider the chance of a mischance. The impulses of the passions cause prudence to slip, and there is the risk of ruin. A moment of **wrath**[1] or of pleasure carries you on farther than many hours of calm, and often a short diversion may put a whole life to shame. The cunning of others uses such moments of temptation to search the recesses of the mind: they use such thumbscrews as are wont to test the best caution. Moderation serves as a **counterplot**[2], especially in sudden emergencies. Much thought is needed to prevent a passion **taking the bit between the teeth**[3], and **he is doubly wise who is wise on horseback**[4]. He who knows the danger may with care pursue his journey. Light as a word may appear to him who throws it out, it may import much to him that hears it and **ponders on**[5] it.

---

5. ponder over 沈思，深思

208・不要死於愚蠢

聰明之人通常會在失去理智後死掉，而愚蠢之人則是在獲得理智之前就死掉了。死於愚蠢，就是死於過度思考。有些人因其過分敏感，思考過多而死，而另一些人則是什麼都不想，不知道什麼是感慨，但是卻活得好好的。前者是因事事憂慮而愚蠢，後者則是因其從不知悔恨憂慮為何物而愚蠢。過分聰明而暴亡是愚蠢的，這就造成了一些人因為懂得太多而死，而另一些人因其懂得不多而活著。雖然有很多人死於愚蠢，但真正的蠢人卻很少會死。

209・把自己從芸芸眾生中解脫出來

這樣做需要一種特殊的冷靜和策略。芸芸眾生的愚蠢被約定俗成變成了權威，人可以抗拒個體的無知，但是卻抵抗不住群體的力量。在這之中有一種普遍的偏見就是：沒有誰會對自己的福氣滿足，即使那是福中之福；也沒有誰對自己的才智不滿，即使他們非常愚蠢。再者是，他們對自己的命運不滿，而對別人的卻垂涎三尺。更有甚者，人們喜歡厚古薄今，坐這山望那山，過去的似乎總是更好，而遠處的事物看起來更完美和珍貴。對什麼都嗤之以鼻之人與對什麼都抱有悲觀態度之人一樣愚蠢。

ccviii Do Not Die of the Fools' Disease.

T he wise generally die after they have lost their reason: fools before they have found it. To die of the fools' disease is to die of too much thought. Some die because they think and feel too much: others live because they do not think and feel: these are fools because they do not die of sorrow, the others because they do. A fool is he that dies of too much knowledge: thus some die because they are too knowing, others because they are not knowing enough. Yet though many die like fools, few die fools.

ccix Keep Yourself Free from Common Follies.

T his is a special stroke of policy. They are of special power because they are general, so that many who would not be led away by any individual folly cannot escape the universal failing. Among these are to be counted the common prejudice that any one is satisfied with his fortune, however great, or unsatisfied with his intellect, however poor it is. Or again, that each, being discontented with his own lot, envies that of others; or further, that persons of today praise the things of yesterday, and those here the things there. Everything past seems best and everything distant is more valued. He is as great a fool that laughs at all as he that weeps at all.

210・學會對待真相

說 出真相是非常危險的,但作為一個好人又不能不講,這就需要高超的技巧。善解人意的醫生設法讓真相變為更容易被接受的甜化劑,若是直接把真相告知那些當事人,對他們來說會是萬分痛苦。這需要高超成熟的技巧和得體的舉止。同樣的真相既可以讓人聽後開心,也會讓人勃然大怒。今天的事最好是看起來很久以前就發生了。對於聰明人,暗示一句就已足夠,若實在還不行,那就沉默吧。對於王公貴族,千萬不要直接給他們吃苦藥,最好是包上糖衣來迷惑他們。

---

1. quintessence [kwɪn`tɛsns] n. (某事物的)典範
2. to the ground 徹底地
3. draught [dræft] n. (藥水等一次的)服用量
4. gild [gɪld] v. 鍍金

ccx Know How to Play the Card of Truth.

❯ Tis dangerous, yet a good man cannot avoid speaking it. But great skill is needed here: the most expert doctors of the soul pay great attention to the means of sweetening the pill of truth. For when it deals with the destroying of illusion it is the **quintessence**[1] of bitterness. A pleasant manner has here an opportunity for a display of skill: with the same truth it can flatter one and fell another **to the ground**[2]. Matters of today should be treated as if they were long past. For those who can understand a word is sufficient, and if it does not suffice, it is a case for silence. Princes must not be cured with bitter **draughts**[3] ; it is therefore desirable in their case to **gild**[4] the pill of disillusion.

211・天堂裏萬般皆樂

地獄裏萬般皆苦，人生活於兩極之間的塵世，可以說兼具兩個世界的苦與樂。福禍多變，人不可能終身享福，也不會終身受苦。塵世本虛無，沒有價值，可是因為天堂在前面等待，塵世才有了諸多的意義。以淡泊之心看待世事的冷暖浮沉才是最謹慎的生存之道。真正的智者對新奇之物往往漠然處之。人生如戲，有開幕自有閉幕，且劇中複雜總會慢慢解決，因此聰慧之人需注意，在落幕之際給自己一個好的結局。

212・技藝在身切勿盡示於人，
應學會保留

這是大師的經驗之談。在傳授學生時，大師都會精明地保留一手，他們也以此為傲。只有深藏你的拿手絕技，你才能永保大師地位。傳授知識時必須講究策略技巧，只講知識本身就夠了，沒必要指出其出處。透過此法，你就能讓別人一直尊敬並依賴你。不管是娛樂還是教學，都要遵循這個技巧，在別人對你滿心期待的過程中逐步完善，點點滴滴地展示你的造詣。含蓄節制向來是人生制勝的法寶，對那些居於高位之人尤其如此。

ccxi In Heaven All Is Bliss;

i n Hell all misery. On earth, between the two, both one thing and the other. We stand between the two extremes, and therefore share both. Fate varies: all is not good luck nor all mischance. This world is merely zero: by itself it is of no value, but with Heaven in Front of it, it means much. Indifference at its ups and downs is prudent, nor is there any novelty for the wise. Our life gets as complicated as a comedy as it goes on, but the complications get gradually resolved: see that the curtain comes down on a good denoument.

ccxii Keep to Yourself the Final Touches of Your Art.

T his is a maxim of the great masters who pride themselves on this subtlety in teaching their pupils: one must always remain superior, remain master. One must teach an art artfully. The source of knowledge need not be pointed out no more than that of giving. By this means a man preserves the respect and the dependence of others. In amusing and teaching you must keep to the rule: keep up expectation and advance in perfection. To keep a reserve is a great rule for life and for success, especially for those in high place.

213・善用矛盾

查明事情真相的主要方法就是利用矛盾，讓別人處於尷尬境地，而自己卻置身於外。這是真正的「拇指夾」，往往能激發他人的情緒。委婉的質疑是秘密的催吐劑。它是打開心門的鑰匙，巧妙地對心理和意志進行雙重訊問。對於他人高深莫測的話語故意狡猾地表現出不屑一顧，你就能追蹤其隱藏最深的秘密，並將這些秘密點點滴滴地引到他們的舌尖，最後落入你精心編織的網。不要引起他人對你的注意，這樣別人就不會過分防備你，而讓他心底的秘密盡情流露，否則你無法瞭解他的內心世界。假裝的懷疑態度是最靈巧的打開他人心靈的鑰匙，利用好奇心知道你想知道的。同樣，在學習上亦是如此，優秀的學生會反駁他的老師，這種做法是最聰明的，這樣可以使得老師更加透徹，不遺餘力地為你講解。適當的反駁老師，反而使他的教誨更加完善。

---

1. tepid [ˋtɛpɪd] adj. 溫熱的，不太熱烈的
2. emetic [ɪˋmɛtɪk] n. 催嘔劑
3. bait [bet] n. 餌，誘惑物
4. inscrutable [ɪnˋskrutəbl] adj. 難以了解的，不能預測的
5. picklock [ˋpɪk͵lɑk] n. 撬鎖工具

ccxiii Know How to Contradict.

A chief means of finding things out – to embarrass others without being embarrassed. The true thumbscrew, it brings the passions into play. **Tepid**[1] incredulity acts as an **emetic**[2] on secrets. It is the key to a locked-up breast, and with great subtlety makes a double trial of both mind and will. A sly depreciation of another's mysterious word scents out the profoundest secrets; some sweet **bait**[3] brings them into the mouth till they fall from the tongue and are caught in the net of astute deceit. By reserving your attention the other becomes less attentive, and lets his thoughts appear while otherwise his heart were **inscrutable**[4] . An affected doubt is the subtlest **picklock**[5] that curiosity can use to find out what it wants to know. Also in learning it is a subtle plan of the pupil to contradict the master, who **thereupon**[6] **takes pains**[7] to explain the truth more thoroughly and with more force, so that a moderate contradiction produces complete instruction.

---

6. thereupon [ˌðɛrəˈpɑn] adv. 於是，因此
7. take pains 盡力，耐心

214 · 蠢事不可再犯

人們常常總會為了糾正一個錯誤一而再，再而三的再做另一件錯事；或者是為了彌補對別人的無禮而再次冒犯他。謊話一旦開頭，就會一發不可收拾，因為一個謊言需要更多的謊言來支撐，做蠢事亦是如此。最糟糕的是你不得不與蠢事鬥爭，而比蠢事更糟糕的是你不能把它掩蓋起來。為過錯辯護需要付出更大的代價。大智者亦會犯錯，但不會一錯再錯，就像是滑倒一樣，是奔跑之際的大意所造成的，而非站立之時故意所為。

---

1. annuity [əˋnjuətɪ] n. 年金，養老金

ccxiv Do Not Turn One Blunder into Two

I t is quite usual to commit four others in order to remedy one, or to excuse one piece of impertinence by still another. Folly is either related to, or identical with the family of Lies, for in both cases it needs many to support one. The worst of a bad case is having to fight it, and worse than the ill itself is not being able to conceal it. The **annuity**[1] of one failing serves to support many others. A wise man may make one slip but never two, and that only in running, not while standing still.

215・謹防城府很深之人

商人善於採用的策略就是故意分散他人心志，降低其警惕，從而加以打擊。人心志一旦分散，便很容易受挫。那些圖謀不軌者為了得到想要的，善於隱藏其真實意圖。為了在最後關頭獨佔鰲頭，他們甘願暫時屈居第二。如果不被察覺，這種方法鮮有失敗。既然敵人謀我之心昭然若揭，我們就應該時時保持注意。如果他們為了掩蓋自己的計畫而甘居第二，你一定要成為第一個揭露他陰謀的人。謹慎可以幫助識別這種人的花招，還能幫助注意到他為了達到目的而使用的託辭。他往往不將槍口直接對準目標，而是虛晃一槍，然後靈巧地轉身直接向獵物射去。掌握自己的容忍限度，在必要之時讓他們知道你已經看穿了他們的花招。

---

1. dissemble [dɪˋsɛmbḷ] v. 掩飾，掩藏
2. attain [əˋten] vt. 達到，獲得
3. spurt [spɝt] n. （努力或速度）突然增加，迸發

ccxv Watch Him that Acts on Second Thoughts.

I t is a device of business men to put the opponent off his guard before attacking him, and thus to conquer by being defeated: they **dissemble**[1] their desire so as to **attain**[2] it. They put themselves second so as to come out first in the final **spurt**[3]. This method rarely fails if it is not noticed. Let therefore the attention never sleep when the intention is so wide awake. And if the other puts himself second so to hide his plan, put yourself first to discover it. Prudence can discern the artifices which such a man uses, and notices the pretexts he puts forward to gain his ends. He aims at one thing to get another: then he turns round smartly and fires straight at his target. It is well to know what you grant him, and at times it is desirable to give him to understand that you understand.

216 · 學會表達自己

這不僅要求你思路清晰，而且要求你思維活躍。有些人善於醞思，但卻經常難產，因為欠缺清晰的表達方式，那麼觀念、思想、決斷的成果就永難誕生。有些人就像肚大口小的酒壇一樣，儘管有想法，但卻不能很好地表達出來；而有些人雖表達得淋漓盡致，但所說多於所想。意志需要作出決斷，思想需要表達出來，同時擁有二者則天賦非凡。思路清晰，能言善辯的人倍受人稱讚與歡迎；然而思緒雜亂無章之人也經常受人尊敬─僅僅因為其思想很難被理解。有時為了避免過於粗俗，需要採取含糊其辭之法。但是，如果我們說的不著邊際，那別人又怎麼會明白呢？

217 · 可以化敵為友，亦能化友為敵

在相信今日的朋友之時，要想到他們可能明天就是你的對手，而且對你來說是最具威脅性的對手。既然這些事在現實中確實會發生，就應有所防備。我們不應因友誼而解除武裝，否則，等到斷交時，他們會拿起武器來攻擊我們。另一方面，對於敵人，和解之門應始終敞開，如果這還是慷慨之門，那麼你就更安全。之前復仇的快感有時到了今日反會變成折磨，傷害他人的快感有時也會變成痛苦。

---

1. vivacity [vaɪˋvæsətɪ] n. 活潑　2. vent [vɛnt] n. 通風孔，出煙孔
3. reconciliation [ˌrɛkənˌsɪlɪˋeʃən] n. 和解，調和

ccxvi Be Expressive.

This depends not only on the clearness but also on the **vivacity**[1] of your thoughts. Some have an easy conception but a hard labour, for without clearness, the children of the mind, thoughts and judgments, cannot be brought into the world. Many have a capacity like that of vessels with a large mouth and a small **vent**[2]. Others again say more than they think. Resolution for the will, expression for the thought: two great gifts. Plausible minds are applauded: yet confused ones are often venerated just because they are not understood, and at times obscurity is convenient if you wish to avoid vulgarity; yet how shall the audience understand one that connects no definite idea with what he says?

ccxvii Neither Love nor Hate, forever.

Trust the friends of today as if they will be enemies tomorrow, and that of the worst kind. As this happens in reality, let it happen in your precaution. Do not put weapons in the hand for deserters from friendship to wage war with. On the other hand, leave the door of **reconciliation**[3] open for enemies, and if it is also the gate of generosity so much the more safe. The vengeance of long ago is at times the torment of today, and the joy over the ill we have done is turned to grief.

218・做事切勿固執，要學會應用知識

固執就像是大腦的毒瘤，又像是衝動的小孩，從來都會把事情搞砸。有些人在任何事情上都會挑起事端，行事風格就像土匪。他們做什麼事情都一定要成功，根本不懂得與人和睦相處。這種人如果成了統治者，危害更大。他們會使政府內部派系林立，朋黨相爭，搞得天翻地覆，他們還會把理應當作孩子看的人當作仇敵。他們行事鬼鬼祟祟，一旦有所成，就認為是自己的策略奏效。一旦人們認清了他們的乖張本性，就會群起反抗，推翻他們不切實際的計畫。如此一來，他們不僅一事無成，還留下了一堆爛攤子，因為他們所做的一切都只是讓人失望。人們看見他們就搖頭，不再信任他們。對於這樣的魔鬼，我們只能避而遠之，就算是荒蠻之地的野蠻人也比他們令人作嘔的本性讓人好受。

---

1. excrescence [ɪk`skrɛsns] n. 瘤，贅生物
2. banditti [`bændɪtɪ] n. 匪徒（bandit 的複數形式）
3. perverse [pɚ`vɝs] adj. 人性的，一意孤行的
4. chimerical [kaɪ`mɛrɪkəl] adj. 空想的
5. heap up 堆起來

ccxviii Never Act from Obstinacy But from Knowledge.

All obstinacy is an **excrescence**[1] of the mind, a grandchild of passion which never did anything right. There are persons who make a war out of everything, real **banditti**[2] of intercourse. All that they undertake must end in victory; they do not know how to get on in peace. Such men are fatal when they rule and govern, for they make government rebellion, and enemies out of those whom they ought to regard as children. They try to effect everything with strategy and treat it as the fruit of their skill. But when others have recognised their **perverse**[3] humour all revolt against them and learn to overturn their **chimerical**[4] plans, and they succeed in nothing but only **heap up**[5] a mass of troubles, since everything serves to increase their disappointment. They have a head turned and a heart spoilt. Nothing can be done with such monsters except to flee from them, even to the **Antipodes**[6], where the savagery is easier to bear than their loathsome nature.

6. Antipodes　安蒂波德斯群島（Antipodes Islands），屬於新西蘭的亞南極群島。主要包括以下幾部分：安蒂波德斯島（Antipodes Island）、博蘭斯島（Bollans Island）、向風群島（the Windward Islands）、奧德-里斯島（Orde Lees Island）、背風島（Leeward Island）、南島（South Islet）以及其他一些小島。

219・不要以偽善而聞名

雖然人生在世不能缺少智謀，但也不要以偽善而聞名。謹慎遠勝於投機取巧。雖然不一定人人都會以誠待人，但每個人都喜歡別人對自己以誠相待。莫要讓誠摯變成天真，也勿讓睿智變成狡猾。因明智而獲得尊敬遠勝於因陰險而為人所懼怕。真誠之人易受人尊敬愛戴，但也會被欺騙。最好的辦法就是把你認為是欺騙的東西揭露出來。真摯坦白興盛於黃金時代，而現今這個冷酷的時代充斥的卻是狡詐和敵意。知道何者當為是一種榮譽，它能激發信心；但如果被視為偽善，則會被人當成騙子，失去別人的信任。

220・不穿獅皮，則披狐皮

順應時代潮流是為了去引領潮流。人生在世，如果你能如願以償，你的名聲就不會受損。如果強攻不能達到，不妨運用技巧。此路不通就換一條路，可以走以勇氣開闢的光明大道，或者走以機智鋪設的終極捷徑。智謀與蠻力相比，前者總是取勝，機敏也總是比一味的大膽更有效。如果你不能如願以償得到某個東西，那就學會鄙視它吧。

---

1. 指希臘神話中的和平、興隆和幸福的時期。
2. foxpelt [`fɑkspɛlt]n. 狐皮
3. highway [`haɪ,we] n. 公路，大路
4. bypath [`baɪ,pæθ] n. 小路

ccxix Do Not Pass for a Hypocrite,

t hough such men are indispensable nowadays. Be considered rather prudent than astute. Sincerity in behaviour pleases all, though not all can show it in their own affairs. Sincerity should not degenerate into simplicity nor sagacity into cunning. Be rather respected as wise than feared as sly. The open-hearted are loved but deceived. The great art consists in disclosing what is thought to be deceit. In **the golden age**[1] simplicity flourished, in these days of iron cunning. 'The reputation of being a man who knows what he has to do is honourable and inspires confidence, but to be considered a hypocrite is deceptive and arouses mistrust.

ccxx If You Cannot Clothe Yourself in Lionskin Use Foxpelt[2].

T o follow the times is to lead them. He that gets what he wants never loses his reputation. Cleverness when force will not do. One way or another, the king's **highway**[3] of valour or the **bypath**[4] of cunning. Skill has effected more than force, and astuteness has conquered courage more often than the other way. When you cannot get a thing then is the time to despise it.

221 · 勿要置自己或他人於尷尬境地

有些人做事會使自己和別人都很難保持尊嚴，他們總是瀕於愚蠢的邊緣。這種人你相識容易，擺脫卻很難。他們一天到晚自尋煩惱。他們的幽默文不對題。他們總是反對一切。總是做出錯誤的判斷，並且批判一切。最能考驗我們審慎心的是那些一無是處卻挑剔一切的人。在缺乏教養的國度裏，充斥著各種怪物。

---

1. on the point of　正要…的時候
2. indecorum [ˌɪndɪˋkorəm] n. 缺乏教養，粗魯的言行

ccxxi Do Not Seize Occasions to Embarrass Yourself or Others.

T here are some men stumbling-blocks of good manners either for themselves or for others: they are always **on the point of**[1] some stupidity. You meet with them easily and part from them uneasily. A hundred annoyances a day is nothing to them. Their humour always strokes the wrong way since they contradict all and every. They put on the judgment cap wrong side foremost and thus condemn all. Yet the greatest test of others' patience and prudence are just those who do no good and speak ill of all. There are many monsters in the wide realm of **indecorum**[2].

222・謹慎的遲疑是審慎的表現

舌頭就像一頭野獸，一旦沒有了管束，就再難馴伏。舌頭是心靈的脈搏，智者用它來判斷我們的心靈是否健康，細心之人用它來感知自己的心聲。但不幸的是那些本應最謹慎的人卻往往最不謹慎。智者會盡力讓自己避免困境和煩惱，表現出成熟的自制力。智者會十分謹慎，公正如門神，警戒如阿各斯人。莫摩斯會讓手上長眼睛，而不是在胸膛上開扇窗戶。

223・勿做怪人

既不要故弄玄虛，也不要心不在焉。一些人有些明顯的特質，這會讓他們做出一些古怪的行為。這些古怪只是缺陷，而不是長處。正如有些人因為極醜而為人所知，古怪之人也會因其古怪行為方式令人厭煩而聞名。這些行為就像是給他們古怪貼上了標籤一樣，給他們帶來嘲諷或是招來敵意。

---

1. Janus 兩面神。古羅馬神話中的門神，有兩個面孔，朝著相反的方向。
2. Argus 阿各斯，希臘神話中的百眼巨人。
3. Momus 莫摩斯，希臘神話中的挑剔和嘲弄之神。
4. repellant [rɪˋpɛlənt] adj. 令人厭惡的，令人反感的
5. atrocious [əˋtroʃəs] adj. 惡劣的，糟糕的

ccxxii Reserve Is Proof of Prudence.

T he tongue is a wild beast; once let loose it is difficult to chain. It is the pulse of the soul by which wise men judge of its health: by this pulse a careful observer feels every movement of the heart. The worst is that he who should be most reserved is the least. The sage saves himself from worries and embarrassments, and shows his mastery over himself. He goes his way carefully, a **Janus**[1] for impartiality, an **Argus**[2] for watchfulness. Truly **Momus**[3] had better placed the eyes in the hand than the window in the breast.

ccxxiii Be Not Eccentric,

n either from affectation nor carelessness. Many have some remarkable and individual quality leading to eccentric actions. These are more defects than excellent differences. And just as some are known for some special ugliness, so these for something **repellant**[4] in their outward behaviour. Such eccentricities simply serve as trademarks through their **atrocious**[5] singularity: they cause either derision or ill-will.

224 · 不要違背事物的本性

不管事物以怎樣的面貌出現。萬物都有優美的一面，也有醜惡的一面。如果你抓的是刀刃，最好的武器也會傷害到你；如果那你抓的是刀柄，敵人的長矛也能很好的保護你。很多事情是痛苦的，但只要我們考慮到事情有其利的一面，那它還是可以帶來幸福。事情總是會有利弊、正反兩面，聰明之人的聰明就在於他們能夠看到事情有利的一面。不同的角度可以有不同的事實真相，應該從好的角度去看待事物，同時又不混淆好與壞。這就是為什麼有些人在任何事情上都能找到滿足，而另外一些人找到的則總是悲哀。懂得這一道理，則能逢凶化吉，安身立命，這是生活的一大要則，古往今來事事如此。

225 · 知道自己的缺陷

人類在擁有最顯著優點的同時，都會有其對應的缺點。如果缺點被貪欲滋養，則會成為統治你的暴君。戰勝它的辦法就是小心謹慎的對待它。先自我反省，缺點一旦被意識到，尤其是當事人像旁觀者一樣審視自己的缺點時，它就會很快被克服。想掌控自我，就須瞭解自我，學會自省，戰勝最大的缺點，其他缺點就會不戰而降。

---

1. against the grain 格格不入　2. seamy [ˋsimɪ] adj. 醜惡的
3. blade [blɛd] n. 刀刃，刀片　4. commence [kəˋmɛns] v. 開始，著手
5. manifesto [ˌmænəˋfɛsto] n. 宣言，聲明　6. come to an end 結束

ccxxiv Never Take Things Against the Grain[1],

N o matter how they come. Everything has a smooth and a **seamy**[2] side, and the best weapon wounds if taken by the **blade**[3], while the enemy's spear may be our best protection if taken by the staff. Many things cause pain which would cause pleasure if you regarded their advantages. There is a favourable and an unfavourable side to everything, the cleverness consists in finding out the favourable. The same thing looks quite different in another light; look at it therefore on its best side and do not exchange good for evil. Thus it haps that many find joy, many grief, in everything. This remark is a great protection against the frowns of fortune, and a weighty rule of life for all times and all conditions.

ccxxv Know Your Chief Fault.

T here lives none that has not in himself' a counterbalance to his most conspicuous merit: if this be nourished by desire it may grow to be a tyrant. **Commence**[4] war against it, summoning prudence as your ally, and the first thing to do is the public **manifesto**[5], for an evil once known is soon conquered, especially when the one afflicted regards it in the same light as the onlookers. To be master of oneself one should know oneself. If the chief imperfection surrender, the rest will **come to an end**[6].

226・博取他人好感

許多人的言行並非出自真心，而是不得已而為之。讓人相信壞事很容易，因為壞事本來就很容易讓人相信，雖然有時它確實讓人難以置信。一個人即使再有本事，再出色，也有賴於他人的看法。一些人認為正義在自己這邊就行，其實這是遠遠不夠的，因為還需要有人支援。讓他人愉悅往往付出很少，但獲益卻很多。言語可以換來行動。世界就像是一個大房子，隱藏再深的小房間一年之中也總有一天會派上用場，到時候你自然會懷念它的價值，不管這價值多麼微小。人們往往是根據自己的情感來談論事情的。

---

1. ill [ɪl] adj. 壞的，惡意的

ccxxvi Take Care to Be Obliging.

M ost talk and act, not as they are, but as they are obliged. To persuade people of **ill**[1] is easy for any, since the ill is easily credited even when at times it is incredible. The best we have depends on the opinion of others. Some are satisfied if they have right on their side, but that is not enough, for it must be assisted by energy. To oblige persons often costs little and helps much. With words you may purchase deeds. In this great house of the world there is no chamber so hid that it may not be wanted one day in the year, and then you would miss it however little is its worth. Every one speaks of a subject according to his feelings.

227・切勿執著於第一印象

人們往往把他們對事物的最初印象看成明媒正娶的正室,而把後來的印象作為偏房。但是往往錯覺捷足先登,然後真相遂難容身。不要讓最初目標來滿足你的意志,也不要讓第一印象佔據你的頭腦,這樣是很膚淺的。很多人就像新買的酒杯,總會沾滿最先入杯的酒味,而不管這酒是好是壞。如果這種膚淺被他人洞察以後,他們就會惡意地算計你,此時這種膚淺將是致命的。他們會把事情染上你容易輕信的顏色。因此我們一定要拿出時間來對事物再三考慮。就像亞歷山大一樣,**始終留一隻耳朵傾聽事情的另一面**。要注意事情的第二、第三個版本。輕易為第一印象所限制,說明你缺乏能力,這最終會導致你成為情緒的奴隸。

1. concubine [ˋkɑŋkjʊˌbaɪn] n. 妾,情婦,姘婦
2. lodging [ˋlɑdʒɪŋ] n. 寄宿處,寄宿
3. cask [kæsk] n. 桶,木桶
4. mischief [ˋmɪstʃɪf] n. 有意的損害
5. credulous [ˋkrɛdʒʊləs] adj. 輕信的

ccxxvii Do Not Be the
Slave of First Impressions.

S ome marry the very first account they hear: all others must live with them as **concubines**[1]. But as a lie has swift legs, the truth with them can find no **lodging**[2]. We should neither satisfy our will with the first object nor our mind with the first proposition: for that were superficial. Many are like new **casks**[3] who keep the scent of the first liquor they hold, be it good or bad. If this superficiality becomes known, it becomes fatal, for it then gives opportunity for cunning **mischief** [4] ; the ill-minded hasten to colour the mind of the **credulous**[5]. Always therefore leave room for a second hearing. Alexander always kept one ear for the other side. Wait for the second or even third edition of news. To be the slave of your impressions argues want of capacity, and is not far from being the slave of your passions.

228・不要製造醜聞

更不要傳播醜聞，那樣就是等於誹謗。不要以別人為代價來突顯你的機智幽默，傷害他人很容易，但卻讓人憎恨。每個人都想著如何報復你，背後說你的惡言惡語。他們人多勢眾，而你只有一個人，所以最終你會失敗。不要對那些醜聞津津樂道，也絕不要把它當成話題而高談闊論。一個搬弄是非的人是為人們所深惡痛絕的，即使有高尚之人與之交往，他們也只是欣賞他那敏銳的洞察力而不是搬弄是非的習慣。說長道短的人會聽到別人說他的更不堪入耳的話。

229・合理規劃生活

勿要只靠運氣，而是要小心謹慎，深謀遠慮。沒有娛樂的生活苦不堪言，就像旅途中整天看不到一家旅店。要用廣博的知識來為你的生活增添色彩。為了創造美好的生活，我們應做的第一件事就是和古人對話，我們出生於世，是來知人知己的。真正的好書能夠幫助我們成長為真正的人。第二件事是與人交流，仔細觀察和留意世界上所有美好的事物。世上所有美好的事物並不都在同一個地方。造化之神已經分好了他的禮品，有時候他會把最好的嫁妝放在最偏僻的地方。第三件事在你本身，成為一個哲學家是人生最大的幸福。

---

1. monger [ˋmʌŋgɚ] n. 喜歡說（支持）壞事的人 2. witty [ˋwɪtɪ] adj. 富於機智的 3. backbiter [ˋbæk,baɪtɚ] n. 背後誹謗者 4. manifold [ˋmænə,fold] adj. 多種形式的，多方面的 5. dower [ˋdaʊɚ] n. 嫁妝，天賦 6. felicity [fəˋlɪsətɪ] n. 幸福，幸運

ccxxviii Do Not Be a Scandal-monger[1].

S till less pass for one, for that means to be considered a slanderer. Do not be **witty**[2] at the cost of others: it is easy but hateful. All men have their revenge on such an one by speaking ill of him, and as they are many and he but one, he is more likely to be overcome than they convinced. Evil should never be our pleasure, and therefore never our theme. The **backbiter**[3] is always hated, and if now and then one of the great consorts with him, it is less from pleasure in his sneers than from esteem for his insight. He that speaks ill will always hear worse.

ccxxix Plan out Your Life Wisely,

n ot as chance will have it, but with prudence and foresight. Without amusements it is wearisome, like a long journey where there are no inns: **manifold**[4] knowledge gives manifold pleasure. The first day's journey of a noble life should be passed in conversing with the dead: we live to know and to know ourselves: hence true books make us truly men. The second day should be spent with the living, seeing and noticing all the good in the world. Everything is not to be found in a single country. The Universal Father has divided His gifts, and at times has given the richest **dower**[5] to the ugliest. The third day is entirely for oneself. The last **felicity**[6] is to be a philosopher.

230・及早睜開你的眼

並非能見之人均睜著眼，亦非睜眼之人均能看見。遲來的醒悟只會是有憂無樂。有些人在沒有什麼可看之時才去看，在他們喪失家業之後才醒悟過來，發現自己身在何處。想讓一個缺乏意志力的人醒悟過來是困難的，而讓沒有醒悟的人立志則更難。周圍的人們對他們就像路遇盲人一般，與其捉迷藏，讓他們成為別人的笑柄。因為他們對忠告充耳不聞，所以他們也不會睜開眼睛去看。有些人會十分推崇這種盲目，因為他們正是靠這個生存。一匹馬屬於瞎眼的主人是不幸的，因為它永遠也不會變得柔順健壯。

1. betimes [bɪˋtaɪmz] adv. 及早，及時
2. come up to 達到（預期標準），比得上
3. come to oneself 甦醒，醒悟
4. buff [bʌf] n. 迷
5. steed [stid] n. [詩]馬，戰馬

ccxxx Open Your Eyes Betimes[1].

Not all that see have their eyes open, nor do all those see that look. To **come up to**[2] things too late is more worry than help. Some just begin to see when there is nothing more to see: they pull their houses about their ears before they **come to themselves**[3] . It is difficult to give sense to those who have no power of will, still more difficult to give energy to those who have no sense. Those who surround them play with them a game of blind man's **buff**[4], making them the butts of others, and because they are hard of hearing, they do not open their eyes to see. There are often those who encourage such insensibility on which their very existence depends. Unhappy **steed**[5] whose rider is blind: it will never grow **sleek**[6].

---

6. sleek [slik] adj. 平直光滑的

231・未成之事，勿示於人

凡事只有在其成形完美後才能讓人欣賞，這樣一來，看的人才能感到賞心悅目。萬事起初之時都不成形，此時隨便示人，只會給人殘缺的形象。即使在完成之後再看，也會因想起它以前未完成之時的樣子而影響人們的欣賞。一口吞下一大塊食物，我們固然難以分辨其中的具體成分，但是卻可以讓我們的味覺得到滿足。一切事物在形成之前什麼都算不上，就算是它們在形成的過程當中，仍然什麼也不是。即使參觀一道最可口的菜的烹調過程也會使你倒胃口。真正的大師很細心，不會讓其作品在成形的階段就為人所見。他們也許是向自然學習的，未成之事，勿示於人。

---

1. misshapen [mɪsˋʃepən] adj. 變形的，畸形的
2. deformity [dɪˋfɔrmətɪ] n. 變形，畸形
3. gulp [gʌlp] n. 吞嚥
4. Dame Nature = Mother Nature　自然的力量

ccxxxi Never Let Things Be Seen Half-finished.

They can only be enjoyed when complete. All beginnings are **misshapen**[1], and this **deformity**[2] sticks in the imagination. The recollection of having seen a thing imperfect disturbs our enjoyment of it when completed. To swallow something great at one **gulp**[3] may disturb the judgment of the separate parts, but satisfies the taste. Till a thing is everything, it is nothing, and while it is in process of being it is still nothing. To see the tastiest dishes prepared arouses rather disgust than appetite. Let each great master take care not to let his work be seen in its embryonic stages: they might take this lesson from **Dame Nature**[4], who never brings the child to the light till it is fit to be seen.

232 · 學會務實

生活僅僅靠思想是不夠的，還應該有行動。最聰明的人最容易受騙，是因為他們可能會懂得許多不同於尋常的知識，但卻對生活中最普通、最必要的常識一無所知。他們整日忙於思考那些崇高而偉大的事務，以至於沒有時間關注身邊的小事。由於他們對生活的基本知識——其他人無一不精的領域——竅不通，淺薄的芸芸眾生認為他們很無知。因此，讓聰明的人稍稍實踐一下吧，以使其不被欺騙、嘲諷。懂得如何處理日常事務或許不是人生的最高要務，但卻是生活必備的能力。學以致用，否則知識又有什麼益處呢？如今，真正的學問在於懂得生活之道。

---

1. out-of-the-way [ˋaʊtəvðəˋwe] adj. 偏僻的，非凡的
2. multitude [ˋmʌltəˌtjud] n. 多數，群眾

ccxxxii Have a Touch of the Trader.

L ife should not be all thought: there should be action as well. Very wise folk are generally easily deceived, for while they know **out-of-the-way**[1] things they do not know the ordinary things of life, which are much more needful. The observation of higher things leaves them no time for things close at hand. Since they know not the very first thing they should know, and what everybody knows so well, they are either considered or thought ignorant by the superficial **multitude**[2]. Let therefore the prudent take care to have something of the trader about him – enough to prevent him being deceived and so laughed at, Be a man adapted to the daily round, which if not the highest is the most necessary thing in life. Of what use is knowledge if it is not practical, and to know how to live is nowadays the true knowledge.

233 · 不要錯識他人的品味

以免弄巧成拙，令人討厭，而非得到感激。有人試圖贏得別人的好感，卻因不瞭解對方的性格而惹人討厭。同樣一件事對某些人是恭維，對另一些人則是冒犯，你本來想幫他人的忙，然而卻讓他人受到傷害。讓人惱怒往往會比讓人高興付出更大的代價，因為取悅他人漫無方向，白送了禮不說，還丟掉了別人的感激。如果你不知道他人的性格和品味，你就不知道怎樣去取悅他人。正因為如此，有些人自以為在讚美別人，卻被他人當成了侮辱，從而自取其辱。還有人認為他們是在透過談吐來展示魅力，結果卻是惹人厭煩。

---

1. morsel [`mɔrsl] n. （食物）一口，少量
2. take no account of 不考慮，不重視
3. flattery [`flætərɪ] n. 諂媚，捧場話，恭維話，諂媚的舉動
4. compass [`kʌmpəs] n. 羅盤，指南針
5. loquacity [lo`kwæsətɪ] n. 多話，饒舌

ccxxxiii Let Not the Proffered Morsel[1] Be Distasteful;

O therwise it gives more discomfort than pleasure. Some displease when attempting to oblige, because they **take no account of**[2] varieties of taste. What is **flattery**[3] to one is an offence to another, and in attempting to be useful one may become insulting. It often costs more to displease a man than it would have cost to please him: you thereby lose both gift and thanks because you have lost the **compass**[4] which steers for pleasure. He who knows not another's taste, knows not how to please him. Thus it haps that many insult where they mean to praise, and get soundly punished, and rightly so. Others desire to charm by their conversation, and only succeed in boring by their **loquacity**[5].

234・不要將你的名譽託付給別人，除非他以名譽為抵押

沉默對雙方都有好處，而坦露秘密會將雙方都置於險境。如果名譽面臨威脅，你一定要找個夥伴，這樣每個人才會為了自己的名譽小心保護他人的名譽。個人隱私最好不要輕易向人透露，一旦透露，就應巧妙安排，小心翼翼，讓其以信譽擔保。兩人只有休戚相關，利害與共，你的同伴才不致用已知的秘密來做不利於你的事情。

---

1. turn king's evidence 出庭提供同案犯的罪證

ccxxxiv Never Trust Your Honour to Another, unless You Have His in Pledge.

A rrange that silence is a mutual advantage; disclosure a danger to both. Where honour is at stake you must act with a partner, so that each must be careful of the other's honour for the sake of his own. Never entrust your honour to another; but if you have, let caution surpass prudence. Let the danger be in common and the risk mutual, so that your partner cannot **turn king's evidence**[1].

235・善於求人

有些人善於運用此道，有些人拙於運用此道。有人天生就不知道如何說「不」，對這種人，你不需要任何手段和心機就可應付。而對那些出口即「不」的人，你就需要些高超的技巧，並且需要選擇恰當的時機。一定要在他們心情愉快，興致高昂，靈魂與肉體都覺得愜意的時候提出請求，但願這時候對方的精明沒有預料到你的意圖。過著快樂日子的人是樂於施恩的，因為快樂從人的內心外化為樂善好施。如果你看到在你前面已經有人遭到拒絕，那麼你就不要再提什麼要求了，因為「不」字一旦出口，那再說起來便會毫無顧忌。求於悲愴者必不成功。只要是被求之人非卑鄙下流，知恩而不圖報之人，那你先施恩於此人乃為上策。

1. propitious [prə`pɪʃəs] adj. 吉利的，合適的
2. repast [rɪ`pæst] n. 餐

ccxxxv Know How to Ask.

With some nothing easier: with others nothing so difficult. For there are men who cannot refuse: with them no skill is required. But with others their first word at all times is No; with them great art is required, and with all the **propitious**[1] moment. Surprise them when in a pleasant mood, when a **repast**[2] of body or soul has just left them refreshed, if only their shrewdness has not anticipated the cunning of the applicant. The days of joy are the days of favour, for joy overflows from the inner man into the outward creation. It is no use applying when another has been refused, since the objection to a No has just been overcome. Nor is it a good time after sorrow. To oblige a person beforehand is a sure way, unless he is mean.

236・先施恩，再求回報

此乃精明之策。在別人幫你之前就先幫助別人，這樣可以證明你樂於助人的品性。先施人以恩有很大的好處：雪中送炭的幫忙會讓你幫的人以後加倍地回報你。而同樣的幫助如果是事後給予只能換來別人一句感謝的話，而算不上是施恩。這種轉化是很微妙的，最初是你在償還債務，後來債務卻轉到了債主的頭上。當然，這種方法只能施與有教養的人。對於無賴之徒，給他的好處是使他噤聲不言的馬嚼，而不是使他有所表示的馬刺。

---

1. promptness [prɑmptnɪs] n. 敏捷，機敏
2. honorarium [ˌɑnəˈrɛrɪəm] n. （對習俗或法律上不應取酬的服務的）酬勞

ccxxxvi Make an Obligation Beforehand of What Would Have to Be a Reward Afterwards.

This is a stroke of subtle policy; to grant favours before they are deserved is a proof of being obliging. Favours thus granted beforehand have two great advantages: the **promptness**[1] of the gift obliges the recipient the more strongly; and the same gift which would afterwards be merely a reward is beforehand an obligation. This is a subtle means of transforming obligations, since that which would have forced the superior to reward is changed into one that obliges the one obliged to satisfy the obligation. But this is only suitable for men who have the feeling of obligation, since with men of lower stamp the **honorarium**[2] paid beforehand acts rather as a bit than as a spur.

237 · 不要知曉上級的秘密

或許你會覺得你們可以分梨而食，然而事實卻是你能分得的不過是梨皮。許多人會因為分享了別人的秘密而不得善終，他們就像麵包做的湯匙，很快就與湯一樣落入被吃掉的下場。君主王公向你訴說秘密，對你來說並非什麼特權，他只是為了緩解壓力。要知道許多人打碎鏡子是因為鏡子照出了他們的醜惡。同樣我們也不能忍受那些見過我們真正醜惡面目的人，如果你看到了他人醜陋的一面，那別人看你的目光絕不會友善。沒有人會感激我們曾見過他人的隱私，對那些位高權重之人更是如此，除非你給過他們好處，而不是他們給你好處。和朋友分享你的秘密也非常危險。你把秘密告訴他人，那就會使自己陷入奴隸的境地，這是任何權貴都無法容忍的。為了找回失去的自由，他們會不惜一切代價，視正義和公理為無物。因此自己的秘密不能講，他人的秘密不能聽。

---

1. paring [ˋpɛrɪŋ] n. 削下的皮
2. sop [sɑp] n. 麵包片
3. beholden [bɪˋholdən] adj. 對⋯表示感謝

ccxxxvii Never Share the Secrets of Your Superiors.

Y ou may think you will share pears, but you will only share **parings**[1]. Many have been ruined by being confidants: they are like **sops**[2] of bread used as forks, they run the same risk of being eaten up afterwards. It is no favour in a prince to share a secret: it is only a relief. Many break the mirror that reminds them of their ugliness. We do not like seeing those who have seen us as we are: nor is he seen in a favourable light who has seen us in an unfavourable one. None ought to be too much **beholden**[3] to us, least of all one of the great, unless it be for benefits done him rather than for such favours received from him. Especially dangerous are secrets entrusted to friends. He that communicates his secret to another makes himself that other's slave. With a prince this is an intolerable position which cannot last. He will desire to recover his lost liberty, and to gain it will overturn everything, including right and reason. Accordingly neither tell secrets nor listen to them.

238・瞭解自己缺少什麼

許多人如果能瞭解自己缺少什麼，其人格就可以臻於完美，他也能夠成為名人。有些人身上有很明顯的缺點，如果能將其改正，他們就會成為更出色的人。有的人為人處事不夠莊重嚴肅，使其才華黯淡失色；有的人不夠親切，而親切正是他們身邊的人最嚮往的東西，尤其是當他們位高權重的時候；有些人缺乏組織能力；另一些人不善於克制自己。對於這些所有的缺陷，謹慎者可以多加注意，使其變成人的第二天性。

239・不要吹毛求疵

做事理智十分重要。懂的知識太多，思維之武器就會變鈍，因為刀刃磨得太利，非彎即斷。瞭解常識性的知識就可以了，不要深究。冗長的評論會引起爭端，有理性的判斷最好，它會讓我們不脫離手上的工作。

---

1. do justice to 公平對待，適當處理
2. captious [`kæpʃəs] adj. 吹毛求疵的，挑剔的

ccxxxviii Know What Is Wanting in Yourself.

M any would have been great personages if they had not had something wanting without which they could not rise to the height of perfection. It is remarkable with some that they could be much better if they could he better in something. They do not perhaps take themselves seriously enough to **do justice to**[1] their great abilities; some are wanting in geniality of disposition, a quality which their entourage soon find the want of, especially if they are in high office. Some are without organising ability, others lack moderation. In all such cases a careful man may make of habit a second nature.

ccxxxix Do Not Be Captious[2].

I t is much more important to be sensible. To know more than is necessary blunts your weapons, for fine points generally bend or break. Common-sense truth is the surest. It is well to know but not to niggle. Lengthy comment leads to disputes. It is much better to have sound sense, which does not wander from the matter in hand.

240・裝瘋賣傻

最聰明之人時常會利用此計，即所謂的大智若愚。你不必真的無知，假裝如此即可。在愚人面前顯示智慧，在智者面前暴露愚蠢都是沒用的。見人說人話，見鬼說鬼話。裝作愚蠢的人並不蠢，而忍受愚蠢的人才是真的蠢。天生的愚蠢是真蠢，裝蠢只是智慧到達一定境界的表現，而不是真蠢。要讓大家都喜歡你，那你必須穿上頭腦最簡單的動物的皮。

241・經得住被人開玩笑，
但不要開他人的玩笑

前者會顯示出你的氣度，後者則可能為你招致不悅。因為玩笑而爭吵怒罵如同動物一般，甚至連動物都不如。巧妙的玩笑令人心情愉悅，欣然接受，是明智之舉。若你表現出不悅，那只會自討沒趣。最好的做法是置之不理，適可而止。玩笑往往容易節外生枝，沒有什麼比開玩笑更需要技巧和精力的了。所以**開玩笑之前，要弄清楚別人的承受度**。

---

1. pitch [pɪtʃ] n. 程度
2. raillery [`relərɪ] n. 善意的戲弄，逗弄
3. snarl [snɑrl] vi. 咆哮，怒吼
4. tact [tækt] n. 機智，乖巧

ccxl Make Use of Folly.

T he wisest play this card at times, and there are times when the greatest
wisdom lies in seeming not to be wise. You need not be unwise, but
merely affect unwisdom. To be wise with fools and foolish with the wise
were of little use. Speak to each in his own language. He is no fool who
affects folly, but he is who suffers from it. Ingenuous folly rather than the
pretended is the true foolishness, since cleverness has arrived at such a
pitch[1]. To be well liked one must dress in the skin of the simplest of animals.

ccxli Put up with Raillery[2], But Do Not Practise It.

T he first is a form of courtesy, the second may lead to embarrassment.
To **snarl**[3] at play has something of the beast and seems to have more.
Audacious raillery is delightful: to stand it proves power. To show oneself
annoyed causes the other to be annoyed. Best leave it alone; the surest way
not to put on the cap that might fit. The most serious matters have arisen
out of jests. Nothing requires more **tact**[4] and attention. Before you begin to
joke know how far the subject of your joke is able to bear it.

242・善始善終

有些人做事一開始熱血沸騰，幹勁十足，卻不能持之以恆，有了目標卻從未將之實現，最終只是敷衍了事。他們不能贏得讚譽，因為他們做事不能善始善終，每件事情都半途而廢。脾氣急躁的人最容易這樣，這也正是西班牙人的弱點，相反地耐心則是比利時人的優點。後者能夠圓滿完成所做之事，而前者則會半途而廢，不了了之。做事沒有毅力的人千辛萬苦克服了困難，但卻僅僅滿足於克服眼前的困難，他們不懂如何堅持到最後的勝利。他們說自己能做到，只是不願去做，其實這只說明了他們根本做不到，或是他們沒有毅力和恆心。值得去做的事，為何不做完呢？不值得做的事，為何還要去做呢？對於聰明的獵人來說，他們不會因發現獵物而洋洋得意，而是要最終抓獲獵物。

---

1. palter [`pɔltɚ] vi. 含糊其詞，敷衍了事
2. Spaniard [`spænjɚd] n. 西班牙人
3. Belgian [`bɛldʒən] n. 比利時人
4. surmount [sɚ`maʊnt] vt. 戰勝，超越，克服
5. flush [flʌʃ] vt. （因激動而）臉紅

ccxlii Push Advantages.

S ome put all their strength in the commencement and never carry a thing to a conclusion. They invent but never execute. These be **paltering**[1] spirits. They obtain no fame, for they sustain no game to the end. Everything stops at a single stop. This arises in some from impatience, which is the failing of the **Spaniard**[2], as patience is the virtue of the **Belgian**[3]. The latter bring things to an end, the former come to an end with things. They sweat away till the obstacle is surmounted, but content themselves with **surmounting**[4] it: they do not know how to push the victory home. They prove that they can but will not: but this proves always that they cannot, or have no stability. If the undertaking is good, why not finish it? If it is bad, why undertake it? Strike down your quarry, if you are wise; be not content to **flush**[5] it.

243 · 做人不能太善良

人應兼備毒蛇的狡詐與鴿子的純真。再也沒有比欺騙誠實人更容易的事了。從不說謊之人很容易相信他人，從不騙人之人則很信任他人。被人欺騙往往不是因為愚蠢，而是因為善良。有兩種人能自我保護不受傷害：一種是透過自己親身經歷得到教訓的人；另一種則是從他人的經歷中有所領悟的人。要時刻懷有一顆謹慎之心防備別人設下的陷阱，不要過於好心使得陰險之人有機可乘。你的性格中應既有蛇的狡詐，亦有鴿子的純真，這樣的你不是魔鬼，而是天才。

---

1. candour [`kændɚ] n. 直率，公正
2. subtlety [`sʌtltɪ] n. 機敏，狡猾
3. prodigy [`prɑdədʒɪ] n. 天才（特指神童）

ccxliii Do Not Be Too Much of a Dove.

A lternate the cunning of the serpent with the **candour**[1] of the dove. Nothing is easier than to deceive an honest man. He believes in much who lies in naught; who does no deceit, has much confidence. To be deceived is not always due to stupidity, it may arise from sheer goodness. There are two sets of men who can guard themselves from injury: those who have experienced it at their own cost, and those who have observed it at the cost of others. Prudence should use as much suspicion as **subtlety**[2] uses snares, and none need be so good as to enable others to do him ill. Combine in yourself the dove and the serpent, not as a monster but as a **prodigy**[3] .

244.求得別人幫助之時使其感激自己

有些人善於把受他人之惠反變成施恩於人，本來他們正在接受恩惠，但他們卻使之看起來好像在施予恩惠。有的人十分狡猾，本來是在求人，但給他人的感覺卻是他們在給人榮幸。他們善於使自己獲利，但卻讓別人感到榮幸，他們掌控事情非常精明。別人為他做事，卻會讓他人覺得是他在為別人做事。他們手段高明，會打亂主客的次序，顛倒受惠與施恩，讓人分不清誰是施惠者，誰又是受惠者。他們透過廉價的讚揚來獲得他們需要的東西；透過表示他們自己喜歡某件東西，讓人覺得給予他會是件榮幸的事情。他們利用對別人的謙卑來獲得人情，本來該他們自己對他人表示感激，但最終卻讓別人覺得是受了他的恩惠。他們就是透過這樣的手段，變被動的受惠為主動的施恩，這種花招說明了他們雖不通文法，但卻很擅長運用權術。這真是妙不可言。如果你能當場識破其狡詐，阻止他反客為主，讓名譽歸於當得之人，讓利益歸於當得之主，那就證明你才是高明之人。

1. bestow [bɪ`sto] vt. 給予，授予
2. transpose [træns`poz] vt. 調換，顛倒順序，移項
3. beholden [bɪ`holdən] adj. 欠⋯人情
4. conjugate [`kɑndʒə‚get] v. 使變化
5. grammarian [grə`mɛrɪən] n. 文法家，文法教師，文法學者

ccxliv Create a Feeling of Obligation.

Some transform favours received into favours **bestowed**[1], and seem, or let it be thought, that they are doing a favour when receiving one. There are some so astute that they get honour by asking, and buy their own advantage with applause from others. They manage matters so cleverly that they seem to be doing others a service when receiving one from them. They **transpose**[2] the order of obligation with extraordinary skill, or at least render it doubtful who has obliged whom. They buy the best by praising it, and make a flattering honour out of the pleasure they express. They oblige by their courtesy, and thus make men **beholden**[3] for what they themselves should be beholden. In this way they **conjugate**[4] "to oblige" in the active instead of in the passive voice, thereby proving themselves better politicians than **grammarians**[5] . This is a subtle piece of finesse; a still greater is to perceive it, and to **retaliate**[6] on such fools' bargains by paying in their own coin, and so coming by your own again.

---

6. retaliate [rɪˋtælɪˌet] v. 報復,反擊

245 · 有獨到的見解

方能證明你才識過人。我們並不看好那些從來沒有反對意見的人，這說明他不愛別人，只愛自己。不要被阿諛奉承所蒙蔽，並為之付出代價，而是應譴責這種行為。此外，當你受他人責難，尤其是他們總是把你的好處說成壞處時，你可以將其視為對你的讚美。相反地，當你的言行能夠取悅所有人時，你應該感到不安，因為這表明你的言行微不足道。要知道完美之人微乎其微。

246 · 無求莫諫言

即使他人確實需要你的幫助，你給予的幫助哪怕多一點點也是錯，好比在不恰當的時候為自己辯解反而更會為難了自己；身體安然無恙卻替人家抽血化驗，這樣會讓人覺得你心懷惡意；出人意料的致歉則容易引起他人的猜疑。明智之人面對他人的猜疑從來都面不改色，不去自尋煩惱。他會憑藉自己正直的行為來消除別人對自己的不信任。

---

1. take credit for 因…而得到好評

ccxlv Original and out-of-the-way Views

a re signs of superior ability. We do not think much of a man who never contradicts us that is no sign he loves us, but rather that he loves himself. Do not be deceived by flattery, and thereby have to pay for it: rather condemn it. Besides you may **take credit for**[1] being censured by some, especially if they are those of whom the good speak ill. On the contrary, it should disturb us if our affairs please every one, for that is a sign that they are of little worth. Perfection is for the few.

ccxlvi Never Offer Satisfaction Unless It Is Demanded.

A nd if they do demand it, it is a kind of crime to give more than necessary. To excuse oneself before there is occasion is to accuse oneself. To draw blood in full health gives the hint to ill-will. An excuse unexpected arouses suspicion from its slumbers. Nor need a shrewd person show himself aware of another's suspicion, which is equivalent to seeking out offence. He had best disarm distrust by the integrity of his conduct.

247 · 求知多一點，享樂少一點

有些人不這麼認為。他們認為安逸的生活勝於忙碌的工作。其實真正屬於我們的只有時間，縱使一個人一無所有，但他還擁有時間。把寶貴的生命浪費在大量機械的工作上，或是浪費在繁重的工作上，都是莫大的不幸。不要放大佔有欲從而心生妒忌，否則你會打亂生活、耗盡心神。有人想將此理應用到求知上。只有知道了這個道理，一個人才算真正活過。

248 · 不要結交熱衷新潮之人

有些人總是喜歡追求新潮，從而喪失理性，走向極端。他們的欲望很難得到滿足，不論什麼樣的新事物，都會吸引他們的眼球，以前的則被統統丟棄。到頭來一無所獲，因為他們總是很快丟棄得到的東西。對他們的評價則是眾口不一。有人說作為心腹之交，他們並不可靠，因為他們就像永遠長不大的孩子，心性不專。由於他們的情感和意志極不穩定，因此他們的思想躊躇不定，人生路上時走時停，忽左忽右。

---

1. profusion [prə`fjuʒən] n. 豐富，大量
2. heap up 堆起來，積累
3. wax [wæks] n. 增大，變大
4. obliterate [ə`blɪtə,ret] vt. 忘掉，抹去
5. volition [vo`lɪʃən] n. 意志

ccxlvii Know a Little More, Live a Little Less.

S ome say the opposite. To be at ease is better than to be at business. Nothing really belongs to us but time, which even he has who has nothing else. It is equally unfortunate to waste your precious life in mechanical tasks or in a **profusion**[1] of important work. Do not **heap up**[2] occupation and thereby envy: otherwise you complicate life and exhaust your mind. Some wish to apply the same principle to knowledge, but unless one knows one does not truly live.

ccxlviii Do Not Go with the Last Speaker.

T here are persons who go by the latest edition, and thereby go to irrational extremes. Their feelings and desires are of **wax**[3]: the last comer stamps them with his seal and **obliterates**[4] all previous impressions. These never gain anything, for they lose everything so soon. Every one dyes them with his own colour. They are of no use as confidants; they remain children their whole life. Owing to this instability of feeling and **volition**[5], they halt along cripples in will and thought, and totter from one side of the road to the other.

249・先做重要的事

有些人最初時只顧娛樂，最後弄得自己焦頭爛額。在條件允許的情況下，重要的事情應該放在首位，次要事情次之。有的人則期盼不勞而獲，不戰而勝。有的人起初學了一些不重要的事，卻將那些能帶給他名譽和利益的事留到了晚年。另一些人則是剛剛小有財富就跳槽離開。由此可見，無論求知，還是生活，方法是最重要的。

250・何時正話反說

當與心懷不軌的人交談時。有些人總是正話反說，他們的「不是」即「是」，「是」即「不是」。如果他們貶低某事，則說明他們對此事評價甚高。他們想擁有的東西總是別人輕視的東西。讚揚某事不一定非要讚揚它的優點，在有些人面前不能稱讚他的優點，而要稱讚他的缺點。因為讚美他的缺點就意味著他沒有缺點。

---

1. accessory [æk`sɛsərɪ] n. 附件，零件
2. contrariwise [`kɑntrɛrɪ,waɪz] adv. 反之，頑固地
3. depreciate [dɪ`priʃɪ,et] v. （使）貶值，輕視

ccxlix Never Begin Life with What Should End It.

Many take their amusement at the beginning, putting off anxiety to the end; but the essential should come first and **accessories**[1] afterwards if there is room. Others wish to triumph before they have fought. Others again begin with learning things of little consequence and leave studies that would bring them fame and gain to the end of life. Another is just about to make his fortune when he disappears from the scene. Method is essential for knowledge and for life.

ccl When to Change the Conversation.

When they talk scandal. With some all goes **contrariwise**[2] : their No is Yes, and their Yes No. If they speak ill of a thing it is the highest praise. For what they want for themselves they **depreciate**[3] to others. To praise a thing is not always to speak well of it, for some, to avoid praising what's good, praise what's bad, and nothing is good for him for whom nothing is bad.

251 · 施以人道宛如神道之不在，
施以神道恰似人道之不存。

互古不變之真理：對此毋庸置疑。

252 · 既不要只為自己活
也不要只為他人活

這兩種態度都非常蠻橫專制。如果你一心為自己，就想把一切據為己有。這類人不願做出一丁點讓步，不願損失一丁點利益。他們幾乎沒有對他人的感恩之心，而是將成功全歸於自己的幸運，會漸失人心，沒人願意幫助他們。有時不妨為別人考慮，這樣別人也會為你考慮。「若擔任公職，你一定要做一名人民公僕，要不然就讓位賢能者」。一位老婦人對哈德良如是說。然而還有些人完全為他人活著，這種想法既愚蠢又容易讓人走入極端，這樣的人是不幸的，甚至沒有一天、一個小時真正屬於他們自己，他們無時無刻不想著別人，如此看來，他們就是眾人的奴隸。求知亦是如此，有人知道關於別人的一切，卻對自己一無所知。一個明智的人知道別人找他不是單純為了找他，而是為了他們自己的利益，希望能從他身上有所收穫。

---

1. jot [dʒɑt] n. 少量，少額，稍許　2. tittle [ˋtɪtl] n. 一點　3. crutch [krʌtʃ] n. （跛子用的）拐杖　4. berth [bɝθ] n. 鋪位　5. burthen [ˋbɝðən] n. 負荷，重荷，負擔　6. 引自 Georg Ebers 的小說 The Emperor。哈德良（76～138）：羅馬皇帝，117～138在位。

ccli Use Human Means as if There Were No Divine Ones, and Divine as if There Were No Human Ones.

A masterly rule: it needs no comment.

cclii Neither Belong Entirely to Yourself nor Entirely to Others.

B oth are mean forms of tyranny. To desire to be all for oneself is the same as desiring to have all for oneself. Such persons will not yield a **jot**[1] or lose a **tittle**[2] of their comfort. They are rarely beholden, lean on their own luck, and their **crutch**[3] generally breaks. It is convenient at times to belong to others, that others may belong to us. And he that holds public office is no more nor less than a public slave, or let a man give up both **berth**[4] and **burthen**[5], as the old woman said to **Hadrian**[6] . On the other hand, others are all for others, which is folly, that always flies to extremes, in this case in a most unfortunate manner. No day, no hour, is their own, but they have so much too much of others that they may be called the slaves of all. This applies even to knowledge, where a man may know everything for others and nothing for himself. A shrewd man knows that others when they seek him do not seek him, but their advantage in him and by him.

253・凡事點到為止

多數人並不看重他們已知的東西，而是看重那些未知的東西。要讓東西受人重視，就要花費一些心思，即人們不明白的東西往往受到重視。要想受人尊重，你必須在與你打交道的人面前表現得更智慧，更謹慎，但是要適度，無贅言。在明智之人面前談論常識問題毫無必要，在大眾面前談論詳盡的細節還是有必要的。不要留給他們指責你的機會，而是讓他們揣摩你的心思。很多人說不清自己為何讚揚別人，原因在於他們將自己不知的東西視為神秘之物，倍加推崇，聽到別人稱讚，自己也對它大加讚賞。

---

1. elaboration [ɪˌlæbəˋreʃən] n. 詳盡說明，闡述
2. drift [drɪft] n. （話語的）大意，要旨

ccliii Do Not Explain Overmuch.

M ost men do not esteem what they understand, and venerate what they do not see. To be valued things should cost dear: what is not understood becomes overrated. You have to appear wiser and more prudent than he requires with whom you deal, if you desire to give him a high opinion of you: yet in this there should be moderation and no excess. And though with sensible people common sense holds its own, with most men a little **elaboration**[1] is necessary. Give them no time for blame: occupy them with understanding your **drift**[2]. Many praise a thing without being able to tell why, if asked. The reason is that they venerate the unknown as a mystery, and praise it because they hear it praised.

254・小問題不可忽視

問題不是出了一個後就沒有了，而是接踵而來，幸運的事情亦是如此。幸運與不幸通常會與自己的同類聚集一起，因此人們都想遠離不幸，接近幸運，甚至無知的鴿子也明白要朝著最白的鴿籠飛。人不幸時什麼事都做不成，不論是本身、言辭抑或其運氣都不順，因此千萬不要驚醒沉睡中的不幸女神。當不幸來臨時，你摔一跤事小，但致命的損失會接踵而至，你不知何時是盡頭。正因沒有完美的幸福，也無徹底的厄運，所以對於天災需耐心，對於人禍需審慎。

---

1. hence [hɛns] ad. 【書】因此，由此
2. prudence [`prudns] n. 審慎，慎重

ccliv Never Despise an Evil, However Small,

for they never come alone: they are linked together like pieces of good fortune. Fortune and misfortune generally go to find their fellows. **Hence**[1] all avoid the unlucky and associate with the fortunate. Even the doves with all their innocence resort to the whitest walls. Everything fails with the unfortunate – himself, his words, and his luck. Do not wake Misfortune when she sleeps. One slip is a little thing: yet some fatal loss may follow it till you do not know where it will end. For just as no happiness is perfect, so no ill-luck is complete. Patience serves with what comes from above; **prudence**[2] with that from below.

255・每天行善一點點，持之以恆

不要給予太多，使人無法回報。給予太多不是給予，而是出售。不要耗盡別人的感激之情，當他們發現無法回報所受之恩時，便不再跟你來往。若想失去他們，你只需讓他們欠你很多便可達到目的。若他們償還不起，便會自覺地走得很遠，甚至與你為敵也不願做你永遠的債務人。好比雕像從來不想見到他面前的雕刻師，受恩的人也不希望總見到他的恩人。切記施恩的微妙所在：只有人們迫切需要而又成本少的恩惠才是人們喜歡的。

---

1. dregs [drɛgz] n. 渣滓，糟糠
2. debtor [ˋdɛtɚ] n. 債務人
3. sculptor [ˋskʌlptɚ] n. 雕刻家

cclv Do Good a Little at a Time, But Often.

O ne should never give beyond the possibility of return. Who gives much does not give but sells. Nor drain gratitude to the **dregs**[1], for when the recipient sees all return is impossible he breaks off correspondence. With many persons it is not necessary to do more than overburden them with favours to lose them altogether: they cannot repay you, and so they retire, preferring rather to be enemies than perpetual **debtors**[2]. The idol never wishes to see before him the **sculptor**[3] who shaped him, nor does the benefited wish to see his benefactor always before his eyes. There is a great subtlety in giving what costs little yet is much desired, so that it is esteemed the more.

256・有備無患

要防範那些魯莽之徒、無信之人、虛假之人以及各種愚蠢的人。世上這樣的人很多，謹慎的做法是避免和這類人接觸。每天都要保證自己已經全副武裝，足以應付這些愚蠢之徒的攻擊。時刻準備應付這樣的事情，不要讓他人的粗魯毀壞了自己的聲譽。做人須謹慎，不可魯莽無禮。人際關係之路障礙重重，千溝萬壑，你的名聲很可能毀於一旦。最好的辦法就是找條捷徑，學習一下聰明的尤利西斯，在這樣的事上裝傻是很有效的，再加上禮貌待人，基本上就可以解決問題了。通常來說，這是擺脫困境的唯一途徑。

---

1. perfidy [ˋpɝfədɪ] n. 不忠，背信
2. contingency [kənˋtɪndʒənsɪ] n. 偶然，意外事故
3. Ulysses 尤利西斯

cclvi Go Armed Against Discourtesy,

a nd against **perfidy**[1], presumption, and all other kinds of folly. There is much of it in the world, and prudence lies in avoiding a meeting with it. Arm yourself each day before the mirror of attention with the weapons of defence. Thus you will beat down the attacks of folly. Be prepared for the occasion, and do not expose your reputation to vulgar **contingencies**[2]. Armed with prudence, a man cannot be disarmed by impertinence. The road of human intercourse is difficult, for it is full of ruts which may jolt our credit. Best to take a byway, taking **Ulysses**[3] as a model of shrewdness. Feigned misunderstanding is of great value in such matters. Aided by politeness it helps us over all, and is often the only way out of difficulties.

257・慎於斷交

因為遭遇過後我們的名譽總要受損。任何人如果不是朋友，很可能成為我們致命的敵人。很少有人對我們有利，幾乎人人都對我們不利。與甲蟲決裂後，鷹即使在朱庇特懷裏築巢都感到危機四伏。暗處的敵人會藉助明處敵人之手煽風點火，引發爭鬥，他們躲在暗處觀望。你冒犯的朋友會成為你最棘手的敵人，他們把自己的失敗歸因於別人的錯誤，無論別人說什麼都像針對他似的，發生的事就像他預想的那樣。所有人都責備我們，說我們開始時沒遠見，最後又沒忍耐力，而且做事不謹慎。當你覺得必須和某人斷交時，與其突然斷交，彼此吵得面紅耳赤，不如心照不宣，逐漸淡化感情。這是有關如何明智絕交的箴言。

1. rupture [ˋrʌptʃɚ] n. 破裂，決裂，敵對
2. paw [pɔ] n. 手掌，手爪
3. breach [britʃ] n. 破裂，裂口
4. slacken [ˋslækən] v. 鬆弛，放慢，減弱
5. wrath [ræθ] n. 憤怒

cclvii Never Let Matters Come to a Rupture[1],

f or our reputation always comes injured out of the encounter. Every one may be of importance as an enemy if not as a friend. Few can do us good, almost any can do us harm. In Jove's bosom itself even his eagle never nestles securely from the day he has quarrelled with a beetle. Hidden foes use the **paw**[2] of the declared enemy to stir up the fire, and meanwhile they lie in ambush for such an occasion. Friends provoked become the bitterest of enemies. They cover their own failings with the faults of others. Every one speaks as things seem to him, and things seem as he wishes them to appear. All blame us at the beginning for want of foresight, at the end for lack of patience, at all times for imprudence. If, however, a **breach**[3] is inevitable, let it be rather excused as a **slackening**[4] of friendship than by an outburst of **wrath**[5]: here is a good application of the saying about a good retreat.

258・找人分擔煩惱

你才不會感到孤獨，即使身處險境也不必獨自承受全部痛苦。有人認為如果他們憑藉自己的職位獲得了所有成功的榮譽，那麼理所應當由自己忍受失敗的恥辱。這樣做沒有人原諒他們，沒有人幫他們分擔責任。如果兩人並肩做事，那麼厄運和暴民都不敢前來冒犯。明智的醫師不能治癒病人時，會以諮詢問題的名義找人幫忙處理屍體，一起分擔重擔和哀傷。如果你獨自承擔不幸，不幸會變得加倍難挨。

---

1. consultation [ˌkɑnsəlˋteʃən] n. 請教，諮詢
2. corpse [kɔrps] n. 屍體
3. woe [wo] n. 悲哀

420

cclviii Find Out Some One
to Share Your Troubles.

Y ou will never be all alone, even in dangers, nor bear all the burden of
hate. Some think by their high position to carry off the whole glory of
success, and have to bear the whole humiliation of defeat. In this way they
have none to excuse them, none to share the blame. Neither fate nor the
mob are so bold against two. Hence the wise physician, if he has failed to
cure, looks out for some one who, under the name of a **consultation**[1], may
help him carry out the **corpse**[2]. Share weight and **woe**[3], for misfortune falls
with double force on him that stands alone.

259・預見危險，化險為夷

避開危險要比對付危險明智得多。把對手轉為自己的密友，把本來要誹謗自己的人變成自己名譽的保護者，是出奇的精明。懂得如何施恩於人，這樣對手才不會陷害你，因為他心裏充滿了對你的感激之情。用這個方法可以化苦為樂，所以嘗試去化險為夷，化敵為友吧！

260・你不能完全屬於別人，
也沒有人能完全屬於你

無論是親情、友情或愛情都不能有這個效果。把心交給一個人和關心一個人截然不同，即使是最親密的結合也會有隔閡，沒有這層隔閡，就會打破交友的原則。朋友總會把一些秘密隱藏在心底，即使兒子也有不願向父親吐露的心事。對一個人隱瞞的一些事也許會對另一個人傾訴，反之亦然。說我們吐露了一切也同時隱瞞了一切，只是針對不同的人而已。

---

1. regard [rɪˋgɑrd] n. 關心，關注

cclix Anticipate Injuries and Turn Them into Favours.

I t is wiser to avoid than to revenge them. It is an uncommon piece of shrewdness to change a rival into a confidant, or transform into guards of honour those who were aiming attacks at us. It helps much to know how to oblige, for he leaves no time for injuries that fills it up with gratitude. That is true savoir-faire to turn anxieties into pleasures. Try and make a confidential relation out of ill-will itself.

cclx We Belong to None and None to Us, Entirely.

N either relationship nor friendship nor the most intimate connection is sufficient to effect this. To give one's whole confidence is quite different from giving one's **regard**[1]. The closest intimacy has its exceptions, without which the laws of friendship would be broken. The friend always keeps one secret to himself, and even the son always hides something from his father. Some things are kept from one that are revealed to another and vice versa. In this way one reveals all and conceals all, by making a distinction among the persons with whom we are connected.

261 · 不要執迷不悟

很多人犯了大錯才知道承擔責任，因為起初他們就走錯了路並堅信只有一路向前才能證明他們的毅力。雖然表面上為自己開脫，而實際上在內心深處，他們懊悔自己犯下的錯誤。犯錯的開始，人們只是以為他們疏忽大意，最後則認為他們愚蠢至極。一時的輕率許諾和錯誤決定其實不應該真正地限制住我們，然而有些人卻繼續執迷不悟，他們寧願是永遠的傻瓜啊。

262 · 學會忘記

與其說這要憑藉技巧，倒不如說要藉助運氣。最該忘掉的事往往是我們記得最深刻的事。有時記憶不僅蠻橫，而且愚蠢，我們需要它時它從不光顧，不需要它時卻不請自來。我們悲傷痛苦時，記憶無比深刻，我們回憶美好時光時，記憶卻消失殆盡。通常治癒這類「疾病」的最好藥方就是忘記，我們往往會不記得「忘記」這個藥方。不過我們可以培養良好的記憶習慣，因為記憶既可把人帶入天堂，也可把人帶入地獄。快樂的人是個例外，他們只是單純地享受簡簡單單的快樂。

---

1. unruly [ʌnˋrulɪ] adj. 不守規矩的，難駕馭的
2. leave sb in the lurch 臨危捨棄某人
3. inferno [ɪnˋfɝno] n. 陰間，地獄

cclxi Do Not Follow up a Folly.

Many make an obligation out of a blunder, and because they have entered the wrong path think it proves their strength of character to go on in it. Within they regret their error, while outwardly they excuse it. At the beginning of their mistake they were regarded as inattentive, in the end as fools. Neither an unconsidered promise nor a mistaken resolution are really binding. Yet some continue in their folly and prefer to be constant fools.

cclxii Be Able to Forget.

It is more a matter of luck than of skill. The things we remember best are those better forgotten. Memory is not only **unruly**[1], **leaving us in the lurch**[2] when most needed, but stupid as well, putting its nose into places where it is not wanted. In painful things it is active, but neglectful in recalling the pleasurable. Very often the only remedy for the ill is to forget it, and all we forget is the remedy. Nevertheless one should cultivate good habits of memory, for it is capable of making existence a Paradise or an **Inferno**[3]. The happy are an exception who enjoy innocently their simple happiness.

263・很多東西只需感受，不必擁有

人們總覺得別人的東西比自己的東西要好。一樣東西的美好只有第一天屬於擁有它的人，之後就屬於其他人了。當一樣東西屬於別人時，我們會有雙倍的快樂，因為我們既不用擔心弄壞它，又有新鮮感。無論任何東西，總是在我們沒有時感到它更好，甚至別人井裏的水對我們來說也如同仙釀。擁有一樣東西不僅會使人失去快樂，還會大增煩惱，到底是把它借出去還是保存起來。事實上，當你擁有它的時候，不管你是在替別人保管，或是在防範別人，總是多了些敵人，少了些朋友。

264・不能馬虎度日

命運總是喜歡惡作劇，只要你稍不留意，它就會抓住機會捉弄你。我們的才智、審慎、勇氣，甚至美貌時刻都要準備好接受命運的考驗。自認為最有信心的時候往往很有可能做出丟臉的事；最應小心謹慎時往往會變得毫無防範之心；總有一些沒考慮到的因素讓我們輸得很慘。軍事中一條策略是在未事先準備的訓練中就要做到盡善盡美。舉行閱兵的時間眾所周知，但究竟選擇哪天來閱兵往往是最出人意料的，因為只有這樣才能在嚴峻的考驗中展現將士的英勇。

cclxiii Many Things of Taste One Should Not Possess Oneself.

One enjoys them better if another's than if one's own. The owner has the good of them the first day, for all the rest of the time they are for others. You take a double enjoyment in other men's property, being without fear of spoiling it and with the pleasure of novelty. Everything tastes better for having been without it: even water from another's well tastes like nectar. Possession not alone hinders enjoyment: it increases annoyance whether you lend or keep. You gain nothing except keeping things for or from others, and by this means gain more enemies than friends.

cclxiv Have No Careless Days.

Fate loves to play tricks, and will heap up chances to catch us unawares. Our intelligence, prudence, and courage, even our beauty, must always be ready for trial. For their day of careless trust will be that of their discredit. Care always fails just when it was most wanted. It is thoughtlessness that trips us up into destruction. Accordingly it is a piece of military strategy to put perfection to its trial when unprepared. The days of parade are known and are allowed to pass by, but the day is chosen when least expected so as to put valour to the severest test.

265 · 給下屬分派有挑戰性的工作

當人們遇到亟待解決的困難時，他們的才能會馬上被激發出來，正如人掉進水中，出於對溺死的恐懼從而學會了游泳一樣。很多人都是這樣發現了自己的勇氣、知識和技巧，若沒有這樣的機會，而且缺乏進取心，這些能力可能會被永遠埋沒。困境為我們提供了出人頭地的機會，當一個高尚的人看到自己的名譽陷入了困境，他能完成千萬人才能做得到的事情。天主教女王伊莎貝爾深諳這一道理（以及很多其他道理），她對精明的大船長哥倫布寵愛有加，從而使他贏得了名望，還有許多人在女王的寵愛下都名垂青史，萬古流芳。正是憑藉這種手法，她成就了眾多偉人。

---

1. Queen Isabella 伊莎貝爾一世（1451～1504），支持哥倫布航行大西洋的西班牙王后。她所作出的一系列重大決策，對西班牙和拉丁美洲發生了長達幾個世紀的影響。

2. 指哥倫布

cclxv Set Those under You Difficult Task.

M any have proved themselves able at once when they had to deal with a difficulty, just as fear of drowning makes a swimmer of a man, In this way many have discovered their own courage, knowledge, or tact, which but for the opportunity would have been for ever buried beneath their want of enterprise. Dangers are the occasions to create a name for oneself; and if a noble mind sees honour at stake, he will do the work of thousands. **Queen Isabella**[1] the Catholic knew well this rule of life, as well as all the others, and to a shrewd favour of this kind from her the **Great Captain**[2] won his fame, and many others earned an undying name. By this great art she made great men.

266・萬事皆有度，善良勿過頭

如果你從來不發脾氣，那就有點過頭了。那些沒有任何感情的人不是真實的人，他們那樣做往往不是由於怠惰，而通常是由於無能。在合宜的情況下表達強烈的感受是一種很有個性的行為。小鳥還會捉弄稻草人呢！苦樂參半也是一種不錯的味道，絕對甜的糖果只是孩子和白癡的食物。若是一個人為了追求絕對的善良而深陷麻木狀態，那是非常危險的。

267・甜言蜜語，溫文爾雅

箭刺透的是人的身體，而惡言惡語中傷的則是人的心。好的糕餅能讓人吐氣如蘭。懂得如何推銷自己是人生中偉大的藝術。很多事情都是用話語來完成的，憑藉話語就能讓你擺脫困境。面對趾高氣揚的人，高貴的語氣能給人帶來勇氣和力量。讓你的嘴裏時刻充滿甜言蜜語吧！即使是心懷叵測之人也能被征服。想要惹人喜愛，說話必須溫柔和氣。

---

1. scarecrow [ˋskɛrˌkro] n. 稻草人
2. silken [ˋsɪlkən] adj. 圓滑的，柔和的
3. Sugared [ˋʃʊgəd] adj. 加糖的，甜蜜甘美的
4. pastry [ˋpestrɪ] n. 麵粉糕餅，餡餅皮

cclxvi Do Not Become Bad
from Sheer Goodness.

That is, by never getting into a temper. Such men without feeling are scarcely to be considered men. It does not always arise from laziness, but from sheer inability. To feel strongly on occasion is something personal: birds soon mock at the **scarecrow**[1]. It is a sign of good taste to combine bitter and sweet. All sweets is diet for children and fools. It is very bad to sink into such insensibility out of very goodness.

cclxvii Silken[2] Words, Sugared[3] Manners.

Arrows pierce the body, insults the soul. Sweet **pastry**[4] perfumes the breath. It is a great art in life to know how to sell wind. Most things are paid for in words, and by them you can remove impossibilities. Thus we deal in air, and a royal breath can produce courage and power. Always have your mouth full of sugar to sweeten your words, so that even your ill-wishers enjoy them. To please one must be peaceful.

268・聰明之人早做事，
愚蠢之人晚做事

蠢人和聰明人做同樣的事，不同在於做事的時間。聰明人在恰當的時候做，而蠢人在不恰當的時候做。如果從一開始就顛三倒四，那麼到最後也是如此。該敲打頭頂他卻去抓腳跟，該向左轉他卻向右，他做事就像個孩子。能讓他走上正路的方法只有一個，那就是逼迫他去做他原本可以心甘情願去做的事。相反地，聰明人能夠看到遲早要做的事，並且能夠欣然去做，這樣就獲得了尊敬。

---

1. topsyturvy [ˈtɑpsɪˈtɝvɪ] adj. 顛倒的，亂七八糟的
2. of one's own accord 自願地

cclxviii The Wise Do at Once
What the Fool Does at Last.

B oth do the same thing; the only difference lies in the time they do it: the one at the right time, the other at the wrong. Who starts out with his mind **topsyturvy**[1] will so continue till the end. He catches by the foot what he ought to knock on the head, he turns right into left, and in all his acts is but a child. There is only one way to get him in the right way, and that is to force him to do what he might have done **of his own accord**[2]. The wise man, on the other hand, sees at once what must be done sooner or later, so he does it willingly and gains honour thereby.

269·利用你的新鮮感

一般來說，新人會較受重視。與眾不同的新鮮感會博得眾人的喜愛，令人耳目一新。比起人們早已熟悉的出類拔萃者，初來乍到的平庸之人能獲得更多好評，因出類拔萃者的能力已經衰減。但是，新鮮感帶來的榮耀不會長久。幾天之後，人們對你的尊重就所剩無幾。要學會利用人們對你的第一印象，在短暫的歡迎會中抓住有用之人的心。人們的新鮮感一旦過去，激情就會冷卻，新鮮感也會膩掉，成為人們覺得習以為常的東西。萬物皆有其時，萬物終將消亡。

270. 不要逆潮流而動

有的東西既然能取悅眾人，就必有其好處，雖然人們說不出喜歡它的原因，但就是發自內心的喜歡。品味另類的人總不討人喜歡，而且一旦出錯，就會遭人嘲笑。逆潮流而動只會使自己名譽受損，對你不屑的物件構不成絲毫傷害，人們還會鄙棄你和你的低級品味。如果你發現不了一件東西的美，也不用說出來，更不要立即譴責它。通常來講，低級的品味往往源自知識的貧乏。眾口一詞的東西若不是事實，就是人們希望成為事實的東西。

cclxix Make Use of the Novelty of Your Position;

or men are valued while they are new. Novelty pleases all because it is uncommon, taste is refreshed, and a brand new mediocrity is thought more of than accustomed excellence. Ability wears away by use and becomes old. However, know that the glory of novelty is short-lived: after four days respect is gone. Accordingly, learn to utilise the first fruits of appreciation, and seize during the rapid passage of applause all that can be put to use. For once the heat of novelty over, the passion cools and the appreciation of novelty is exchanged for satiety at the customary: believe that all has its season, which soon passes.

cclxx Do Not Condemn Alone that Which Pleases All.

here must be something good in a thing that pleases so many; even if it cannot be explained it is certainly enjoyed. Singularity is always hated, and, when in the wrong, laughed at. You simply destroy respect for your taste rather than do harm to the object of your blame, and are left alone, you and your bad taste. If you cannot find the good in a thing, hide your incapacity and do not damn it straightway. As a general rule bad taste springs from want of knowledge. What all say, is so, or will be so.

271．所知不多，就力求走最安全的路線

做不到機智過人，就做一個踏實可靠的人。訓練有素的人可以去冒險，放縱自己的想像力。但如果你一無所知而去冒險，就等於自尋死路。這種情況下最好是按照規矩來，要知道覆水難收。不瞭解情況，就不要走別人沒走過的路，不管是瞭解內幕還是被蒙在鼓裏，穩當總比獨樹一格要好得多。

272．販售東西，附贈殷勤

使你覺得購買他的東西是一種應盡的義務。自私自利者的索求與慷慨大方者的贈予相比有天壤之別。禮貌殷勤雖然不能憑空變出禮物，卻能讓人感動萬分，慷慨大方則會讓人感激有加。對於高尚的人來說，別人送給他的東西他會加倍珍惜。你等於一物賣兩次，但價格不同，一次是貨物本身的價值，一次是你的盛情的價值。當然，殷勤有禮對無賴不過是瞎話一場，因為他們聽不懂有教養的語言。

---

1. gibberish [ˈdʒɪbərɪʃ] n. 胡扯，令人費解的話

cclxxi In Every Occupation if You Know Little Stick to the Safest.

If you are not respected as subtle, you will be regarded as sure. On the other hand, a man well trained can plunge in and act as he pleases. To know little and yet seek danger is nothing else than to seek ruin. In such a case take stand on the right hand, for what is done cannot be undone. Let little knowledge keep to the king's highway, and in every case, knowing or unknowing, security is shrewder than singularity.

cclxxii Sell Things by the Tariff of Courtesy.

You oblige people most that way. The bid of an interested buyer will never equal the return gift of an honourable recipient of a favour. Courtesy does not really make presents, but really lays men under obligation, and generosity is the great obligation. To a right-minded man nothing costs more dear that what is given him: you sell it him twice and for two prices: one for the value, one for the politeness. At the same time it is true that with vulgar souls generosity is **gibberish**[1], for they do not understand the language of good breeding.

273・瞭解相交之人的性格

這樣你才會瞭解他們的意圖。先瞭解對方的性情，再獲知事情的起因和結果，你大致就可以猜出對方的動機。憂鬱的人所預想的都是不幸；喜歡誹謗之人看到的只是流言蜚語，他們總是看不到善的一面，而惡的一面也就很容易地在其心裏紮根；**受情緒控制的人不能如實的看待事物，他們心中只有激情沒有理智。**人人都根據自己的情感或脾氣來表達看法而遠離真相本身。**應該學會如何琢磨他人的表情，才能解讀其靈魂深處的想法和意圖。**記住：總愛發笑之人是蠢人；不苟言笑之人則是偽君子。需小心應付那些愛八卦之人，他不是個嘮叨鬼就是個奸細。不要指望從面惡的人那裏得到什麼好處，這類人常常覺得上蒼從不眷顧他們，所以他們常為此報復自然。美貌通常會與愚蠢同行。

---

1. spell out 講清楚，清楚地說明
2. babbler [`bæblɚ] n. 說話模糊不清者，嘮嘮叨叨

cclxxiii Comprehend Their Dispositions with Whom You Deal,

S o as to know their intentions. Cause known, effect known, beforehand in the disposition and after in the motive. The melancholy man always foresees misfortunes, the backbiter scandals; having no conception of the good, evil offers itself to them. A man moved by passion always speaks of things differently from what they are; it is his passion speaks, not his reason. Thus each speaks as his feeling or his humour prompts him, and all far from the truth. Learn how to decipher faces and **spell out**[1] the soul in the features. If a man laughs always, set him down as foolish; if never, as false. Beware of the gossip: he is either a **babbler**[2] or a spy. Expect little good from the misshapen: they generally take revenge on Nature, and do little honour to her, as she has done little to them. Beauty and folly generally go hand in hand.

274 · 要有吸引力

恰當的施禮於人會帶來不可思議的魔力，它能讓一個人總是有吸引力。那令人愉快的特質就像是一塊磁石，能給你帶來善意，但不能帶來善行。儘管如此，你還是要向所有人展示你的魅力。美德要有優雅相助才好，因為氣質優雅可以讓人心甘情願地接受你，這也是統治別人的最好辦法。如果人們發現你的魅力，將是你的運氣，但這種運氣還需要修養相助，因為天賦和後天的修養結合在一起將產生意想不到的效果。魅力能招來善意的說明，使你無往不利。

---

1. subtle [sʌt!] a. 不可思議的，微妙的，難捉摸的
2. courtesy [`kɝtəsɪ] n. 禮貌，好意，殷勤

cclxxiv Be Attractive.

It is the magic of **subtle**[1] **courtesy**[2] use the magnet of your pleasant qualities more to obtain goodwill than good deeds, but apply it to all. Merit is not enough unless supported by grace, which is the sole thing that gives general acceptance, and the most practical means of rule over others. To be in vogue is a matter of luck, yet it can be encouraged by skill, for art can best take root on a soil favoured by nature. There goodwill grows and develops into universal favour.

275・要合群，但不要逾禮

不要總是裝作一副老成持重的樣子，不要惹人厭煩，這是保持豪爽風度所必需的。你可以在行為舉止上做些讓步，以便贏得人們的喜歡。你可能會時時地出入大多數人出入的場所，但是你不可逾禮而為。對於在公眾場合出醜的人，人們會認為他的私生活也不怎麼自律。一日之樂所失去的可能用一生的辛苦都無法彌補。但是也不要成為離群索居的人，這樣就等於嘲弄他人的行為；也不要表現得過分正經，做適合於自己性別的事吧：就算是宗教上的假正經也會讓人覺得滑稽可笑。做男人的要領就是要像個男子漢。女人可以模仿男人，但男人若是模仿女人則不是什麼優點了。

---

1. prude [prud] n. （在性方面）過分拘謹的人
2. prudery [`prudərɪ] n. 裝規矩，假正經的行為

cclxxv Join in the Game as far as Decency Permits.

D o not always pose and be a bore: this is a maxim for gallant bearing. You may yield a touch of dignity to gain the general good-will: you may now and then go where most go, yet not beyond the bounds of decorum. He who makes a fool of himself in public will not be regarded as discreet in private life. One may lose more on a day of pleasure than has been gained during a whole life of labour. Still you must not always keep away: to be singular is to condemn all others. Still less act the **prude**[1] – leave that to its appropriate sex: even religious **prudery**[2] is ridiculous. Nothing so becomes a man as to be a man: a woman may affect a manly bearing as an excellence, but not vice versa.

276·完善品格

俗話說：人之性情在天性和後天努力下7年一變。讓其朝著更好的方向發展，那麼，你的品味也會隨之變得更加高雅。過了第一個7年以後，就到了理智的年齡，從此以後，務使每一個7年精益求精。注意這種自然的改變，順勢求進，也同時希望別的方面有所長進。人們會隨著地位或職業的變化而改變行為舉止。有時候這種變化直到成熟之際才會為人所察覺。人啊，20歲如孔雀，30歲如獅子，40歲如駱駝，50歲如蛇精，60歲如狗，70歲如猴，到了80歲時什麼都不像了。

---

1. lustre [ˈlʌstɚ] n. 光彩，光澤
2. peacock [ˈpikɑk] n. 孔雀

cclxxvi Know How to Renew Your Character,

With the help both of Nature and of Art, Every seven years the disposition changes, they say. Let it be a change for the better and for the nobler in your taste. After the first seven comes reason, with each succeeding **lustre**[1] let a new excellence be added. Observe this change so as to aid it, and hope also for betterment in others. Hence it arises that many change their behaviour when they change their position or their occupation. At times the change is not noticed till it reaches the height of maturity. At twenty Man is a **Peacock**[2], at thirty a Lion, at forty a Camel, at fifty a Serpent, at sixty a Dog, at seventy an Ape, at eighty nothing at all.

277・展示自我

這樣才會讓你的才能更加耀眼。每人都會遇到一展才華的機會，你要學會善加利用，因為並不是每天都可以這麼走運。有些人充滿幹勁，隨便做什麼都可以大大展示一番，開個展都綽綽有餘。如果能力能配上各色才藝展現出來，人們就會驚為奇蹟。有些民族知道怎樣吸引眼球，在這方面，西班牙人最出眾。這個世界剛被創造，就有光使它顯示出來。展示可以彌補缺陷，可以錦上添花，可以讓萬物有另一種生存狀態，尤其是該物品格真正卓越的時候。上帝一方面創造了完美的事物，另一方面又提供了展示這一方法，離開了對方，另一方只能是失敗的。展示也要一定的技巧，即使是最優異的事物也有賴於環境，需要時機。如果不得其時，其巧妙之處便很難表現出來。在展示自己特長時，不應過於矯揉造作，否則容易流於炫耀，炫耀容易招致嘲笑和輕蔑。展示也應以謙虛的態度流露，以免流於粗俗。露才過甚，為智者所不恥。**有時無言勝有言，不經意的展示更讓人動心。聰明的隱藏是贏得讚揚的最好途徑**，因為人們對不瞭解的東西總是抱有好奇心。不要一下子展露你所有的本領，要慢慢來，層層推進。贏得一次輝煌後再次精進，使人在為你鼓掌喝彩時，期盼後頭有更多的好戲。

---

1. miraculous [mɪˋrækjələs] adj. 奇蹟的，不可思議的
2. abortive [əˋbɔrtɪv] adj. 流產的，夭折的
3. opportune [ˌɑpɚˋtjun] adj. 合適的時機
4. border on 接近
5. pique [pik] vt. 激起（好奇心）

cclxxvii Display Yourself.

❯ Tis the illumination of talents: for each there comes an appropriate moment; use it, for not every day comes a triumph. There are some dashing men who make much show with a little, a whole exhibition with much. If ability to display them is joined to versatile gifts, they are regarded as **miraculous**[1]. There are whole nations given to display: the Spanish people take the highest rank in this. Light was the first thing to cause Creation to shine forth. Display fills up much, supplies much, and gives a second existence to things, especially when combined with real excellence. Heaven that grants perfection, provides also the means of display; for one without the other were **abortive**[2]. Skill is however needed for display. Even excellence depends on circumstances and is not always **opportune**[3]. Ostentation is out of place when it is out of time. More than any other quality it should be free of any affectation. This is its rock of offence, for it then **borders on**[4] vanity and so on contempt: it must be moderate to avoid being vulgar, and any excess is despised by the wise. At times it consists in a sort of mute eloquence, a careless display of excellence, for a wise concealment is often the most effective boast, since the very withdrawal from view **piques**[5] curiosity to the highest. 'Tis a fine subtlety too not to display one's excellence all at one time, but to grant stolen glances at it, more and more as time goes on. Each exploit should be the pledge of a greater, and applause at the first should only die away in expectation of its sequel.

278・不要在任何事情上
損毀自己的名譽

聲 名狼藉時，你的優點也會變成缺點。惡名源於離群與獨處，這總受到批判，因此獨處之人會被大家孤立起來。濃妝豔抹會讓美貌聲名掃地，因為它冒犯了人們的審美習慣。孤傲只會引起人們更多的反感。然而有些惡人千方百計做各種壞事，以使自己可以遺臭萬年。就算是真正智慧的人，如果不懂得謙虛，也會落得一個浮誇之名。

279・不要回應駁斥你的人

你 首先需弄清楚他是賣弄聰明還是本身庸俗惡劣。駁斥行為並不總是出於固執己見，還有可能是陰謀詭計。對此，需格外留神，前者會讓你受困，而後者則會讓你涉險。對於奸細，再小心都不為過。當有人拿著窺探你心思的萬能鑰匙時，與其對抗，不如將心房的鑰匙留在鑰匙孔內。

---

1. coxcombry [ˋkɑksˏkomrɪ] n. 過分注重衣著者
2. infamy [ˋɪnfəmɪ] n. 聲名狼藉，醜名，醜行
3. loquacity [loˋkwæsətɪ] n. 多話，饒舌
4. obstinacy [ˋɑbstənəsɪ] n. 固執
5. countercheck [ˋkɑʊntəˏtʃɛk] n. 阻擋，對抗，妨礙

cclxxviii Avoid Notoriety in All Things.

E ven excellences become defects if they become notorious. Notoriety arises from singularity, which is always blamed: he that is singular is left severely alone. Even beauty is discredited by **coxcombry**[1], which offends by the very notice it attracts. Still more does this apply to discreditable singularities. Yet among the wicked there are some that seek to be known for seeking novelties in vice so as to attain to the fame of **infamy**[2]. Even in matters of the intellect want of moderation may degenerate into **loquacity**[3].

cclxxix Do Not Contradict the Contradicter.

Y ou have to distinguish whether the contradiction comes from cunning or from vulgarity. It is not always **obstinacy**[4], but may be artfulness. Notice this: for in the first case one may get into difficulties, in the other into danger. Caution is never more needed than against spies. There is no such **countercheck**[5] to the picklock of the mind as to leave the key of caution in the lock.

280・誠實守信

講 誠信的交易已經一去不復返，信任被人拋棄，很少有人會言而有信，當今社會就是付出得越多，回報得越少。普天之下，惡言惡行肆虐。有人怕某些人背信忘義；有人怕其他人善變；有人怕被欺騙。留意別人的不良行為不是為了模仿，而是為了保護自己不受其害。最怕的就是這種不恥的行為會讓大家正義的言行有所動搖，但高尚的人並不因為看到別人怎麼做而忘記自己應該怎樣做。

281・贏得智者的好感

真 正傑出的人物所說的一句平淡的「是」，也比一群粗俗之人的掌聲更有價值。為什麼要為缺少見識的人的稱讚而沾沾自喜呢？智者的話語中包含了非凡的見解，所以他們的讚揚能夠給你帶來長久的滿足。聖人安提戈努斯把自己的名聲全部歸於宙斯，柏拉圖也認為亞里斯多德抵得上他所有的學生。有些人只管填飽肚子，毫不介意吃的是粗劣之物。即使是君主也需要有人為他們豎碑立傳，他們對作家之筆的恐懼甚於醜婦恐懼畫家之筆。

---

1. override [ˌovəˋraɪd] vt. 視為比…更重要
2. chaff [tʃæf] n. 穀殼，糠
3. Zeus 宙斯，眾神之父
4. albeit [ɔlˋbiɪt] conj. 雖然

cclxxx Be Trustworthy

H onourable dealing is at an end: trusts are denied: few keep their word: the greater the service, the poorer the reward: that is the way with all the world nowadays. There are whole nations inclined to false dealing: with some treachery has always to be feared, with others breach of promise, with others deceit. Yet this bad behaviour of others should rather be a warning to us than an example. The fear is that the sight of such unworthy behaviour should **override**[1] our integrity. But a man of honour should never forget what he is because he sees what others are.

cclxxxi Find Favour with Men of Sense.

T he tepid Yes of a remarkable man is worth more than all the applause of the vulgar: you cannot make a meal off the smoke of **chaff**[2]. The wise speak with understanding and their praise gives permanent satisfaction. The sage Antigonus reduced the theatre of his fame to **Zeus**[3] alone, and Plato called Aristotle his whole school. Some strive to fill their stomach **albeit**[4] only with the breath of the mob. Even monarchs have need of authors, and fear their pens more than ugly women the painter's pencil.

282・以不露面來贏得聲望

如果露面變得有損聲譽，那深居簡出反而會增加你的聲望。不露面者，人們會當其為雄獅，一露面則可能被看成可笑之物。天分只有充分運用才能發芽生長，人們看到的往往只是外表皮毛，看不見精髓所在。想像力的步伐遠遠快於視覺，聽覺能夠遏制想像力，破除幻覺。想保持名聲，就要通過公眾輿論的考驗。鳳凰涅槃重生，它們總是利用這暫時的消失讓人們對其復出抱持期待。

---

1. parturition [ˌpɑrtjʊˋrɪʃən] n. 分娩，生產

cclxxxii Make Use of Absence to Make Yourself More Esteemed or Valued.

I f the accustomed presence diminishes fame, absence augments it. One that is regarded as a lion in his absence may be laughed at when present as the ridiculous result of the **parturition**[1] of the mountains. Talents get soiled by use, for it is easier to see the exterior rind than the kernel of greatness it encloses. Imagination reaches farther than sight, and disillusion, which ordinarily comes through the ears, also goes out through the ears. He keeps his fame that keeps himself in the centre of public opinion. Even the Phoenix uses its retirement for new adornment and turns absence into desire.

283·善於探索與發現

是 具備很高天賦的證明，哪些天才不帶一些瘋狂呢？如果說善於探索發現是一種天賦，那麼選擇合適的方法則是理智的標誌。發現需要特別的勇氣，因此少有發生。因為多數人精於探究已被發現之事物，而只有很少人能夠發現與創造，這少數人卓越超群，盛名持久。新奇之物引人好奇，如能獲得成功，則倍添光彩。但是在需要判斷力時，追新求異十分危險，因為事物常常包含很多似是而非的東西。只有在才智方面追求新奇值得稱許。如果探索成功，那麼發現者與被發現者都應當獲得應有的認可。

284·勿多管閒事

這 樣才不會受人怠慢與侮辱。欲得他人尊重，需先自重。對自己的出場要嚴格一些，不要輕易做事情，要知道只有他人需要你時，你才會受到善待。只去受人邀請之地，不要不請自來。如果只按自己的意願行事，事敗則必會招人怨恨，自取其辱，就算事成也無人感激。**多管閒事之人總會成為他人責備的對象。**管了不該管的事，大多只能狼狽而歸。

---

1. importunate [ɪmˈpɔrtʃənɪt] adj. 纏擾不休的，胡攪蠻纏的
2. slight [slaɪt] vt. 輕視，玩忽，怠慢

cclxxxiii Have the Gift of Discovery.

I t is a proof of the highest genius, yet when was genius without a touch of madness? If discovery be a gift of genius, choice of means is a mark of sound sense. Discovery comes by special grace and very seldom. For many can follow up a thing when found, but to find it first is the gift of the few, and those the first in excellence and in age. Novelty flatters, and if successful gives the possessor double credit. In matters of judgment novelties are dangerous because leading to paradox, in matters of genius they deserve all praise. Yet both equally deserve applause if successful.

cclxxxiv Do Not Be Importunate[1],

a nd so you will not be **slighted**[2]. Respect yourself if you would have others respect you. Be sooner sparing than lavish with your presence. You will thus become desired and so well received. Never come unasked and only go when sent for. If you undertake a thing of your own accord you get all the blame if it fails, none of the thanks If it succeeds. The importunate is always the butt of blame; and because he thrusts himself in without shame he is thrust out with it.

285‧勿被他人厄運拖累

看那些深陷泥淖的人，他們總是拉別人下水，以便給自己找個夥伴共同承擔不幸。他們四處尋求幫助，而恰恰是在他們風光時不理睬他們的人此時伸出了援助之手。營救溺水之人時須特別小心，不要讓自己處於危險境地。

286‧不要欠太多人情

否則你會淪為他人的奴隸。有些人天生就比別人更幸運，故他們生來就廣為行善，讓別人受惠於他。當你受到誘惑時，可能會拋棄一些自由來換取某樣事物，但事實上自由更加珍貴。我們應該更加注重讓自己獨立，而不是花太多精力吸引別人來尋求自己的幫助。握有權力的唯一好處就在於你可以利用它做更多更大的善事。總而言之，不要把別人履行責任當作是幫忙，因為幫忙只是他計畫的一部分，真正的目的是讓別人依靠他。

cclxxxv Never Die of Another's Ill-luck.

N otice those who stick in the mud, and observe how they call others to their aid so as to console themselves with a companion in misfortune. They seek some one to help them to bear misfortune, and often those who turned the cold shoulder on them in prosperity give them now a helping hand. There is great caution needed in helping the drowning without danger to oneself.

cclxxxvi Do Not Become Responsible for All or for Every One,

O therwise you become a slave and the slave of all. Some are born more fortunate than others: they are born to do good as others to receive it. Freedom is more precious than any gifts for which you may be tempted to give it up. Lay less stress on making many dependent on you than on keeping yourself independent of any. The sole advantage of power is that you can do more good. Above all do not regard responsibility as a favour, for generally it is another's plan to make one dependent on him.

287 · 情緒激動時不要行動

如果不這樣做，你就會失去一切。那些缺乏自制的人不能代表自己。激情總會使人喪失理智，這時候應去找一個明慎的第三者，一個未被激情所左右的人給自己一些建議。有道是當局者迷，旁觀者清。你一旦察覺到自己情緒衝動，就要控制脾氣並使火氣消退。否則一旦熱血沸騰，則會迸發，短暫的爆發與失控會讓我們後悔不已，甚至讓別人心存怨恨。

288 · 順應時勢，順勢求成

我們的所作所想等都應當順應時勢而為。當時機對時就立即行動，要知道時不我待。處世接物不要被某些人為的規定所束縛，除非關乎道德。也不要讓你的意願被一些固定條件束縛，因為你不屑一顧之物明天或許會令你難以割捨。有人心懷不切實際的幻想，竟然期望時勢能遷就自己，而不是改變自己去順應時勢。明智的人知道謹慎的要旨在於調整自己去順應時勢，順勢求成。

---

1. looker-on [ˌlʊkəˋɑn] n. 觀看者，旁觀者
2. repentance [rɪˋpɛntəns] n. 後悔，悔改
3. cardinal [ˋkɑrdnəl] adj. 主要的，最重要的
4. subscribe [səbˋskraɪb] v. 簽（名）
5. steering [ˋstɪrɪŋ] n. 操縱，掌舵，指導

cclxxxvii Never Act in a Passion.

I f you do, all is lost. You cannot act for yourself if you are not yourself, and passion always drives out reason. In such cases inter-pose a prudent go-between who can only be prudent if he keeps cool. That is why **lookers-on**[1] see most of the game, because they keep cool. As soon as you notice that you are losing your temper beat a wise retreat. For no sooner is the blood up than it is spilt, and in a few moments occasion may be given for many days' **repentance**[2] for oneself and complaints of the other party.

cclxxxviii Live for the Moment.

O ur acts and thoughts and all must be determined by circumstances. Will when you may, for time and tide wait for no man. Do not live by certain fixed rules, except those that relate to the **cardinal**[3] virtues. Nor let your will **subscribe**[4] fixed conditions, for you may have to drink the water to-morrow which you cast away to-day. There be some so absurdly paradoxical that they expect all the circumstances of an action should bend to their eccentric whims and not vice versa. The wise man knows that the very polestar of prudence lies in **steering**[5] by the wind.

289・貶低一個人最有效的辦法莫過於讓他知道他和別人沒什麼兩樣

當一個人被認為與他人無異時,他也走下了名譽的神壇。輕浮是傳聲揚名最大的障礙。羞怯的人依然還會被當作人看待,而輕浮的人則得不到常人所應有的尊敬。輕浮最能讓人喪失尊重,因為它與受人敬重的品格完全相反。輕浮之人即使到了老年,仍無內涵可言,儘管歲月的磨練本應當讓其謹慎。輕浮這一缺點非常普遍,往往招來他人的極端蔑視。

---

1. frivolity [frɪ`vɑlətɪ] n. 輕薄,輕率
2. levity [`lɛvətɪ] n. 輕率,輕浮,不穩定,多變

cclxxxix Nothing Depreciates a Man More Than to Show He Is a Man like Other Men.

T he day he is seen to be very human he ceases to be thought divine. Frivolity is the exact opposite of reputation. And as the reserved are held to be more than men, so the frivolous are held to be less. No failing causes such failure of respect. For **frivolity**[1] is the exact opposite of solid seriousness. A man of **levity**[2] cannot be a man of weight even when he is old, and age should oblige him to be prudent. Although this blemish is so common it is none the less despised.

290・同時獲得人們的喜愛和尊敬，實屬幸事

通常欲受人尊敬，則不可被人喜愛得太殷切。愛比恨更感性。喜愛與敬重難以和諧相容。因此，你的目標是不可太令人懼，亦不可太令人愛。愛戀之情使彼此過分熟稔，而越是相信和瞭解一個人就越不容易尊敬他。甯受人敬愛，而不是被人喜愛，因為喜愛會大眾化。

291・學會判斷他人

智者會以敏銳的觀察力與良好的判斷力來防範他人的惡意。想要揣測他人的意圖，需要擁有極強的判斷能力。瞭解他人的品性比瞭解礦石和草藥的特性更為重要。這是人生中最為微妙的事情。聽音可辨金，聞言則可以辨人。言辭可以流露出一個人的品格，行為則更能證明。揣測他人時需要特別小心謹慎，須深刻觀察加上敏銳的鑑別能力，才能做出正確的決定。

---

1. recede [rɪ`sid] vi. 降低，縮減

ccxc 'Tis a Piece of Good Fortune to Combine Men's Love and Respect.

G enerally one dare not be liked if one would be respected. Love is more sensitive than hate. Love and honour do not go well together. So that one should aim neither to be much feared nor much loved. Love introduces confidence, and the further this advances, the more respect **recedes**[1]. Prefer to be loved with respect rather than with passion, for that is a love suitable for many.

ccxci Know How to Test.

T he care of the wise must guard against the snare of the wicked. Great judgment is needed to test that of another. It is more important to know the characteristics and properties of persons than those of vegetables and minerals. It is indeed one of the shrewdest things in life. You can tell metals by their ring and men by their voice. Words are proof of integrity, deeds still more. Here one requires extraordinary care, deep observation, subtle discernment, and judicious decision.

智慧書

292 · 讓你自身的
素質優於你的職責需要

而不應相反。不論職位多高，你本身的素質都要比之更高。隨著職位的升高，你的才能需要不斷地拓展。與之相反的是，氣度狹小之人容易失去自信，並會因其地位下降，名氣降低陷入悲傷。偉大的奧古斯都看重的並不是自己是君王，而是自己成為了一代偉人。在這方面，高尚的靈魂總能找到自己的位置，自信的人也總能找到發揮才能的機會。

293 · 論成熟

成熟之輝昭然於外表，但更見於人的風度。黃金的價值現於其物質重量，人的價值則現於其精神力量。成熟讓一個人的能力完全發揮，贏得他人的尊重。泰然自若之舉止是成熟心靈的門面。這並非輕浮之人以及愚蠢之人的麻木不仁，而是一種沉著的威嚴。有此種成熟境界者出言必睿智，行事必成功。成熟成就人，成熟的程度和人格的完善程度成正比。當你的行動不再幼稚而變得莊重時，自然而然就能產生一種威嚴感。

---

1. dilate [daɪˋlet] vi. 擴大，膨脹　2. Augustus: 奧古斯都，為羅馬帝國的開國君主，統治羅馬長達43年，被人尊稱為「奧古斯都」，意思是「令人敬畏的有威嚴的人」。　3. well-grounded 基礎牢固的，有充分根據的　4. costume [ˋkɑstjum] n. 裝束，服裝　5. bearing [ˋbɛrɪŋ] n. 舉止，風度　6. oration [oˋreʃən] n. 演說，致辭

464

ccxcii Let Your Personal Qualities Surpass Those of Your Office,

et it not be the other way about. However high the post, the person should be higher. An extensive capacity expands and **dilates**[1] more and more as his office becomes higher. On the other hand, the narrow-minded will easily lose heart and come to grief with diminished responsibilities and reputation. The great **Augustus**[2] thought more of being a great man than a great prince. Here a lofty mind finds fit place, and **well-grounded**[3] confidence finds its opportunity.

ccxciii Maturity.

t is shown in the **costume**[4], still more in the customs. Material weight is the sign of a precious metal; moral, of a precious man. Maturity gives finish to his capacity and arouses respect. A composed **bearing**[5] in a man forms a facade to his soul. It does not consist in the insensibility of fools, as frivolity would have it, but in a calm tone of authority. With men of this kind sentences are **orations**[6] and acts are deeds. Maturity finishes a man off, for each is so far a complete man according as he possesses maturity. On ceasing to be a child a man begins to gain seriousness and authority.

294 · 客觀提出觀點

人們往往都是根據自己的利益而持有種種觀點,並且自認為持之有故,言之成理。大多數人的判斷總是受情緒所影響。我們常見兩個人針鋒相對,各執己見,都認為自己言之有理。但真理是真實無欺的,絕無兩張面孔。在這種困境下,要機智和審慎地加以處理,因為對對方觀點的判斷可能會影響自己觀點的客觀性,**要設身處地思考一下,研究別人為何會持這種觀點。如此一來,你才不會盲目地譴責他人或盲目地自我辯護。**

---

1. prudent ['prudnt] a. 審慎的,小心的

ccxciv Be Moderate in Your Views.

E very one holds views according to his interest, and imagines he has abundant grounds for them. For with most men judgment has to give way to inclination. It may occur that two may meet with exactly opposite views and yet each thinks to have reason on his side, yet reason is always true to itself and never has two faces. In such a difficulty a **prudent**[1] man will go to work with care, for his decision of his opponent's view may cast doubt on his own. Place yourself in such a case in the other man's place and then investigate the reasons for his opinion. You will not then condemn him or justify yourself in such a confusing way.

295・事未完成，勿邀功

往往是沒有資格邀功請賞之人才宣揚自己的功勞。他們把沒有的事說得神乎其技，不著邊際。他們就像一隻變色龍，一心只想贏得他人的掌聲，卻只會令人捧腹大笑。虛榮之心令人討厭，而這種行為則更加讓人嘲笑。有的人就如螞蟻儲糧一樣四處攀爬，去竊得榮譽。對於真正成大事者，成就越大，越不宣揚。心安理得地做自己的事，讓別人去說吧。功勞盡可能拱手相送，萬不可待價而沽。不要找一些貪婪之人為你歌功頌德，這只會讓智慧之人取笑你罷了。做人應擁有英雄之品性，而非只談表面。

1. chameleon [kə`miljən] n. 變色龍
2. filch [fɪltʃ] vt. 偷竊（不貴重的東西）
3. scrap [skræp] n. 殘羹剩飯
4. venal [`vinl] adj. 貪污的

ccxcv Do Not Affect What
You Have Not Effected.

Many claim exploits without the slightest claim. 'With the greatest coolness they make a mystery of all. **Chameleons**[1] of applause they afford others a surfeit of laughter. Vanity is always objectionable, here it is despicable. These ants of honour go crawling about **filching**[2] **scraps**[3] of exploits. The greater your exploits the less you need affect them: content yourself with doing, leave the talking to others. Give away your deeds but do not sell them. And do not hire **venal**[4] pens to write down praises in the mud, to the derision of the knowing ones. Aspire rather to be a hero than merely to appear one.

296 · 高貴的品性

才能造就高貴之人。一個具有高貴品性之人比一群庸碌無為之輩更具價值。曾有一個人親手製作他的全部物品,甚至包括家用器皿,他力求做到盡善盡美。偉大之人也應該嚴格要求自己的品德及靈魂。上帝擁有永恆和無限;英雄也應該偉大莊嚴,這樣他的一切行動,甚至他的一切言辭才能顯得超凡脫俗,有王者之風。

297 · 行動之時要感覺處於注視之中

行為謹慎之人知道別人現在看著他或將會看見他,知道隔牆有耳、壞事傳千里的道理。即使他單獨一個人行事,也像是全世界的人都在一旁注視他。他明白,事情總會有真相大白之時,他在行動的時候像有許多目擊證人在場,這些證人將來必會出來證實此事。不怕全世界人注視的人,必不會怕鄰居的窺視。

---

1. utensil [ju`tɛnsl] n. 器具
2. nay [ne] adv. <古>否,不
3. pervade [pɚ`ved] v. 遍及

ccxcvi Noble Qualities.

Noble qualities make noblemen: a single one of them is worth more than a multitude of mediocre ones. There was once a man who made all his belongings, even his household **utensils**[1], as great as possible. How much more ought a great man see that the qualities of his soul are as great as possible. In God all is eternal and infinite, so in a hero everything should be great and majestic, so that all his deeds, **nay**[2], all his words, should he **pervaded**[3] by a transcendent majesty.

ccxcvii Always Act as if Your Acts Were Seen.

He must see all round who sees that men see him or will see him. He knows that walls have ears and that ill deeds rebound back. Even when alone he acts as if the eyes of the whole world were upon him. For as he knows that sooner or later all will be known, so he considers those to be present as witnesses who must afterwards hear of the deed. He that wished the whole world might always see him did not mind that his neighbours could see him over their walls.

298・三樣事使人超凡脫俗

天堂有三樣事使人超凡脫俗，那就是超凡的智慧、深刻的判斷力以及令人愉悅、得體的品味。能夠思考是件好事，而能正確思考就更好了。我們不是用脊柱而是用大腦思考，不用大腦思考的人會面臨很多麻煩。正確思考是理性的產物。20歲的人意志力最強，30歲的人才智最豐富，40歲的人判斷力最果敢。有的人悟性閃耀光芒，如同山貓一樣刺眼，在黑暗處最能看見其思維推理之精；有人則長於切中要害，面對最繁瑣的事也條理清楚，秩序井然。這是多麼豐富的才智啊！至於良好的品味，能調劑一切，使一個人的生活充滿樂趣。

---

1. prodigy [ˈprɑdədʒɪ] n. 不凡，奇蹟

ccxcviii Three Things Go to a Prodigy[1].

T hey are the choicest gifts of Heaven's prodigality – a fertile genius, a profound intellect, a pleasant and refined taste. To think well is good, to think right is better: 'tis the understanding of the good. It will not do for the judgment to reside in the backbone: it would be of more trouble than use. To think aright is the fruit of a reasonable nature. At twenty the will rules; at thirty the intellect; at forty the judgment. There are minds that shine in the dark like the eyes of the lynx, and are most clear where there is most darkness. Others are more adapted for the occasion: they always hit on that which suits the emergency: such a quality produces much and good; a sort of fecund felicity. In the meantime good taste seasons the whole of life.

299・使人常有饑餓感

瓊漿玉液只宜沾沾唇邊,事物的價值是用所需的量來衡量的。例如有人口渴,可以為之解渴,不可為其止渴。物以稀為貴,美好的東西越少越美好。事物來第二回,其價值就會頓減。饜足了的快樂是危險的:它們甚至使那些永恆卓越的事物也受到嘲弄。使人愉悅的重要法則是刺激人的胃口,使其保持飢餓。如果想刺激食欲,最好只吃半飽,以免飽食之後喪失了對美味的興致。自己爭取來的歡樂享受起來會更加歡愉。

---

1. slake [slek] v. 消除
2. quench [kwɛntʃ] vt. 結束,熄滅,淬火
3. repletion [rɪˋpliʃən] n. 充滿,飽滿

ccxcix Leave off Hungry.

O ne ought to remove even the bowl of nectar from the lips. Demand is the measure of value. Even with regard to bodily thirst it is a mark of good taste to **slake**[1] but not to **quench**[2] it. Little and good is twice good. The second time comes a great falling off. Surfeit of pleasure was ever dangerous and brings down the ill-will of the Highest Powers. The only way to please is to revive the appetite by the hunger that is left. If you must excite desire, better do it by the impatience of want than by the **repletion**[3] of enjoyment. Happiness earned gives double joy.

300・一言以蔽之：當一個聖徒

一切人生要義盡在於此。美德是眾善之鏈，是一切快樂和幸福的中心。美德會使人謹慎、明辨、機敏、通達、明智、勇敢、慎重、誠實、快樂、可敬、真實……總之，可以使你成為一個功德圓滿之人。有三件東西可以使人獲得幸福，那就是健康、聖潔和智慧。

美德猶如宇宙之太陽，而這個太陽有一半是由良心所構成的。美德是如此美麗可愛，她討得了上帝的恩寵，也贏得了芸芸眾生的喜愛。沒有什麼比美德更可愛，也沒有什麼比邪惡更可恨。只有美德是真實存在的，其他一切都是虛假的。衡量一個人的偉大是依據其美德而非取決於他所擁有的財富。**擁有美德便擁有了一切。她在世時受人愛戴，死後也讓人銘記於心。**

---

1. sagacious [sə`geʃəs] adj. 有洞察力的，有遠見的，精明的，敏銳的

ccc In One Word, Be a Saint.

S o is all said at once. Virtue is the link of all perfections, the centre of all the felicities. She it is that makes a man prudent, discreet, **sagacious**[1], cautious, wise, courageous, thoughtful, trustworthy, happy, honoured, truthful, and a universal Hero. Three HHH's make a man happy – Health, Holiness, and a Headpiece.

Virtue is the sun of the microcosm, and has for hemisphere a good conscience. She is so beautiful that she finds favour with both God and man. Nothing is lovable but virtue, nothing detestable but vice. Virtue alone is serious, all else is but jest. A man's capacity and greatness are to be measured by his virtue and not by his fortune. She alone is all-sufficient. She makes men lovable in life, memorable after death.

Memo

Memo

國家圖書館出版品預行編目（CIP）資料

智慧書：300篇亙古不朽的睿智箴言／
巴爾塔沙‧葛拉西安著；盛世教育翻譯.
--初版.--臺北市：笛藤，2011.12
面；公分 中英對照
譯自：The art of worldly wisdom
ISBN 978-957-710-584-4（平裝）.--
ISBN 978-957-710-608-7（精裝）
1. 格言

192.8   100026010

《典藏精裝版》

智慧書 300篇亙古不朽的睿智箴言　　　　　定價380元

2013年3月26日 初版第2刷

著　　者：巴爾塔沙‧葛拉西安(Baltasar Gracián)

翻　　譯：盛世教育

封面設計：碼非創意

總 編 輯：賴巧凌

發 行 所：笛藤出版圖書有限公司

地　　址：台北市萬華區中華路一段104號5F

電　　話：(02)2388-7636

傳　　真：(02)2388-7639

總 經 銷：聯合發行股份有限公司

地　　址：新北市新店區寶橋路235巷6弄6號2樓

電　　話：(02)2917-8022‧(02)2917-8042

製 版 廠：造極彩色印刷製版股份有限公司

地　　址：新北市中和區中山路2段340巷36號

電　　話：(02)2240-0333‧(02)2248-3904

訂書郵撥帳戶：八方出版股份有限公司

訂書郵撥帳號：19809050

© Dee Ten Publishing Co., Ltd.　繁體字版本